Structural Anthropology Zero

Claude Lévi-Strauss

Structural Anthropology Zero

Edited and with an Introduction by Vincent Debaene

Translated by Ninon Vinsonneau and Jonathan Magidoff

polity

Originally published in French as *Anthropologie structurale zéro. Préfacé et édité par Vincent Debaene* © Editions du Seuil, 2018. Collection *La librairie du XXIe siècle*, sous la direction de Maurice Olender.

This English translation © Polity Press, 2022

Polity Press
65 Bridge Street
Cambridge CB2 1UR, UK

Polity Press
101 Station Landing
Suite 300
Medford, MA 02155, USA

All rights reserved. Except for the quotation of short passages for the purpose of criticism and review, no part of this publication may be reproduced, stored in a retrieval system or transmitted, in any form or by any means, electronic, mechanical, photocopying, recording or otherwise, without the prior permission of the publisher.

ISBN-13: 978-1-5095-4497-4 – hardback
ISBN-13: 978-1-5095-4498-1 – paperback

A catalogue record for this book is available from the British Library.

Library of Congress Cataloging-in-Publication Data
Names: Lévi-Strauss, Claude, author. | Debaene, Vincent, editor
Title: Structural anthropology zero / Claude Levi-Strauss ; edited and with an introduction by Vincent Debaene ; translated by Ninon Vinsonneau and Jonathan Magidof.
Description: Cambridge, UK ; Medford, MA : Polity Press, 2021. | Translation of: Anthropologie structurale zéro. | Includes bibliographical references and index. | Summary: "Writings from Lévi-Strauss's sojourn in the United States in the 1940s that shed new light on the thinking of one of the world's greatest anthropologists"-- Provided by publisher.
Identifiers: LCCN 2021002218 (print) | LCCN 2021002219 (ebook) | ISBN 9781509544974 (hardback) | ISBN 9781509544981 (paperback) | ISBN 9781509544998 (epub) | ISBN 9781509548064 (pdf)
Subjects: LCSH: Structural anthropology. | Structural anthropology--History.
Classification: LCC GN362 .L44813 2021 (print) | LCC GN362 (ebook) | DDC 301--dc23
LC record available at https://lccn.loc.gov/2021002218
LC ebook record available at https://lccn.loc.gov/2021002219

Typeset in 10.5 on 12 pt Times New Roman
by Fakenham Prepress Solutions, Fakenham, Norfolk NR21 8NL
Printed and bound in Great Britain by TJ Books Ltd, Padstow, Cornwall

The publisher has used its best endeavours to ensure that the URLs for external websites referred to in this book are correct and active at the time of going to press. However, the publisher has no responsibility for the websites and can make no guarantee that a site will remain live or that the content is or will remain appropriate.

Every effort has been made to trace all copyright holders, but if any have been overlooked the publisher will be pleased to include any necessary credits in any subsequent reprint or edition.

For further information on Polity, visit our website:
politybooks.com

Contents

Note on this Edition		vii
List of Illustrations		ix
Introduction by Vincent Debaene		1

History and Method   **33**
I   French Sociology   35
II   In Memory of Malinowski   63
III   The Work of Edward Westermarck   65
IV   The Name of the Nambikwara   77

Individual and Society   **81**
V   Five Book Reviews   83
VI   Techniques for Happiness   92

Reciprocity and Hierarchy   **101**
VII   War and Trade among the Indians of South America   103
VIII   The Theory of Power in a Primitive Society   117
IX   Reciprocity and Hierarchy   132
X   The Foreign Policy of a Primitive Society   135

Art   **149**
XI   Indian Cosmetics   151
XII   The Art of the Northwest Coast at the American Museum of Natural History   158

South American Ethnography   **165**
XIII   The Social Use of Kinship Terms among Brazilian Indians   167
XIV   On Dual Organization in South America   179

XV	The Tupi-Kawahib	188
XVI	The Nambikwara	199
XVII	Tribes of the Right Bank of the Guaporé River	214

Map 227
Sources 228
Notes 231
Index 246

A Note on this Edition

This collection is organized into five non-chronological parts. Indeed, the only chronology we might have relied on is that of the official publication dates of the articles it comprises. And in those troubled years, and over such a brief period of time, this could not be expected to have revealed much, either about their actual date of publication or that of their composition or conception. A thematic organization suggested itself for two additional reasons: first, to remain faithful to the "structural anthropologies" model, as Lévi-Strauss himself had conceived it for his own volumes; and, second, to avoid the assembled articles being received as mere "heritage." For the point was not to collect the juvenilia of a great author or to shed light on the genesis of his oeuvre but, rather, to make more easily available forgotten and little-known texts that have lost none of their relevance today – and which the current state of the world may well have made newly pertinent.

The references for the original publications are provided at the end of the volume. Twelve of the seventeen articles were originally published in English, and it is unclear whether Lévi-Strauss wrote them directly in English – perhaps with some assistance – or if he translated them himself from an original French text. These original English texts have been edited for clarity and consistency for the present volume. Their initial publication was, in some cases, followed by the publication of an original French version (chapters I and XII) or else of a French translation of the original English version by Lévi-Strauss himself (chapter VIII). The original French versions of chapters II and XI have been lost, and so the texts included here are slightly edited English translations by Patricia Blanc from 1942. Concerning the names of tribes, we standardized usage and spelling when there were variations from one text to the next.

We have endeavored to include the illustrations that accompanied these articles in their original publication, although this has in some cases proven technically impossible. The quality of the plates of photographs that illustrated chapters XV, XVI and XVII was too poor for them to be reproduced, and we have included only those photographs for which we were able to find quality reproductions. The illustrations for chapter XII combine original images (those we managed to locate) and recent photographs of the objects that appeared in the 1943 version.

This volume would not have been possible without the friendly support and encouragement of Monique Lévi-Strauss, who spurred me to resume work on this project, and the precious exchanges and discussions with Laurent Jeanpierre and Frédéric Keck, whose original idea it was. My warmest thanks to all three. This work also owes a lot to various people who generously reread the preface and translations or who lent assistance on certain specific points: Marie Desmartis, Eléonore Devevey, Frédéric Keck, Emmanuelle Loyer, Gildas Salmon, Thomas Hirsch and Samuel Skippon. Finally, Maurice Olender kept a benevolent watch over the entire process and offered invaluable suggestions, as a reader always keen to maintain the "right distance."

Illustrations

The photographs in this volume are by Claude Lévi-Strauss.
All © Editions du Seuil and Claude Lévi-Strauss.

Figure 1 Kaduveo child with painted face   154
Figure 2 Motif by a Kaduveo woman   155
Figure 3 Motif by a Kaduveo woman   156
Figure 4 Life in a Tupi-Kawahib village: a monkey being skinned   190
Figure 5 Life in a Tupi-Kawahib village: production of corn beer   191
Figure 6 Life in a Tupi-Kawahib village: a Tupi-Kawahib
          mother and her baby   193
Figure 7 Life in a Tupi-Kawahib village: a child carrier   194
Figure 8 Nambikwara family shelter   203
Figure 9 Nambikwara woman piercing a mother-of-pearl earring   204
Figure 10 Nambikwara man wearing a jaguar skin headdress   205
Figure 11 Nambikwara man weaving a bracelet   207
Figure 12 Indians of the Pimenta Bueno River   217
Figure 13 Indians of the Pimenta Bueno River   218
Figure 14 Indians of the Pimenta Bueno River   219
Figure 15 Huari ax (copied from Nordenskiöld, 1924b, fig. 26)   220
Figure 16 Guaporé musical instruments: left, *Amniapä* trumpet;
           upper right, *Guaratägaja* bird whistle; bottom right, *Arua*
           double pan flute (copied from Snethlage, 1939)   223
Figure 17 Macurap pseudo-panpipe (copied from Snethlage,
           1939)   224
Figure 18 Huari flutes made of bone (copied from
           Nordenskiöld, 1924b, fig. 43)   224

Introduction by Vincent Debaene

"Your thought is not yet mature." According to Claude Lévi-Strauss, this is how Brice Parain, then assistant and editorial advisor to the illustrious publisher Gaston Gallimard, explained his decision not to publish the collection of articles entitled *Structural Anthropology*. In his account Lévi-Strauss does not date the incident but indicates that it took place "before writing *Tristes Tropiques*" – i.e. likely sometime in 1953 or 1954.[1] Beyond his stated motive, Parain – whom Lévi-Strauss would soon describe as among the "opponents of anthropology"[2] – probably did not think very highly of volumes of collected articles in general, often seen as too heterogeneous and repetitive to make for a good read. However, the manuscript of *Structural Anthropology* that Lévi-Strauss submitted to the Plon publishing house – which was ultimately published in 1958, three years after *Tristes Tropiques* – was not simply a compilation of previously published work preceded by a perfunctory preface. Quite the contrary, the collection had a robust structure, dispensing with a lazy chronology in favor of a thematic organization in five parts and seventeen chapters. The volume proceeds from the most fundamental level at which social facts are structured ("Language and Kinship") to "Social Organization" and then to the concrete expressions of these underlying structures, which can be traced in rites and myths ("Magic and Religion"), before turning to creative expression ("Art") and finally to the question of the place of anthropology in both the field of social science and modern education ("Problems of Method and Teaching"). The whole is preceded by an ambitious introduction that outlines the respective roles of anthropology and history, at a time when the latter was emerging as one of the most high-profile and innovative disciplines in the social sciences, as demonstrated by the prominent place it was given within the newly founded "Sixth Section" of the École Pratique des Hautes Études, ancestor of today's École des Hautes Études en Sciences Sociales (Lévi-Strauss himself was a member of the "Fifth Section," devoted to the "Religious Studies").

In retrospect, it seems clear that the publication of *Structural Anthropology* marked a crucial stage in the rise and spread of structuralism. The carefully conceived organization of the book undoubtedly played an essential role in this. It highlighted the extremely innovative character of the thought as well as the theoretical ambition of a body of work that relied on very precise anthropological data even while opening up onto other disciplines (linguistics, history, psychoanalysis, etc.) and the anglophone literature in the field. It thus lent the work a certain force, further enhanced by its programmatic title. It should be recalled that this was by no means a sure bet. Against the sense of inexorability conveyed by retrospective accounts, which lay out a chronology of editorial and institutional successes, it is important to remember that the adjective "structural" was considered at the time to be something of a vulgarism and that the entire enterprise was a bit of a gamble. After all, intellectual history is strewn with stillborn neologisms, conceived in the heat of the moment as banners and manifestos.

Structural Anthropology was thus both more than and altogether different from collections of contributions artificially bound together by a title. This is also true of *Structural Anthropology, Volume II*, which came out in 1973 and whose organization is rather similar to that of the first volume: the "Perspective Views" that explore the history and pre-history of modern anthropology are followed by two sections, entitled "Social Organization" and "Mythology and Ritual," closing with a final (and long) section entitled "Humanism and the Humanities." Here again, the order reflected stages of thought, with chronology playing no part. The book even concludes with the essay "Race and History," which had been first published twenty years earlier, in 1952; however innovative it might have been (and still is), this short treatise on cultural diversity and evolutionism had not found its rightful place within the architecture of the first volume – more affirmative and more disciplinary, less concerned with locating anthropology within a set of reflections that made the destiny of humanity its object – while it provided an ideal complement to meditations on the notions of humanism and progress.

Although its structure differed from that of the two previous volumes, *The View from Afar* – published in 1983 and which Lévi-Strauss would have gladly entitled *Structural Anthropology, Volume III*, had the adjective not by then become trite and "lost its content" due to its status as an intellectual "fashion"[3] – obeyed the same principle. Less strictly anthropological, the book engages more directly with the theories and ideologies of its time, through a discussion of the various forms of constraint that weigh on human activity.

In any case, two conclusions may be drawn. First, the *Structural Anthropology* volumes were indeed conceived as books – i.e. as theoretical interventions into debates that they sought to shape and not as simple collections of essays. Second, the way Lévi-Strauss understood anthropology, its methods and objects, did not evolve much over the course of his career. The only true exception is probably with regard to the status of the distinction between nature and culture: initially presented (in *The Elementary Structures of Kinship*, in 1949) as an anthropological invariant, in line with social science since its origins in the eighteenth century, it became a distinction of "primarily methodological importance," according to his formulation in *The Savage Mind* in 1962.[4] With the exception of this shift, in keeping with his redefinition of the concept of symbol,[5] Lévi-Strauss's thought remained very faithful to a few governing principles, and its evolution has to do more with the diversity of objects to which it was applied than with any change in the "rustic convictions" (to quote *Tristes Tropiques*) that guided his project.

A prehistory of structural anthropology

In 1957, Lévi-Strauss collected the seventeen articles that were to form *Structural Anthropology*, selecting them from among "some one hundred papers written during the past thirty years" (according to the brief preface he wrote for the occasion). In addition to two unpublished contributions, he settled on fifteen articles, the oldest of which had been published in 1944. The idea that Lévi-Strauss neglected the writings of his "youth" in favor of more recent work, which demonstrated greater intellectual maturity, is thus unfounded. Quite the contrary, the table of contents reflects the work of careful selection. This is the first observation at the origin of the present volume, *Structural Anthropology Zero*,[6] which brings together seventeen articles that Lévi-Strauss rejected when he composed the 1958 volume. Some of his decisions are easily enough understood and, indeed, Lévi-Strauss himself offered explanations for them: "I have made a choice, rejecting works of purely ethnographic and descriptive character, as well as others of theoretical scope but the substance of which has been incorporated into my book *Tristes Tropiques*." Other texts, such as "The

Art of the Northwest Coast at the American Museum of Natural History" (chapter XII of the present volume), had probably appeared dated: the sense of wonder was still there, but progress in the discipline had rendered the theoretical point (in this case, diffusionist questions) obsolete. Finally, some of the studies seemed to have been superseded by more recent ones, as for instance "Indian Cosmetics" (chapter XI), which, in 1942, had provided readers of the American surrealist review *VVV* with a detailed description of Kaduveo makeup, the in-depth analysis of which was yet to come in *Tristes Tropiques*. Similarly, the long presentation of "French Sociology" (chapter I) must also have seemed outdated to Lévi-Strauss, superseded by his *Introduction to the Work of Marcel Mauss*, published in 1950.[7]

We were thus left with a loss, which the present collection seeks to remedy. A loss because the final selection effectively excluded many insights – such as, for example, certain passages of "The Theory of Power in a Primitive Society" (chapter VIII), on which Lévi-Strauss amply drew in *Tristes Tropiques*, yet whose remarkable final considerations on the notion of "natural power" were left out; or, to take another example, the very dense discussion of Durkheim's work found in "French Sociology" but that did not find its way into the 1950 study on the work of Mauss – itself an important and difficult article, the much discussed "bible of structuralism," into which the 1945 text on Durkheim provides much insight.[8] But a loss also because Lévi-Strauss's selection left out articles that did not fit with the theoretical project of *Structural Anthropology* yet played a major role in the development of other ideas outside the scope of structuralism. This is the case for both "War and Trade among the Indians of South America" (chapter VII), as well as "The Theory of Power in a Primitive Society." Both of these articles are essential references for social and political theories that take native societies of South America as examples of societies with low levels of material wealth and minimal political organization, and thus social forms that preceded the state and the primitive accumulation of capital – ideas in political anthropology, of which Pierre Clastres is the most notable illustration.[9] The same can be said of the article "The Social Use of Kinship Terms among Brazilian Indians" (chapter XIII). Whereas Lévi-Strauss had partially drawn on it for his minor dissertation *The Family and Social Life of the Nambikwara Indians*, the article was rediscovered by Brazilian scholars in the 1990s and has become, alongside other ethnographic works of the 1940s, a central reference for one of the most important developments in recent anthropology: the reconstruction of Amerindian ontologies through the extension of the notion of affinity with the non-human world. "Initially envisioned as an internal mechanism for the constitution of local groups, affinity has since appeared as a relational dynamic that organizes extra-local relations, articulates people and groups of people beyond kinship, and finally as a language and relational schema between Self and Other, identity and difference."[10]

Finally, we can easily see how "Techniques for Happiness" (chapter VI), an amusing yet profound reflection on modern American society as Lévi-Strauss experienced it from the inside in the 1940s, did not fit into the theoretical collection he had in mind in 1957. Written in 1944 and published a year later in the journal *L'Âge d'Or*, it was subsequently republished in 1946 in a special issue of the journal *Esprit* on "Homo Americanus," alongside contributions by American writers and thinkers (Kenneth Burke, Margaret Mead), as well as by other exiled intellectuals in the United States during the war (Georges Gurvitch, Denis de Rougemont). Its tone anticipated the more "liberated" meditations of the 1970s and 1980s (such as "New York in 1941" in *The View from Afar* and the texts of the posthumous collection *We Are All Cannibals*) but, unlike these, the 1945 article conveyed a sense of concern, even anxiety, with an ample dose of the ambivalence of all participant observation. The text is imbued with a mixture of fascination for and rejection of North American society, which was rather commonplace at the time, but with a content that was quite original. As in the horrified pages of *Tristes Tropiques* on South Asia, it shows the anthropologist fighting his own aversions (for the almighty imperative of social harmony, the generalized infantilization, the impossibility of solitude, etc.) and attempting to overcome them in a theoretical comparison with European societies. If his aversion here is less visceral than in the descriptions of Calcutta crowds, the text also reveals a subjectivity grappling with its own discomfort and which, in an effort to distance itself from a purely reactive (or simply condescending) form of anti-Americanism, tries to grasp as accurately as possible, through formulations that are sometimes spot on, some of the fundamental traits of North American society: the heterogeneity with itself of a society whose "skeletal structure ... is still external" ("alternately amazed and appalled, it discovers itself every day from the outside"); its repudiation of the tragic dimension through a "relentless" sociability; and the ideals of a "childhood without malice," an "adolescence without hatred" and a "humanity without rancor" – a denial of the contradictions of social life that sometimes culminates, through a kind of return of the repressed, in conflicts between communities of an inordinate violence (p. 98).[11]

Notwithstanding his repeated homages to the country that "very probably saved his life," and to its universities and libraries, his genuine and profound misgivings about the United States are palpable, which would be confirmed a few years later by his categorical refusal of offers from Talcott Parsons and Clyde Kluckhohn (with vigorous encouragement from Roman Jakobson) of a position at Harvard. "I knew in my bones that I belonged to the Old World, irrevocably."[12] As with the chapters of *Tristes Tropiques* on Pakistan and Islam – which, although written based on notes from 1950, mention only very fleetingly the massacres and massive population displacements that followed the partition of India – the contemporary reader of "Techniques for Happiness" may also be struck by the silences and blind spots typical of the times and to the position of the observer who, even though called upon to give witness on American society, wonders about the utter estrangement between "generations, sexes and classes" but barely mentions segregation and racial conflict.[13]

The present volume is thus intended to make available important yet often lesser known contributions, most of which were originally published in English in various journals, and many of which have become difficult to find.[14] In addition to their intrinsic interest, the seventeen articles Lévi-Strauss decided to omit in 1958 represent a kind of prehistory of structural anthropology; they allow us, through a process of cross-checking, to grasp better both the theoretical project and its meaning for Claude Lévi-Strauss, the person, in the mid-1950s.

New York, 1941–1947

But there's more. For the present volume is not made simply of residues, of "odds and ends," as Lévi-Strauss liked to say in English. Its coherence is not a negative one only. It is, first and foremost, shaped by a place and a time: New York in the years 1941 to 1947. The articles collected here were all written by Lévi-Strauss during his American, and we could even say New York, period, first as a Jewish refugee – a scholar in exile, saved by the rescue plan for European academics of the Rockefeller Foundation – and then as the cultural attaché of the French embassy. They were published between 1942 and 1949 – i.e. before *The Elementary Structures of Kinship*, whose publication marks a felicitous chronological milestone: it dates (superficially but conveniently) the beginning of structuralism, as well as for Lévi-Strauss himself the moment of definitive return to France and national reintegration through the dissertation ritual and the obtention of a research position at the French national research center (CNRS), even if, in both his personal and professional life, the late 1940s and early 1950s were a troubled period.

These seventeen articles thus reflect a biographical and historical turning point. They reveal the young anthropologist honing his skills and finding his way in American anthropology – a discipline that was older and more established than in France – as a South America specialist, and more specifically of the "lowlands," thus called to distinguish the region from the great Andean civilizations that had garnered most of the attention of researchers on South America until the 1930s. This volume includes five ethnographic articles, three of which are drawn from the major six-volume work *Handbook of South American Indians*, edited by Julian H. Steward (a publication that, as recently as 2001, and despite its shortcomings, Lévi-Strauss did not consider to have been made obsolete by more recent work).[15] These articles provide an ample rejoinder to the reproach, often made of Lévi-Strauss, that the philosopher by training had a "theoretical bias" and that his approach to native peoples was overly abstract and lacked empirical grounding.

In these articles of the 1940s, Lévi-Strauss appears, on the contrary, as a meticulous ethnographer, not at all a theoretician. Coming from philosophy, via sociology, he now wrote as an expert on the tribes of the Brazilian plateau, at a time when the discipline was focused mostly on questions of tribal identification, of mapping territory and describing practices, from a diffusionist perspective, or at least a perspective informed by the history of South American migration and settlement. Indeed, Lévi-Strauss appears very much as a typical anthropologist of his time: he has read all of the existing literature, but his fieldwork experience is limited (a few weeks with the Bororo and the Nambikwara, later recounted in *Tristes Tropiques*). Yet the tributes he paid to Bronisław Malinowski, and even more so to Curt Nimuendajú (chapters I and V) – both accomplished fieldworkers on whom he lavished praise – show that he laid great store by prolonged ethnographic work. Indeed, he sensed that such stays – long, solitary periods of "immersion" in the society under study – would become the norm in the discipline, rightly announcing that, "in the future, anthropological works will probably be classified as 'pre-Malinowskian' or 'post-Malinowskian,' according to the degree to which the author shall have committed himself personally" (p. 64). It remains the case, however, that Lévi-Strauss himself (who, by his own admission, considered himself to be "a library man, not a fieldworker")[16] earned his stripes as an ethnographer through a different and older model of fieldwork – i.e. group expeditions, focused primarily on information gathering, that spent only a few days with the populations – that is reflected in his contributions to the *Handbook*, which all conform to the same model. In these texts, as well as in his first article of 1936 on the Bororo Indians (which had drawn Robert Lowie's attention and led indirectly to his participation in the Rockefeller Foundation rescue operation), the intention is first and foremost descriptive, even when first-hand; it focuses on empirical data (material culture, technologies, life stages), and only very brief reflections on social organization or religious or magical forms. The articles' value lies in the informed distillations they offer of intermittent and heterogeneous sources, often separated by decades, if not centuries.

There is also a strong dimension of initiation in this work for the young French anthropologist, joining a group project in the discipline at a time when taking ethnographic censuses and inventories remained the chief concern of American anthropology, with a prevailing sense of urgency concerning populations threatened by demographic and cultural collapse. Julian H. Steward himself conceived of the *Handbook* as a form of applied anthropology designed to integrate traditional native communities into the new nation-states of the continent. These texts show the degree to which he had assimilated the dominant issues of American anthropology at the time; for that reason, the terminology is sometimes obsolete, especially in the use of the then common notion of "cultural level" and "level of culture," which referred to the degree of complexity of social organization and to the more or less rudimentary character of the material culture under study. Lévi-Strauss would later abandon these kinds of formulations because of the evolutionist connotations they retained, even among American anthropologists keen to steer clear of any evolutionism.

This experience of integration into a foreign disciplinary project had the effect above all of leading Lévi-Strauss – erstwhile professor of sociology at the University of São Paulo, sent to Brazil by the Durkheimian Célestin Bouglé – to take stock of the theoretical tradition from whence he came. Many of the articles in the present volume thus try to situate the French social science tradition, and to determine its particularity, in relation to other national traditions. There is no better example of this than the rigorous literature review "French Sociology" (chapter I), written at the request of Georges Gurvitch for a book that was first published in English under the title *Twentieth Century Sociology*. In this extended study, dedicated to Marcel Mauss, Lévi-Strauss presents the major lights of the discipline, as well as a few figures outside the mainstream, before proceeding to a detailed discussion of Durkheim's work, astutely demonstrating the ways in which it constantly vacillates between a "historical perspective" and a "functional perspective," between the search for primary facts devoid of explanatory value and a social theory that sets ends for itself but cuts itself off from empirical observation. This wavering, as Lévi-Strauss goes on to explain, is based on an implicit assumption of discontinuity between "the psychological and sociological perspectives," between the analysis of representations and that of institutions. It was to be Mauss's undertaking to resolve this dilemma by making symbolic activity not the result but a condition of social life, thus restoring continuity between individual consciousness, group representations and social organization. Lévi-Strauss then delves into his core argument – i.e. a response to the critique levelled at French sociology by the great American anthropologist Alfred Kroeber, who accused it of lacking methodological rigor and of being overly abstract and insufficiently attuned to the concrete realities of fieldwork. This recurring accusation on the part of American anthropologists since the 1920s and continuing to the present day – indeed, Lévi-Strauss himself would become one of its chief targets – clearly exercised the young anthropologist who was about to take up a diplomatic posting and to play a more active role in the "cultural influence" of a country that had not yet fully emerged from war (he was writing in late 1944 or very early 1945). Lévi-Strauss first concedes to Kroeber that the "philosophical ancestry" of the *Année Sociologique* group led its members to neglect fieldwork, but only so as better to point out that the resulting deficiency was about to be remedied: "The next generation of French sociologists, who reached maturity around 1930, has, over the last fifteen years, almost entirely – but no doubt temporarily – given up theoretical work in order to make up for this shortcoming" (p. 50). In support of this claim, he cites the recent ethnographic work of Marcel Griaule, Michel Leiris, Jacques Soustelle, Alfred Métraux, Roger Bastide, Georges Devereux and Denise Paulme, as well as his own.

Lévi-Strauss turns his attention above all to Kroeber's critique of Mauss, a critique which he considered full of "misunderstandings" but that "raised essential questions" and prompted him to mount a forceful theoretical clarification. Kroeber's argument is classic: he reproached Durkheim and Mauss for using categories, such as those of "suicide" and "gift," that were neither indigenous notions nor rigorous concepts on which to base a scientific argument. Lévi-Strauss replied that, unless one is prepared to give up on scientific study as a matter of principle, one had to begin somewhere, with what was given to observation. But he also made clear that these categories were not in any way the end point of the analysis and that, on the contrary, they gradually disappeared from the study. Indeed, they served only to access a deeper level of reality that could not be reached through simple observation but whose explanatory value was greater – the integration of the individual to the group in the case of suicide, the demand for reciprocity in the case of gifting. Against Kroeber, who denied to anthropology the status of a real science, and against American cultural anthropology more broadly, Lévi-Strauss thus reaffirmed the validity of Durkheimian methodological principles ("For our part, we remain convinced that social facts must be studied as things," he would still write in 1948 (p. 85) – it was the atomistic and mechanistic conception of these "things" that he found wanting in Durkheim), as well as the ambition, at once explanatory and universalist, of anthropology.[17] This article (as well as other articles from the period) also expresses for the first time one of Lévi-Strauss's deep concerns, namely the fear that the otherwise legitimate critique of nineteenth-century evolutionism might reduce anthropology to a mere compilation of monograph studies void of any comparative horizon or universal claim: "Are we condemned, like new Danaids, endlessly to fill the sieve-like basket of anthropological science, vainly pouring monograph after monograph, without ever being able to collect a substance with a richer and denser value?" (p. 117). In retrospect, this was to be the main benefit of his prolonged stay in the United States, which made him aware of the rut in which the discipline could get stuck: aimless accumulation. Thus, with an ambition, intelligence and capacity for hard work bordering on madness, he took it upon himself to pull anthropology out of this rut and to infuse it once again with the mission of achieving "a truth endowed with general validity" (p. 117).

There are two points to be made here. First, that many of these articles initially appear anecdotal but in fact represent occasions for more robust theoretical reflection; and, second, this reflection is itself directly linked to Lévi-Strauss's own condition of exile at the time he was writing them. At first glance, many of the pieces gathered here – historical overviews, reviews and tributes – appear not to be making any argument. However, even the tribute to Malinowski makes no secret of Lévi-Strauss's "serious doubts" with regard to the former's theoretical work, paving the way for "History and Anthropology" (the first chapter of *Structural Anthropology*). His critique of Malinowskian functionalism and its tautological character grew stronger over the years (see chapters I and V, in particular). The unexpected, and seemingly curious, rehabilitation of Edward Westermarck (chapter III) can be seen in a similar light. The Finnish sociologist's attempts to account for the prohibition of incest in his 1891 work *The History of Human Marriage* had indeed already been largely discredited, especially by Durkheim and, more broadly, by the critics of nineteenth-century British evolutionism. But in his obituary written in 1945, six years after Westermarck's death (the war accounting for the delay), Lévi-Strauss reviews the criticisms raised by the work only to highlight its merits (its theoretical ambition and erudition, its "insistence on a sociology that could furnish a comprehensive explanation," the link maintained between sociology and psychology, its "dissatisfaction with historical and local explanation") and, more importantly, to reformulate the question in a way that was to play a decisive role in his subsequent work: "At the root of the prohibition of incest lies neither the physiological link of kinship, nor the psychological link of proximity, but the fraternal or paternal link, in its exclusively institutional dimension" (p. 72). In other words, the moral rule that prohibits incest finds its source and explanation in an entirely social imperative – we are thus getting very close to the sensational reversal that later opened *The Elementary Structures of Kinship* and its reading of the incest taboo not as a prohibition but as an obligation to exogamy.

In the same way, technical or anecdotal pieces such as "On Dual Organization in South America" (chapter XIV) or "The Name of the Nambikwara" (chapter IV) provide occasions for theoretical clarification, whether on the historicity of forms of social organization (and the status of the historical hypothesis in anthropology) or on the question of the naming of native tribes, which is often a false problem threatening to engulf anthropology in sterile academic disputes. At first glance, the title of "Reciprocity and Hierarchy" (chapter IX) may appear somewhat misleading, but, beyond the detailed discussions of the terms used to designate the other moieties in Bororo communities, what is at stake is the persistent principle of reciprocity at the root of social life, even when relations of subordination would appear to prevail.

It is in the book reviews that Lévi-Strauss's dialogue with American anthropology is most vigorously pursued. The five reviews (chapter V) included here are all little known and yet of far-reaching significance (and continuing relevance, seventy years after they were first published). Written for *L'Année Sociologique* (a journal founded by Durkheim, whose publication had just resumed after the war), they all focus on works published in the United States – Lévi-Strauss acting as emissary for an American anthropological tradition that was still largely unknown in France. Two of the reviews had indeed already been published in English, but the French adaptations that Lévi-Strauss submitted were often less restrained than the original versions and provided him with an opportunity to launch more forceful attacks on what he saw as the dead ends being pursued by anglophone anthropology – be it functionalism and its "providentialist" tendencies or the American school about to claim the name "culture and personality," which outrageously simplified the relationship between individual psychology and culture and accorded far too much importance to native autobiographies.

In still more incisive fashion, he targeted the so-called "acculturation" studies that were beginning to develop in the United States, which focused on the transformation of native societies that were losing their former ways of life under the influence of a dominant modern civilization. Lévi-Strauss strongly disapproved of the ecumenical functionalist premise that led these groups threatened with demographic and cultural collapse to be considered as objects comparable to traditional societies, on the grounds that they were "functioning" communities. The tone is both pessimistic – Lévi Strauss draws a particularly grim picture of these degraded societies, which is not sparing of individuals – and accusatory – for the relationship of equivalence according to which "all human community is a sociological object, simply by virtue of the fact that it exists" (p. 89), which appears as epistemological tolerance and axiological neutrality, serves in fact to mask the violence of the confrontation; he sees in it an attempt on the part of a civilization to deny responsibility for having imposed on others paths that were not of their own choosing. We can see two forms of history emerging here: on the one hand, a history of borrowings and exchanges between societies and of their development under mutual influence; and, on the other, an external history of destruction, a tragic chronicle of the annihilation of ancient social forms by an exorbitant Western civilization. The first can constitute an object of scientific inquiry and is essential for the anthropologist; the second is a function only of the power imbalances at play and the hubris of a devastating modernity with respect to other cultures, as well as to a natural world it is irreparably defiling.

However, what is most important to understand is that this body of work was profoundly shaped by Lévi-Strauss's expatriation and the particularity of his New York experience during the war years and the years immediately afterwards.[18] Indeed, what all these texts have in common is that they were written either in exile or over the course of a diplomatic career, which, although brief and repeatedly minimized by Lévi-Strauss in subsequent interviews, was far from idle,[19] yet constantly subject to a dynamic of double-estrangement with regard to the intellectual traditions of both home and host country. These years were also ones of professionalization and, more generally, of a reconfiguring of Lévi-Strauss's intellectual and social identity – as well as of his private life, having separated from his first wife on the eve of World War II. This process was aided by his family connections in New York, which facilitated his integration and made it possible for him to circulate between different heterogeneous worlds,[20] as well as his extraordinary capacity for hard work, which enabled him to digest the entirety of the anthropological literature contained in the New York Public Library and to become proficient in the English language (with his local aunt's help) and so, very early on, to write his first articles in English.[21] In this respect, his experience of exile is entirely distinct from that of other, older intellectuals, such as Georges Gurvitch, not to mention André Breton, with whom Lévi-Strauss spent time in New York, and who made it a point of honour to speak only in French.[22] Enjoined, as it were, by his position as a foreigner, with an uncertain status and professional future (he had not yet defended his dissertation), Lévi-Strauss was forced to determine his own intellectual tradition and to hone his own ideas. And herein lies another reason for collecting these articles: not only as tribute to a singular individual experience and historical moment but also as testimony and lesson on the historical and sociological conditions of intellectual invention.

Tabula rasa

These texts of the 1940s, which Lévi-Strauss later chose to set aside, offer a window onto an emerging structuralism, a perspective that rejects seeing it as nothing more than an intellectual fad of the 1960s, as some facile and superficial accounts would have it. Structuralism can thus be viewed as a European movement that was born in the United States, in response to a crisis in functionalism and to the deadlock of American nominalism, which rejected the idea of comparing cultural entities on the grounds that each was irreducible and singular. The teachers and researchers of the École Libre des Hautes Études did not all become structuralists. Yet these exiled intellectuals, many of whom were Jewish, shared a common commitment to a comparative approach. The specifically structuralist project within this general orientation was thus to restore an epistemological status to intercultural comparison.[23] These articles also show that the genesis of structuralism was by no means a linear process. The birth of structural anthropology is too often presented as a kind of "accession," the crowning moment of a glorious sequence that begins with Lévi-Strauss's lack of peer recognition upon returning to France (he was twice rejected by the Collège de France, in 1949 and 1950, and *The Elementary Structures of Kinship* initially met with a lukewarm response), followed by the publication of *Tristes Tropiques* in 1955 and that of *Structural Anthropology* in 1958, and culminating finally in his election to the Collège de France in 1959. However, returning to these older texts helps us to understand that this sequence did not result from the intrinsic power of structuralist theory, ultimately prevailing over all obstacles and opposition. It was, instead, made possible by a work of reconstruction, selection and "repression," undertaken by Lévi-Strauss himself, in relation to certain aspects of his own thought. One essential dimension of his writing, in particular, was excised, namely any role for political commitment in anthropological reflection – a concern that was indeed to disappear entirely from the anthropologist's work from *Structural Anthropology* onward. This is perhaps the most original and striking aspect of the articles collected in this volume.

We now know that political activism played a major part in the life of the young Lévi-Strauss. A member of the French Section of the Workers' International (SFIO) at age eighteen, then secretary of the Groupe d'Études Socialistes from 1927, he founded the Révolution Constructive group in 1931, together with ten of his *agrégation* classmates, to give the party a new intellectual face. While serving as assistant to SFIO deputy Georges Monnet in 1930, he ran unsuccessfully for local office in the town of Mont-de-Marsan, to whose secondary school he had been appointed as a teacher in 1933. The image of Lévi-Strauss as a melancholy anthropologist withdrawn from the world and devoted to the study of vanished civilizations is thus a later construction. The work of intellectual history that, in the 1980s and 1990s, rediscovered the political commitments of his youth did not radically transform his public image. Lévi-Strauss himself dated the end of his political "career" to his unsuccessful electoral run, which he jokingly attributed to a car accident.[24] The Citroën he had bought for the campaign ended up in a ditch, which seemed in retrospect to have marked a turning point: indeed, only a few months later, Lévi-Strauss was sent to teach sociology in Brazil, where he would launch a career in anthropology that had no links with his earlier political ambitions. Yet a careful reading of his 1940s writings shows that, far from having given up on his "political illusions," well into his adulthood, Lévi-Strauss did not separate his scholarly work from his political thinking, in which he was already anticipating the post-war context, as confirmed by his activities in circles associated with the École Libre des Hautes Études as well as in international intellectual networks. His early return to France – the war was not yet over – and his subsequent appointment as cultural attaché show that he had been identified by the Gaullist political machine as a reliable man.

It is through a few incidental remarks that this political dimension is first revealed. For instance, the teleological bent he perceived in Durkheim paradoxically places the founder of sociology together with the reactionary Louis de Bonald. Hence the worried observation: "Obviously, any social order could take such a doctrine as a pretext for crushing individual thought and spontaneity" (p. 56). And yet: "All moral, social and intellectual progress has made its first appearance as a revolt of the individual against the group" (p. 56). This was yet another reason for rejecting Malinowski's functionalism, which indeed retained from Durkheim only the all-powerful group and thereby appeared as a "system of interpretation ... which makes it dangerously possible to justify any regime whatsoever" (p. 64). The critique is epistemological (functionalism leads to circular assertions), but the forcefulness of its tone is due to the potential political consequences of the challenged thesis. Conversely, Westermarck is rehabilitated for theoretical reasons, yet his analytical rigor "confers on his work a critical and politically engaged quality of which he was fully aware." "In his view, moral evolution had a meaning: it was going to bring humanity closer to an ideal of liberalism and rationalism, to free it from its errors and prejudices. ... He considered the relativist critique to be an instrument of spiritual emancipation" (p. 75).

More generally, the circumstances in which these texts were written reveal that they were often part of a collective process of political reflection. Indeed, "The Theory of Power in a Primitive Society" (chapter VIII), which was first published in English in 1944, was originally part of a series of "lectures" on "modern political doctrines" given at the École Libre des Hautes Études, which included presentations on human rights, on the various conceptions of the state, and on the political thought of Louis de Bonald and Charles Maurras. As the jurist Boris Mirkine-Guetzévitch pointed out in the foreword to the publication of these contributions, the series was originally intended as the continuation of another series, on the end of the French Third Republic and its supplantation by the Vichy regime, insisting on the urgent need for scholars from various disciplines to work together and to collaborate in confronting the problems of the day. In the same way, "The Foreign Policy of a Primitive Society" (chapter X) was initially published in the journal *Politique etrangère*, which, beginning in the 1930s, distinguished itself in condemning the delusions of the economic and international policies of Nazi Germany. Suspended in 1939, it had just started publishing again in 1949 when Lévi-Strauss contributed his article, which appeared alongside studies on "the refugee problem," "the United States, the USSR and the Chinese problem," and the position of a soon to be divided Germany. The originality of Lévi-Strauss's article does not lie in the description, already published elsewhere, of the exchanges between Nambikwara bands observed on the Brazilian plateau in August and September of 1938 (to be found in part seven of *Tristes Tropiques*). As the end of the article makes clear, the point was to take the Nambikwara's "foreign policy" as a model because this community "represents one of the most elementary forms of social life" and can thus serve as the basis for a more general reflection on the relations between foreign groups.[25] The ambition of this article – which, on the face of it, describes only the particular situation of the Amerindians of Mato Grosso – lies in a desire to contribute to the reconfiguration of international relations in a world devastated by a second world war and soon to enter into a cold one.

The article is thus filled with statements that spoke to the reader of 1949 in ways that are probably not as clear to us today. This is true of the final lines that condemn the naïve optimism of "our current preoccupations, which would have us think about human problems in terms of open societies, of ever more open societies." This is an allusion to Henri Bergson's reflections, taken up by Karl Popper in his 1945 work *The Open Society and its Enemies*, in which Lévi-Strauss detected the excesses of "Christian and democratic thought," which, by constantly expanding the "limits of the human group," failed to see the need to think of humanity as an ensemble of groups whose tendencies toward excessive aggression as well as collaboration needed to be regulated (p. 147). We should also take the measure, four years after the world became aware of the extermination camps, of the resonance of the following pronouncement: "There is always a point beyond which a man ceases to take part in the essential attributes of humanity ... Yet this denial of human status [in so-called primitive societies] only very rarely takes on an aggressive character. For if humanity is denied to certain groups, they are not comprised of men and, as a consequence, one does not behave in relation to them as one would with other human beings" (p. 145). This is the main argument of the article: the violence of one group toward another is itself a recognition of the possibility of partnership; sheer negation of the other manifests only as lack of interest and "strategies of avoidance." Aggressiveness between two groups must thus be thought of as "a function of another, antithetical, situation – i.e. cooperation" (p. 147). In other words, those who were our enemies yesterday were not so by nature, as a result of some primal aggression inherent in the constitution of any community; indeed, they may become our partners tomorrow, as part of a regulated regime of international cooperation. Against the search for universal principles (which would make war and cooperation "instincts" characteristic of all groups), the Nambikwara example shows us that war and trade are the manifestations of a single principle of exchange operating on a gradient between aggression and cooperation – confirming Mauss's thesis that the exchange of gifts precedes market exchanges. "Thus, what we are dealing with here is a continuum, an institutional chain, that runs from war to trade, from trade to marriage, and from marriage to the merger of social groups" (p. 142).

This was already the central proposition in "War and Trade among the Indians of South America": "conflict and economic exchange in South America represent not only two types of coexisting relations, but also two opposite and indissoluble dimensions of a single social process" (p. 115). The article, published in 1943 in *Renaissance*, the journal of the École Libre des Hautes Études, also reflects the urge to anticipate the post-war and to lay the foundations for future national and European political life – a concern shared by many French intellectuals exiled in New York.[26] What is most striking in retrospect is the optimism of these men, many of them young (Lévi-Strauss was not yet forty), who, in the midst of war but far removed from European horrors, were keen to "work in teams" to reinvent the post-war world. This was reflected in the very name of the journal *Renaissance* (itself founded in 1942), as well as in the promising titles of the many generalist periodicals that blossomed after 1945 taking "civilization" as their principal subject, such as *Chemins du Monde* and *L'Âge d'Or* (a journal launched by the publishing house Calmann-Lévy, which was as ambitious as it was short-lived, and to which Lévi-Strauss initially contributed "Techniques for Happiness"). In addition to offering a prehistory of the first two volumes of *Structural Anthropology*, "volume zero" should be understood in terms of the sense of *tabula rasa* that animated its author and the larger project – shared with many others – of civilizational renewal on fresh foundations.

The welfare state and international cooperation

Lévi-Strauss's political speculations in those years dealt essentially with two themes. First, the issue of the articulation of individuals and the group, which in liberal democracies needed to be rethought, maintaining an equal distance from both class and national affiliation – the former because it reflected the failures of the Soviet model and the latter because the recent past had shown it could find expression only in aggression and lead to war. A close reading of his articles of the time shows that, while he was not necessarily aware of it, Lévi-Strauss's analyses resonated with other contemporary publications in English, especially those developing the notions of "social citizenship" and the welfare state, with a view to maintaining the link between individual and community in mass democracies.[27] From the example of Nambikwara society, in which the chief's generosity is the essential instrument of his power, Lévi-Strauss retained that the group is linked to its chief (in himself devoid of any authority or power of coercion) by a relation of reciprocity that creates obligations for both, the "refusal to give" being analogous to the "confidence motion" presented by governments in parliamentary systems. Power is thus a matter not simply of consent (an affiliation with Rousseau that will be strongly reaffirmed in *Tristes Tropiques*) but of the consent of the group as a group (and not as a collection of individuals). Lévi-Strauss concluded in particular that "the interpretation of the State conceived as a security system, recently revived by discussions of a national insurance scheme (such as the Beveridge plan and others), is not a modern development. It is a return to the fundamental nature of social and political organization" (p. 130).[28] Even if they might appear quite distant, Lévi-Strauss's 1940s observations on the United States are not unrelated to these concerns. The title "Techniques for Happiness" – beyond its touch of European irony with regard to a society that seemed devoted entirely to the material and psychological satisfaction of the individual, itself considered as an adult child – also conveys a keen interest in the "social techniques" deployed to suppress conflict and create a "civilization in which both masses and elites find satisfaction." In the same way as the Nambikwara community, contemporary America represented an "original" and "fertile" sociological experiment, which Europeans "would do well to closely monitor" (p. 99).

The second focus of Lévi-Strauss's political reflections had to do not so much with the relationship of the individual to the group as with that of groups with one another. The two concerns are linked since – and, in this respect, the articles are artifacts of their times – they originate in a conviction, shared by many contemporary thinkers, that the nation-state model had become obsolete. Lévi-Strauss was thus determined to contribute to the reinvention of international relations, at a moment when the road to federalism seemed an inevitability, following the examples of the United States and the USSR, as well as Brazil and Mexico. Here, again, reciprocity appears as the first principle, even when it would seem belied by relations of subordination between the groups under consideration (p. 134). At the international level, this principle not only linked societies to one another via bilateral services but also each of them to the ensemble they formed together, for humanity was not an abstract reality whose unity could be ensured by principles but a "a set of concrete groups between which a constant balance must be found between competition and aggression, through pre-defined mechanisms for buffering the extreme forms that may arise in either direction" (p. 147).

When he wrote these lines, Lévi-Strauss was a cultural attaché, and it is very likely that they bear the mark of his exchanges with Henri Laugier (thanks to whom he had obtained that position), himself the Under Secretary-General of the brand-new United Nations, to whose founding he had contributed. In "The Foreign Policy of a Primitive Society," the ability of Amerindians to recognize rivers as "international waterways" and the strategies they developed to settle rivalries "in a no doubt hostile yet not overly dangerous manner" thus served as models. In the same vein, his description of the "industrial and commercial specializations" of the Xingu tribes is a discreet call for a form of international division of labor, facilitated by diplomats whose role would be similar to the multilingual mediators that were found in each of the villages. It is probably the Nambikwara conception of territory that offered the most fertile ground for contemporary political thought, since Amerindians entirely severed the notion of territory from that of land and thus paved the way for an immaterial definition of community whose unity was no longer determined by borders but by shared values: "For us, the Nambikwara territory covers a specific land area; it is a space bounded by borders. For them, this reality appears as different as the X-ray image of a body would from the image of that same body seen by the naked eye. Territory is nothing in and of itself; it is reduced to a set of modalities, to a system of situations and values that would appear meaningless to a foreigner and might well even go unnoticed" (pp. 143–4).

Rereading these texts of the 1940s, it is clear that the theory of exchange that would be mobilized in *The Elementary Structures of Kinship* – first for its heuristic value and ability to account for highly varied situations – had deep political resonance with very concrete implications. It also shows that, in Lévi-Strauss's eyes, the role of social science had little to do with the one it would eventually come to play in the heyday of structuralist theory, during which, against his will, his name was regularly invoked as a figure of authority in the most varied domains, and those furthest from anthropology. Nor was his position that of an intellectual in the Sartrean sense of the term: his reflections on the links between war and trade do not fit within that philosophical tradition that has had much to say on the question, from Machiavelli to Benjamin Constant, via Hobbes and Montesquieu. It is indeed as an expert that the anthropologist felt licenced to offer political commentary – i.e. because he was a specialist of the comparison between societies, and because his expertise was anchored in an experience of the Amerindians of the Brazilian plateau and not in the mastery of philosophical notions and traditions. Indeed, in his view, this is one of the distinctive features of French anthropology, characterized by a collaboration between sociology and anthropology, whereas in other countries the former – which "calls for people accepting the social order" – is opposed to the latter – as "a haven for individuals poorly integrated into their own surroundings" (p. 36). "Modern sociology was born for the purpose of rebuilding French society after the destruction wrought first by the French Revolution and later by the Prussian War. But, behind Comte and Durkheim, there are Diderot, Rousseau and Montaigne" (p. 36). It would therefore be a mistake to draw a distinction, among French social scientists, between anthropologists who took over social criticism (Montaigne, Rousseau) and sociologists who sought to inspire legislative and governmental decisions (Comte, Durkheim). The applied approach of the latter was never cut off from the fundamental approach of the former, and the articles of the 1940s seek to maintain the link between theoretical argumentation and political initiative. They represent a similar kind of recourse, after a period of troubles, to "social philosophy." In much the same way as Durkheimian philosophy had set out both to study the phenomenon of the social and to rebuild French society after the war of 1870, the Lévi-Strauss of the 1940s hoped to contribute (alongside others) to national and international political renewal in the aftermath of world war. And, here again, expertise was a matter of circumstance and position: that of an exiled Jewish scholar, himself situated between several worlds, just as the indigenous mediators whose praises he sang and who were able "to speak all the languages" of the Brazilian plateau (p. 142).

"National sovereignty is not a good in itself"

The essential question remains: why did this political dimension disappear from the writings of Lévi-Strauss after 1950? More to the point, when he selected the articles that were to form *Structural Anthropology*, why did he retain only those in which this aspect does not appear? And when he incorporated these reflections of the 1940s into other later works, especially *Tristes Tropiques*, why did he "edit" out the more political passages?

There is no simple, unequivocal answer to these questions. There is, of course, the contingent and quickly obsolete dimension of some of his references, but Lévi-Strauss's political reflections were general enough that they could have survived the narrow circumstances of their production. It is important to remember, as he himself often pointed out, that the early 1950s were a period of crisis for him – at the theoretical, personal and professional levels.[29] By his own account, his two consecutive failures at the Collège de France, in 1949 and 1950, were at the root of it: "After this double disaster, I was convinced that I would never have a real career. I broke with my past, rebuilt my private life."[30] To this series of ruptures must be added the sale at auction in 1951 of the collection of Amerindian art he had built in New York, a dispersion which must have been traumatic, not only because it represented a loss but also because, for Lévi-Strauss, "the passionate impulse to collect" was intimately linked to the construction of identity,[31] and this breaking up of the collection symbolized the fragmentation of the personal and psychological unity he had rebuilt in exile. "I live in a grave," he told Monique Roman, who was to become his third wife.[32] In any case, his texts of the 1950s convey a change of mood as well as of tone: the optimistic planning of the political articles of the 1940s (which may be interpreted as a vestige of the reformist Marxism of his younger years)[33] was no longer appropriate. At the end of his life, when he was asked about the disappearance of politics from his intellectual horizon, Lévi-Strauss agreed, upon his interviewer's insistence, to date it not from the early 1930s but from the war, conceding that he had taken part in a few Gaullist meetings in the early 1940s, yet always playing down his diplomatic work as a cultural attaché in New York from 1945 to 1947 and then his activities as a member of UNESCO's International Social Science Council, over which he presided from 1952 to 1961. No need to suspect him of bad faith – such a reconstruction shows, rather, how profound his change of course truly was, its self-evidence retrospectively shaping the past, especially for someone like Lévi-Strauss who frequently narrated his own life experience and whose autobiographical accounts eventually sedimented. In the early 2000s, in the margins of a letter he had written to his parents in September 1942 that declares his intention to write a book unrelated to anthropology which would hark back to his "former conversations with Arthur" (i.e. Arthur Wauters, the Belgian Marxist activist who had initiated him into politics) – a book intended to "clarify a number of ideas," made necessary in his view by the confusion that marred the political discussions of the time – Lévi-Strauss laconically scribbled: "No recollection."[34]

But whatever the date settled on for his break from politics, Lévi-Strauss's explanation remained the same. He consistently evoked his disillusionment following the realization that his political analyses always turned out to be inadequate and his predictions systematically belied by events. He did not have the political "nose" that enabled some to sense new social tendencies and allow their thinking to be shaped accordingly, permitting some scholars also to act sometimes as decision-makers and political players. Hence, at the very apex of his professional recognition and intellectual celebrity, he decidedly and even deliberately withdrew from the concerns of public life and the ideological battles of his day. An anthropologist specializing in vanished pre-Columbian civilizations, he was to dedicate himself to his teaching at the Collège de France and spend summers at his country refuge at Lignerolles, where he "binged on myths" and wrote the four volumes and two thousand pages of the *Mythologiques*, removed from the unrest of the 1960s. It was at this time that he sketched the features of what was to become his public persona from the 1980s until his death.

The hypothesis of a fundamental and belatedly discovered mismatch between his personal temperament and the demands of political action should not be entirely dismissed, but it cannot account for the early 1950s about-face. We should note, first of all, that the disillusionment occurred at a specific time and place, namely France of the Fourth Republic. The anthropologist who had dreamt of renewal and *tabula rasa* was back in his home country thirteen years after his first trip to Brazil in early 1935; in the intervening years he had been back only for short periods, spending a total of ten of the previous thirteen years abroad. During this period, his status and identity had undergone major changes: an ambassador of French thought in Brazil (a university professor while he was not yet thirty years old), then a young and rising anthropologist upon his return to France, he is drafted in 1939 and experiences the "disorderly retreat" of the French army over several months, "from one billet to another" and from "cattle-trucks" to "sheep-folds";[35] his Jewish identity, which he thought he could discount, was thrown back in his face by the law of October 13, 1940, and he became "potential fodder for the concentration camp,"[36] forced to flee into exile; having reached New York after a gruelling crossing, he gradually made his way in the world of American anthropology and forged local intellectual networks; he played an active role within the École Libre des Hautes Études and was appointed cultural attaché immediately after the war. But, upon his return, he found a country that did not want to see itself as having been defeated and that proved more interested in rewriting its history. Former institutional and intellectual divisions resurfaced (he experienced his own failures at the Collège de France as a victory of the "ancients" over the "moderns"), as did the same characters. It was the physical anthropologist Henri Vallois, a specialist in racial taxonomy appointed by the Vichy government in 1943 to replace Paul Rivet at the helm of the Musée de l'Homme, who was elected director of the institution in 1950, over Jacques Soustelle, a renowned anthropologist and a figure of Free France. As a result, Lévi-Strauss resigned from the position as assistant director of the museum which he had held since his return from the United States. This diffuse yet profound unease with regard to France is revealed in many passages of the early chapters of *Tristes Tropiques* – "confessions" he wrote over the course of a few months, in a state of "rage" and "irritation" that he would "never have dared publish if [he] had been competing for a university position."[37]

The narrow-mindedness condemned by Lévi-Strauss was perfectly illustrated in the French refusal to open the national community "on the basis of equal rights" to the "twenty five million Muslim citizens" from the colonies, a timorous isolationism that contrasted with the audacity of the United States a century earlier, when it opened its doors to mass immigration by poor and uneducated Europeans – a successful gamble "which saved America from remaining an insignificant province of the Anglo-Saxon world."[38] This comparison between the two national destinies figures in the very last chapter of *Tristes Tropiques*, written in early 1955, as the Union Française – the political organization of the French colonial empire from 1946 on – was falling apart and the Algerian war was just beginning. For Lévi-Strauss, this debacle was due to the hypocrisy of the system of representation within the Union Française, the so-called double college which, despite a theoretically egalitarian Constitution (since "indigenous" status had been abolished and all Union members had the status of citizens), established a highly unequal system of representation between metropolitan French and colonial populations. This is the only allusion in *Tristes Tropiques* to an issue that was both at the center of French current events and the essential dynamic of the international context at the time of its writing – i.e. decolonization – which has been singled out as conspicuously absent from Lévi-Strauss's anthropology. Thus, neither at the international nor at the national scale had the post-war period kept its promise of a new deal.

At the end of "The Theory of Power in a Primitive Society," Lévi-Strauss cited the very important memo of November 8, 1941, on the "new indigenous policy in French equatorial Africa" by Governor-General Félix Éboué, which he had read in English translation. In it, Éboué recommended a policy of gradual and realistic association which took existing social structures into account, respected traditions and relied on traditional leaders – and it was with regard to the latter point that Lévi-Strauss mentioned it. This memo was to serve as the starting point of the Brazzaville Conference (January 30 to February 8, 1944), which led to the creation of the Union Française. The latter was widely inspired, at least at the level of principle, by the federalist ideal that Lévi-Strauss supported, having seen nationalism as a scourge ever since his early socialist years. In February 1943, writing for a few interlocutors at the US State Department, he argued: "The disintegration of national sovereignty must start from within through a process of federalism, on the one hand, and the creation of economic bodies, on the other, that will undermine the differences between national groups."[39] But by the mid-1950s that ideal was already anachronistic. "Federalism" had become an accusation leveled by the nationalist right and the colonial camp, in particular against Pierre Mendès-France (whom Lévi-Strauss held in high esteem and with whom he met as he was writing *Tristes Tropiques*), and even against Jacques Soustelle, himself an anthropologist by training and a socialist in his youth, who had been appointed Governor General of Algeria in 1955. Independentist leaders, for their part, saw federalism as nothing but an empty catchword, as demonstrated by the hypocrisies of the Union Française – nothing but a way of surreptitiously perpetuating French rule. The principle of nationhood thus resurfaced everywhere, and Lévi-Strauss understood that he had to accept defeat in the face of what he later termed the "powerful engine" against which "no dominating state, not even a federating state, can stand up to for long." However, as he would immediately add, this was "nothing to celebrate" – "national sovereignty is not a good in itself; it all depends on what use is made of it."[40] In this respect, the early 1950s was indeed a moment of disillusionment for Lévi-Strauss, and, when he incorporated the text of "The Theory of Power" into *Tristes Tropiques*, he removed the reference to Félix Eboué and his comments on the necessity of dialogue between anthropologists and colonial administrators.

In his eyes, the history of the world was now determined, and in some sense overwhelmed, by the expansion of Western modernity. No force, no regulatory mechanism could oppose it any longer. "We have placed the colonized people" in a "tragic position": they are "forced to choose between ourselves or nothing."[41] This accounts for the absence of the colonial question from the work of Lévi-Strauss, since this return of the nation-state forced him to make a distinction between, on the one hand, "small traditional societies, protected by their own isolation from the ravages of civilization, with no other ambition than to live apart" from capitalist modernity and, on the other hand, peoples who wanted to "take part on an equal footing in international life and to become full members of industrial society, in relation to which they can only feel like latecomers."[42] The two do not belong to the same history or call for the same approach. In this respect, the turning point was probably "The Foreign Policy of a Primitive Society" (chapter X) which articulated for the first time the idea on which *Race and History* was to conclude in 1952, and which was to become the central thesis, albeit in a much more pessimistic mode, of *Race et Culture* – namely the relative incommensurability of cultures and the need to maintain differences between groups. Making the "notion of humanity ... coextensive with all human beings peopling the surface of the earth" was progress, but the foreign policy of the Nambikwara reminds us of the need for each group to continue to "think of itself as a group, in relation to and in opposition with other groups," for this balance is the only way out of the alternative between "total war," from which we had only just emerged in 1949, and "the utopian ideal of total peace" (p. 147).

The early 1950s was thus marked less by a withdrawal from politics as by a change of scale in thinking, as well as, it must be said, a rise in pessimism. For it was then that the "unilateral system" of Western civilization as a whole, and the fetishism of progress, became the targets of Lévi-Strauss's critique. It was also then that he began to apply the thermodynamic metaphor of entropy to global history, in the rich sense the term entropy had recently acquired from information sciences and cybernetic theory – i.e. the multiplication of exchanges between human groups flattens and equalizes an enclosed world – and condemns it to disorganization.[43] This did not prevent him from continuing for a few more years to act as an expert within the newly founded UNESCO, whose headquarters were in Paris, not far from the Musée de l'Homme. He was on the panel of scholars the organization formed in December of 1949 to reflect on what was to become UNESCO's first *Declaration on Race*;[44] in August 1950, he went on a four-month mission to India and Pakistan to investigate "the state of the teaching of the social sciences in Pakistan"; and, at the behest of Alfred Métraux – who directed a collection of publications entitled "Race and Racism" – he wrote *Race and History*, which was published in 1952, at the same time as he became head of the UNESCO International Social Science Council. As Wiktor Stoczkowski has noted (and as opposed to Lévi-Strauss's own later account), he was very actively involved, at least during the first few years, even if his interventions betrayed a certain scepticism regarding the principles governing the organization.[45] It was within this framework that his thinking on a "generalized humanism"[46] developed from his critique of traditional humanism, which was in his view poisoned from the start by the "self-love" that had led man to isolate himself from his environment and from the rest of the living world. It was then that he became convinced – sounding incongruous at the time and resonating with disturbing relevance today – that "these recognized rights of humanity as a species will encounter their natural limits in the rights of other species."[47]

The genocide of Amerindians and the destruction of European Jews

Yet this account of the 1950s turning point as a direct consequence of disillusionment remains unsatisfying; there is something too easy and too deliberate about it, which does not quite fit with Lévi-Strauss's intellectual personality. I would like to hazard another possible narrative, one which affords a decisive role to the South Asian experience. The ordeal of his stay in India and Pakistan in the fall of 1950, and the ways it resonated for him, caused an element to resurface that had been hitherto sidestepped in his anthropological thinking: the extermination of European Jewry.

As with other authors and scholars of the war generation, it is very difficult to tell exactly when Lévi-Strauss took the full measure of the Shoah or to gauge its effects on his intellectual life. But there is unquestionably a profound and palpable difference between the American 1940s and the moment of his return to Europe, between the relative optimism of the New York writings, despite the trials of exile, and the tragic prophecies on entropic humanity of the 1950s. A close reading of *Tristes Tropiques* reveals two things: first, events make sense for Lévi-Strauss only in retrospect, they never impart their true significance in the moment; and, second, this significance always comes from a serialization of an event with others, which, in retrospect, appear to him comparable. These are deeply ingrained features of his thought process, as well as characteristics of structural anthropology itself: "social science is no more founded on the basis of events than physics is founded on sense data," as he was to write in *Tristes Tropiques*.[48] It is through the process of contrasting isolated elements that their relevant traits can be determined. Whereas Lévi-Strauss probably discovered the reality of the Shoah in 1945, it was only the traumatizing experience of South Asia that made it painfully thinkable – and that made him realize, reluctantly, that the story was also to some extent his own, however much the assimilated Jewish scholar thought of himself as a "Frenchman of Jewish descent" rather than a "French Jew."[49]

Insufficient attention has been paid to the fact that *Tristes Tropiques*, beyond the opening declaration of hatred of traveling, begins with a description of an Atlantic crossing of "convicts" aboard the *Capitaine-Paul-Lemerle*, the "filthy, overcrowded boat" which transported several hundred refugees, Jewish for the most part, as well as persecuted artists and intellectuals, among them André Breton, Victor Serge, Anna Seghers and Wifredo Lam. What Lévi-Strauss retained from this experience was less the ill treatment by the gendarmes of those they regarded as riffraff than the unbearable lack of privacy and dehumanization of the passengers, packed as "human cargo" for four weeks onto a ship that had only two cabins. The dehumanization was further compounded by the reception given to this shipment of "livestock" by the officers in Fort-de-France, who were "suffering from a collective form of mental derangement" and saw the arrivals as "a cargo of scapegoats" intended to "relieve their feelings," to be insulted and then interned in a concentration camp on the southern part of the island.[50] Too busy at the time to analyze the event, Lévi-Strauss regained his anthropological perspective when he recalled these episodes, now seeing them as situations in which the very conditions of social life were suspended.

The first chapters of *Tristes Tropiques* (which for the reader are then eclipsed by the famous pages and photographs depicting the Amerindians of Brazil) thus present a series of "outbreaks of stupidity, hatred and credulousness which social groups secrete like pus when they begin to be short of space"[51] – a spectacle of arbitrary justice in Martinique, altercations with the Brazilian police in Bahia and with the American police in Puerto Rico, etc. The same images and often the same words – "swarming," "infection," "human cargo" – resurface in the pages on Calcutta and Delhi: dehumanization appears first and foremost as a consequence of a lack of space. The similarity between the experience of being "fodder for the concentration camp"[52] and that of South Asian cities then explicitly emerges in reference to the modern caravansaries of Calcutta – not in the moment, in Lévi-Strauss's travel notes, but retrospectively, in the sequencing of the past that he offered four years later in *Tristes Tropiques*: "As soon as the human cargo has got up and been dispatched to its devotions, during which it begs for the healing of its ulcers, cankers, scabs and running sores, the whole building is washed out by means of hoses so that the stalls are clean and fresh for the next batch of pilgrims. Nowhere, perhaps except in concentration camps, have human beings been so completely identified with butcher's meat."[53]

This memory conjures up another, of an inhumane company town south of Dacca, in which workers who had fled partition were guarded by armed policemen, squeezed into rows of "bare cement rooms, which can be swilled out," rooms that were reminiscent of "poultry yards specially adapted for the cramming of geese."[54] In both cases, housing is reduced to "mere points of connection with the communal sewer" and human life "to the pure exercise of the excretory functions"[55] – excretory functions the performance of which forced passengers on board the *Capitaine-Paul-Lemerle* to accept the indignity of "collective squatting," which seems to have been for Lévi-Strauss the most unbearable aspect of the crossing. There is something absurd about these various images and analogies. They reflect both the difficulty of grasping the unthinkable and a vague sense that this history concerns him very directly as a Jew, however assimilated. Lévi-Strauss does not mention it in his own account, but we know thanks to André Breton that, upon landing at Fort-de-France, he was greeted with anti-Semitic insults by the local gendarmes.[56] Without mentioning it directly in *Tristes Tropiques*, the anthropologist noted: "I knew that, slowly and gradually, experiences such as these were starting to ooze out like some insidious leakage from contemporary mankind, which had become saturated with its own numbers ..., as if its skin had been irritated by the friction of ever-greater material and intellectual exchange brought about by the improvement in communication."[57] Lévi-Strauss was here only rehearsing a common position of his time, according to which the demographic explosion of the human race was the most serious threat to a planet of limited resources.[58] But this led him to a singular position, namely his refusal to grant the Shoah any special status: the barbarity that Europe had experienced could unfortunately not be reduced to "the result of an aberration on the part of one nation, one doctrine, or one group of men. I see them rather as a premonitory sign of our moving into a finite world, such as southern Asia had to face a thousand or two thousand years ahead of us."[59] This is the way to make sense of the curious formulation of 1954, in which Lévi-Strauss states that, in 1941, he "had not suspected at the time [that the crossing aboard the *Capitaine-Paul-Lemerle* would be] so extraordinarily symbolic of the future."[60]

From the 1950s onward, Lévi-Strauss's anthropology thus seemed to be haunted by the memory and the mere possibility of the Shoah (which is, however, never named). There is another sign of this subterranean laboring: the curious emergence, in the 1954 article "Diogène couché," of the figure of Lazarus. In this long article, which is an aggressive response to the attacks of Roger Caillois on *Race and History* (so aggressive, indeed, that Lévi-Strauss always refused to have it republished), the anthropologist is compared to the New Testament figure who, in coming back to life, remains marked by his experience of death: back to civilization, the anthropologist "does not return the same as he was when he left." "The victim of a sort of chronic uprooting, he will remain psychologically mutilated, never again feeling at home anywhere. ... He does not circulate between savage and civilized countries; in whichever direction, he is always returning from the dead ... and, if he does manage to come back, after having reorganized the disjointed elements of his cultural tradition, he remains nonetheless one who is resurrected."[61] In the early 1950s, Lazarus was the most common allegory for referring to and thinking about the survivors returning from the camps. It is present notably in the works of Maurice Blanchot and Jean Cayrol, two authors whose intellectual worlds were quite different from that of Lévi-Strauss, which makes the coincidence all the more unsettling.[62] It was at this same time that Lévi-Strauss wrote *Tristes Tropiques*, which can be seen as subconsciously guided by the analogy between the fate of the surviving European Jews and that of the Amerindians crushed by Western modernity, both "fodder" – "concentration camp fodder" for one, "pathetic creatures caught in the toils of mechanized civilization" for the other,[63] both forced to reorganize the "disjointed limbs" of a cultural tradition in tatters. Shedding light on the principles that preside over such reorganizations will hence become the object of Lévi-Strauss's anthropological work.

It is hard not to see that moment as a turning point, but Lévi-Strauss did not in fact give up on politics; he gave up on his position as an expert in politics and on the ideal of an articulation between scholarly analysis and political prescription. As regards his personal trajectory, the early 1950s in a way repeated the crisis he had experienced upon returning from his Brazilian fieldwork in 1939. Indeed, the return to France from his second Brazilian expedition had been characterized, as is often the case with anthropologists, by an intense personal and intellectual crisis, which led to his separation from his first wife, Dina, and to abortive attempts at writing literature, all of which dealt with the question of vocation and individual accomplishment.[64] A few months later, his escape and exile to New York forced him to undertake the work of personal, professional and theoretical reconstruction.[65] The early 1950s again disrupted his life on every front, and the writing of *Tristes Tropiques*, which coincided with a reconfiguration of his personal life, undoubtedly played a therapeutic role, enabling him to emerge from that state while also laying the bases for a total form of structuralism, one which abandoned any inclination to law-making sociology. From then on, the work of Lévi-Strauss flowed in two veins: one, the search for intelligibility based on the remains of a catastrophic history (and, to his mind, the genocide of Amerindians was not essentially different from the destruction of European Jews)[66] – a search whose governing principle is described in *The Savage Mind* and whose result is the core of the *Mythologiques* volumes, which are based on myths and everything anthropological inquiry has been able to yield in terms of testimonies on ancient practices prior to the Conquest; and, two, sombre reflections on the human species as a whole in relation to its environment and to all living things, which were to form the core of *Race and Culture*, as well as of some of the articles in *The View from Afar* and certain passages of *The Story of Lynx*. In 1949, the anthropologist fancied himself a diplomat who "spoke all the languages" and could contribute to cooperation between societies. Now, with a human species "full of itself" and doomed by its own excesses, he saw himself as an agent working on behalf of non-humans, faithful to the "lessons" he had learned from the small communities he studied, which never considered mankind as "the lord and master of Creation, free to accord itself an exorbitant privilege over all the manifestations of nature and life."[67]

The texts collected in the present volume were written before this bifurcation; they speak to a time when Lévi-Strauss still conceived of history as a force whose course could be influenced. He would subsequently come to abandon this idea, turning instead to a logical order that was to be found against history, at least against the history that was playing out at the global level, conceived as the theatre of confrontation on which the imbalance of forces was such that it led to the annihilation of the communities involved, scattering symbolic forms that could then only be collected in fragments.

This is the ultimate sense of the "zero" that was so essential to the genesis of structuralism: Roman Jakobson's "phoneme zero" and Roland Barthes's "writing degree zero," each of which referred to specific things of course. For Lévi-Strauss, the zero signifier represented the enabling condition for any comparison between distinct symbolic entities. But the term also seemed apt in that it subsumes fundamentally contradictory historical connotations, which suggest renewal and rebirth, of course, but also unthinkable horror, whether we think of Rossellini's *Germany, Year Zero*, Blanchot's man "at point zero,"[68] or Cayrol's man "in the zero state" – not only the promise of *tabula rasa*, for which Lévi-Strauss yearned at the end of the war, but also and at the same time a sense of foreboding for which the impending ecological catastrophe only provides terrifying confirmation: the tragic awareness that civilization carries within itself its own destruction.

History and Method

I

French Sociology

> *To Marcel Mauss, in the constant remembrance of his seventieth birthday spent under a double oppression.*[1]

French sociology was born early, and still suffers from the gap which existed, at the time of its birth, between the boldness of its theoretical intuitions and the lack, or insufficiency, of concrete data. Sociology – both word and thing – was created by Auguste Comte; he conceived it not only as a new science but as the supreme human science, intended to encompass and to crown the work of all other disciplines. Unfortunately, at that time, they did not have much to offer, and Comte's sociology remained suspended between its overarching ambitions and the frailty of its positive basis. To some extent, this difficult situation continued into the first part of the twentieth century. That it has been largely overcome may be seen from the recent renewal of interest in the aims and methods of French sociology exhibited everywhere in the world, especially among English-speaking scholars. While Malinowski's tumultuous support appears, we believe, rather dubious, Radcliffe-Brown's faithfulness is more significant: from the fact that *The Andaman Islanders* starts with a quotation from Henri Hubert's preface to the *Manuel d'histoire des religions* by Chantepie de la Saussaye, to his 1935 paper "On the Concept of Function in Social Science,"[2] he consistently acknowledged the paramount contribution of Durkheim and his companions to the methodology of the social sciences. The strong interest in Durkheim awakened among young American sociologists and anthropologists as a result of Radcliffe-Brown's stay at the University of Chicago is well known.[3] One of its many consequences was the translation of *The Rules of Sociological Method*,[4] forty years after its first publication. It is only fair to say that men such as Redfield did not wait that long to express their keen interest. In the latter's last book, Durkheim is once more referred to as one of his main inspirations.[5] The interest in Durkheim and the Durkheimian school has not subsided in recent years; quite the contrary. It will be enough to mention Lowie's[6] and Parsons's[7] attentive commentaries and the recent publication of articles[8] and even of a book[9] on the subject. Although the main contributions of the French school appeared during the first quarter of the twentieth century – and even during the final years of the [eighteen] nineties – they definitely do not belong to the past.

The main reason for this renewed interest will be made clear later in this chapter. It is due essentially to the fact that French sociology foresaw long ago that sociology is a science of the same type as the other sciences, and that its ultimate end lies in the discovery of general relations between phenomena. But there is another reason which – although less important – should be pointed out from the beginning. In other countries, especially Great Britain and the United States, sociology has long suffered from the existence of bulkheads between it and anthropology. Such outstanding examples as Linton, Redfield and Warner show that this is no longer true; but the fact itself, as well as its inconveniences, was pointed out as recently as a few years ago by A. L. Kroeber: "The persistence with which these two theoretically allied disciplines, born nearly at the same time in western Europe, have in general kept separate from each other, is in itself an interesting problem in cultural history. It suggests that they spring from different sets of impulses and aim at different ends."[10] As Kroeber also shows, this was never the case with French sociology. Should these "different sets of impulses" be seen as referring to the fact that sociology, considered as a technique at the disposal of the group to consolidate its strength and facilitate its functioning, calls for an acceptance of the social order, while anthropology has often provided a haven for individuals poorly integrated into their own surroundings? This may well be. And, if so, we can easily identify the source of the problem raised by the French case. In France, from Montaigne on, social philosophy was nearly always linked to social criticism. The gathering of social data was undertaken to provide arguments against the social order. It is true that modern sociology was born for the purpose of rebuilding French society after the destruction wrought first by the French Revolution and later by the Prussian War. But, behind Comte and Durkheim, there are Diderot, Rousseau and Montaigne. In France, sociology remains the offspring of these first attempts at anthropological thinking.[11]

Some other distinctive characteristics of French sociology should be made clear in order to avoid misunderstandings. French sociology does not consider itself as an isolated discipline, working in its own specific field, but rather as a method, or as a particular attitude toward human phenomena. Therefore, one does not need to be a sociologist in order to do sociology. Many types of studies which, elsewhere, would be referred to as sociology are, in France, successfully conducted under the auspices of other disciplines. This is especially the case for the French school of "human geography" whose members, although trained only as geographers, have nevertheless produced outstanding sociological work, usually monographs dedicated to the human as well as to the ecological aspects of a region or a country. Examples of works by geographers that are deeply impregnated with a sociological spirit, and which can be said to be, in a way, truly sociological, include Jules Sion, *Les Paysans de la Normandie Orientale* (Paris, 1909); Robert Dion, *Essai sur la formation du paysage rural français* (Tours, 1934); Pierre Gourou, *Esquisse d'une étude de l'habitation annamite* and *Les Paysans du Delta Tonkinds* (Paris, 1936). The same tendency is even more marked among geographers of the younger generation: Pierre Monbeig, Jean Gottmann, and others.

This universalism of French sociology has enabled it to contribute to the renewal of several human sciences. More will be said later in this chapter about Simiand's contribution to economics. But even seemingly far-removed disciplines have benefited from the sociological impulse: first of all, linguistics, whose modern European masters Ferdinand de Saussure (*Cours de linguistique générale*, 1916) and Antoine Meillet (*Introduction à l'étude comparative des langues indo-européennes*, Paris, 1903; *La méthode comparative en linguistique historique*, Oslo, 1925; and *Linguistique historique et linguistique générale*, Paris, 2 vols, 1921–36) have repeatedly expressed their agreement with, and their indebtedness to, Durkheim's teaching.

There is, hence, an occasional smugness on the part of French sociology, which has not gone unnoticed by the representatives of the other social sciences, provoking some irritation among them. Because French sociology was able to grasp early on the full breadth of its theoretical scope[12] – long before becoming able to realize it – it was unavoidable that other disciplines, from the starting point of their own methods, would meet it halfway. This process of coming together would have been salutary for everybody (and in many cases it actually was) if, from time to time, sociologists had not assumed the attitude of an overbearing mother witnessing the first steps of her young children and offering them helpful advice. This was not always welcomed by the hard-working practitioners of the other branches who were fully aware of achieving something of their own. Their impatience was sometimes expressed bitterly, for instance, in the case of historians and geographers, in the brilliant but somewhat confused book by Lucien Febvre and Lionel Bataillon, *La Terre et l'évolution humaine* (Paris, 1922);[13] in the more recent discussions between Maurice Halbwachs, a disciple of Durkheim, and Albert Demangeon, simultaneously a great sociologist and a great geographer, although averse to the occasional imperialism of the Durkheim school;[14] and in Marc Bloch's criticism of Simiand's work, which did not prevent the former from producing, in the field of history, outstanding work of a truly sociological character.[15]

In two cases at least – besides that of the linguists – the cooperation and mutual indebtedness was unreservedly embraced by both sides. The first is Henri Hubert, who worked simultaneously in sociology of religion (in cooperation with Mauss) and in history and archaeology with his two books *Le Celtes et l'expansion celtique jusqu'à l'époque de la Tène* and *Les Celtes depuis l'époque de la Tène et la civilisation celtique* (Paris, 1932).[16] The second is Marcel Granet, the head of French sinological studies, whose books are a direct emanation of the Durkheimian school.[17] The adventurous character of his most recent reconstructions[18] should not cause us to forget his illuminating earlier contributions to the study of Chinese social structure. Thus, not only linguistics and geography but also European archaeology and early Chinese history have been fecundated by sociological influence. This influence was so broad that it extended even to the "avant-garde" in art and literature. In the years immediately preceding World War II, the Collège de Sociologie, directed by Roger Caillois, became a meeting place for sociologists, on the one hand, and surrealist painters and poets, on the other. The experiment was a success. This close connection between sociology and every tendency or current having Man, or the study of Man, as its center, is one of the more significant traits of the French school.[19]

It is in this light that the contribution of French sociology to psychology, ethnology, law and economics should be understood. Without dissociating itself from these pre-existing disciplines, sociology has defined a specific approach in each of them. It does not pay great heed to who is carrying out this approach, whether independent scholars or sociologists stricto sensu. As a result, it is somewhat difficult, in a summary account, to disentangle what belongs to sociology proper from the contribution of the other branches. The reader interested in a more complete study will find some guidance in Célestin Bouglé's useful little book *Bilan de la sociologie française contemporaine* (Paris, 1935) and in Georges Davy's work *Sociologues d'hier et d'aujourd'hui* (Paris, 1931).[20]

If there was no place for psychology in Comte's system, Durkheim and Mauss, on the contrary, have constantly insisted on the psychic nature of social phenomena. This was apparent as early as 1898, in Durkheim's article in the *Revue de métaphysique et de morale*, "Représentations individuelles et représentations collectives." This difference comes from the fact that Durkheim perceived the possibility of a new psychology, objective and experimental, permitting the reconciliation of the two aspects of social facts, at the same time "things" and "representations." As was shown by Charles Blondel (*Introduction à la psychologie collective*, Paris, 1928), Comte's opposition was directed less against psychology itself than against the introspective and metaphysical psychology of his time. But Durkheim was not satisfied with stressing the mental side of social processes.[21] He gradually reached the conclusion that they belonged to the realm of ideals and consisted essentially in values.[22]

If Durkheim considers sociology as a kind of psychology, it is, however, a psychology of a special nature, irreducible to individual psychology. This is the meaning of his rejection of Tarde,[23] who contended that all social phenomena can be explained through individual psychological processes – i.e. imitation and innovation. Although Durkheim's criticism of Tarde in *Suicide* (Paris, 1897) is devastating, it will probably appear, in light of the reconciliation, closer every day, between sociology and psychology, that Tarde held at least some clues to the problem, and it would be interesting to proceed to a reappraisal of his almost forgotten work in light of modern ideas on the diffusion of cultures. As pointed out by Blondel (in *Introduction à la psychologie collective*), the opposition between Durkheim and Tarde was not as great as both of them thought.

In recent years, psychology (with psychoanalysis, Gestalt and the study of conditioned reflexes) has contributed more to sociology than it has received from it. In France, however, the opposite trend predominated. While Daniel Essertier was trying to combine the results of Bergsonian psychology and sociology (*Les Formes inférieures de l'explication*; *Psychologie et sociologie*, both published in 1927; *La Sociologie*, 1930), a sociologist such as Halbwachs and a psychologist such as Blondel did not hesitate to reconsider psychological problems in light of sociological data.[24]

The clash occurred on the ground which Durkheim had himself chosen: the problem of suicide. Against Albert Bayet (*Le Suicide et la morale*, Paris, 1923) and Maurice Halbwachs (*Les Causes du suicide*, Paris, 1930) who were following Durkheim's path and extending his analysis to the field of the history of morals and social motivation, respectively, psychiatrists such as François Achille-Delmas and Maurice de Fleury claimed for suicide a strictly psychological and individualistic explanation. It is significant that the synthesis was undertaken by a sociologically minded psychologist, Blondel, in his book *Le Suicide* (1933).

We already know that, in France, sociology and anthropology work together. This cooperation finds an organic expression in the Institut d'Ethnologie de Université de Paris, jointly directed – until 1938 – by Marcel Mauss, Lucien Lévy-Bruhl, and Dr. Paul Rivet, the last also curator of the Musée de l'Homme (Anthropology Museum). The same cooperative spirit inspires the teaching – directed towards more practical ends – of the École Coloniale.[25] Several tendencies should be distinguished, however.

There are first the freelance writers, belonging to a tradition anterior to the constitution of the Durkheim school, and who preferred to follow an independent line rather than rally to the new orthodoxy. Among these, only Emile Nourry (Saintyves) deserves mention here, as his work, strictly folkloric in character, can be linked, if indirectly, to sociology. The case of Arnold van Gennep is different: also a folklorist,[26] he published several books with a wider scope. The best known are *Tabou et totémisme à Madagascar* (1904); *Les Rites de passage* (1909); *Religions, moeurs et légendes* (1908–12); and *L'état actuel du problème totémique* (1920). The work of René Maunier, a jurist interested mainly in North African law and customs, was closer to the Rivet–Mauss group. He is the editor of the *Études de sociologie et d'ethnologie juridique* (since 1931) and his published works include general treatises – *Essai sur les groupements sociaux* (1929); *Introduction au folklore juridique* (1938) and *Sociologie coloniale* (2 vols, 1932–6) – as well as monographs: *La Construction collective de la maison en Kabylie* (1926); "Recherches sur les échanges rituels en Afrique du Nord," *L'Année Sociologique*, 2 (1927); and *Mélanges de sociologie nord-africaine* (1930). His is a challenging and highly original mind. Another figure closely associated with the Durkheim school was Lévy-Bruhl, one of the directors of the Institut d'Ethnologie, although both sides have expressed their theoretical disagreements.[27] His first books on Jacobi and Comte still belong to the field of philosophy. The shift in interest took place with *La Morale et la science des moeurs* (1903), in which he tried to lay out the foundation for an inductive study of morals. From 1910 onward (with *Les Fonctions mentales dans les sociétés inférieures*), he dedicated himself to the description and analysis of the primitive mind: *La Mentalité primitive* (1922); *L'Âme primitive* (1927); *Le Surnaturel et la nature dans la mentalité primitive*

(1931); *La Mythologie primitive* (1935); *L'Expérience mystique et les symboles chez les primitifs* (1938). His work, the significance of which will be analyzed later in this chapter, was received by many as a challenge. While Georges Gurvitch (*Morale théorique et science des moeurs*, 1937) claimed for moral values the same experimental reality as belongs to customs and rules, Paul Rivet and Raoul Allier asserted that the distinctive features of the primitive mind, according to Lévy-Bruhl, can be found also among the civilized. On the other hand, Olivier Leroy (*Essai d'introduction critique à l'étude de l'économie primitive*, 1925) emphasized the positive side in the primitive mind.

In the work of Durkheim and Mauss, sociology and anthropology cannot be separated. The connection is particularly obvious in Durkheim's article "La prohibition de l'inceste," published in the *Année sociologique*'s first volume, and in his books *De la division du travail social* (1893; first American translation by G. S. Simpson, New York, 1933) and *Les Formes élémentaires de la vie religieuse* (1912; first English translation, London, 1915). In collaboration, Durkheim and Mauss published a pioneering essay, "De quelques formes primitives de classification" (*L'Année sociologique*, vol. 6, 1901–2) which, although suffering from oversimplification, makes one regret that others did not follow in the same direction. With Mauss, the anthropological influence becomes predominant. His first publications, in collaboration with Henri Hubert, are dedicated to problems in religious sociology ("Essai sur le sacrifice," *L'Année sociologique*, vol. 2, 1897–8; "Esquisse d'une théorie générale de la magie," ibid., vol. 7, 1902–3; *Mélanges d'histoire des religions*, 1909). Three essays by Mauss have exerted an outstanding influence both on his contemporaries and on sociologists of the younger generation, and they may well be considered as the gems of French socio-anthropological thinking. These are "Les Variations saisonnières dans les sociétés eskimo" (*L'Année sociologique*, vol. 9, 1904–5); "Essai sur le don, forme archaïque de l'échange," ibid., vol. 1, 1923–4); and "Une catégorie de l'esprit humain: la notion de personne celle de 'moi'" (Huxley Memorial Lecture, *Journal of the Royal Anthropological Institute*, 68, 1938). A jurist, Paul-Louis Huvelin, has also contributed to the problem of magic with "La Magie et le droit individuel" (*L'Année sociologique*, vol. 10, 1906) and "Les Tablettes magiques et le droit romain," in *Études d'histoire du droit commercial romain* (ed. Lévy Bruhl, 1929). Mauss's influence extends to theorists as well as to fieldworkers. Among the first, Georges Gurvitch's "La Magie et le droit" (in *Essais de sociologie*, 1938), Roger Bastide's *Elements de sociologie religieuse* (1935) and – in a slightly different field – Roger Caillois's essays on myth and the sacred (*Le Mythe et l'homme*, 1938;

L'Homme et le sacré, 1939) may be cited. Among the second, mention should be made of Alfred Métraux, *La Religion des Tupinamba* (1928); Maurice Leenhardt, *Notes d'ethnologie néo-calédonnienne* (1930) and *Documents néo-calédoniens* (1932); and Marcel Griaule, *Masques dogons* and *Jeux dogons* (1938).

Although Durkheim and Mauss have always proclaimed their diffidence with respect to cultural history, they have inspired historians of civilizations, especially as regards the history of ideas. To Granet's work on Chinese thought and culture, already mentioned, Pierre-Maxime Schuhl's *Essai sur la formation de la pensée grecque* (1934) may be added. In another field, there are the learned but simplistic works of Georges-Henri Luquet: *L'Art néo-calédonien* (1926); *L'Art et la religion des hommes fossiles* (1926); and *L'Art primitif* (1930). Beyond primitive art, sociological inspiration also extended to general aesthetics, for instance in Charles Lalo's books *L'Art et la vie sociale* (1921) and *L'Expression de la vie dans l'art* (1933).

Durkheim was convinced that the anthropological analysis of social phenomena could and should lead to an explanatory synthesis showing how modern forms have grown out of simpler ones. He laid out the methodological principles, of both analysis and synthesis, in his seminal book *Les Régles de la méthode sociologique* (1894; first English translation, 1938). His other early book, *De la division du travail social* (1893), was, in his mind, a first sample of this synthetic reconstruction; it is also – and perhaps for this very reason – his weakest work. Some of his disciples have chosen to follow in the same direction: see Georges Davy, *La Foi jurée* (1922) and Davy and Alexandre Moret, *Des clans aux empires* (1923). In this respect, Mauss has shown more caution: see *La Civilisation: le mot, l'idée* (published by the Centre International de Synthèse, no. 2, 1930).

Finally, Durkheim's synthesis was to be realized in moral conclusions. This aspect of his thought may be found in several books and articles: *Education et sociologie* (1922); *L'Education morale* (1925); "La Détermination du fait moral" (*Bulletin*, Société Française de Philosophie, 1906, repr. in *Sociologie et philosophie*, 1924); "Introduction à la morale" (*Revue philosophique*, 1920); "La Morale professionnelle" (posthumously published in *Revue de métaphysique et de morale*, 1937). Durkheim's morals have been discussed by Gurvitch: "La Morale de Durkheim" (in *Essais de sociologie*, 1938).[28]

Sociology of law was given special attention by Durkheim and his followers. In "Deux lois de l'évolution pénale" (*L'Année sociologique*, vol. 4), Durkheim suggested an approach which was to be followed by two of his disciples: Paul Fauconnet, with *La Responsabilité* (1920), dedicated to a study of the evolution of the notion of responsibility from its early objective forms to its modern individualization; and Georges Davy, with *La Foi jurée* (1922), in which he tried to discover in the potlatch the origins of contract law. In another direction, Albert Bayet (*La Science des faits moraux*, 1935; *La Morale des Gaulois*, 1930) emphasized the conflicts and overlaps between codified law and the non-crystallized morals of the group. In a similar way, Jean Ray (*Essai sur la structure logique du Code civil français*) showed that written law was not the work of abstract reason but the concrete translation of the group's life and needs. In *Le Droit, l'idéalisme et l'expérience* (1922), Davy offered a discussion of the relations between sociology and modern juridical thinking. To the progress of the latter, a highly original mind, Emmanuel Lévy, made a fruitful contribution with his sociological interpretation of such juridical notions as credit and contract: *L'Affirmation du droit collectif* (1903); *Le Fondement du droit* (1929); and *La Vision socialiste du droit* (1926).

However, the main contribution to the sociology of law was that of Georges Gurvitch, both the editor of the *Archives de philosophie de droit et de sociologie juridique* and the author of many books in which he analyzed and followed the historical development of the idea of social rights: *L'Idée du droit social* (1932); *Le Temps présent et l'Idée du droit social* (1932); *L'Expérience juridique* (1936); *Sociology of Law* (New York: Philosophical Library, 1942); and *La Déclaration des droits sociaux* (1944).

In the field of economic sociology, the outstanding figure is François Simiand. He fought against the conception of economics as an abstract, rational science and showed that it cannot be isolated from other disciplines devoted to the study of man, particularly sociology and history.[29] With modern society as its field, the approach of this truly great mind was not unlike Mauss's analysis of primitive groups. In his early book *La Méthode positive en science économique* (1912), Simiand offered a thorough criticism of deductive economics and pointed out the fallacy of the notion of homo economicus. His mimeographed lectures at the Conservatoire National des Arts et Métiers (*Cours d'économie politique ... professé en 1928–29 et 1930–31*, 3 vols) introduce a basic classification: he made a distinction, in economics, between "species" (industry, agriculture, trade ...), "regimes" (cooperation, artisanry ...) and "forms" (concentration, dispersion ...). On this basis, the problems of economics are presented in an entirely new light. In two books published at a twenty-five-year interval, *Le Salaire des ouvriers des mines de charbon en France* (1907) and *Le Salaire, l'évolution sociale et la monnaie* (8 vols, 1932), he developed an interpretation of economic change which was given the name "social monetarism": he put the emphasis on group will, showing how capitalists and workers try to maintain their standard of life and how, accordingly, the general movement of prices depends upon the volume of money. Finally, all fluctuations are linked to variations in gold production. This is made more precise and developed further in *Recherches sur le mouvement générale des prix* (1932) and *Les Fluctuations économiques à longue période et la crise mondiale* (1932). Historians[30] have ironically pointed out what they called sociology's acceptance of the most contingent type of explanation. But, behind gold production, there is the social group and the entire Western culture. Thus, like Mauss, Simiand seeks the explanation in "total facts," not in historical accidents.

An important part of Halbwachs's work can be considered as straddling economics and social morphology. By the latter, Durkheim meant the study of a group's concrete basis (geographic, demographic and structural). This notion was developed by Halbwachs in his book *Morphologie sociale* (1938), a useful summary of what has been done in this direction in other countries. Bouglé's *Essai sur le régime des castes* (1908) was a first effort in social morphology, while Gurvitch tried to discover the basis of a qualitative morphology in "Les Formes de la sociabilité" (in *Essais de sociologie*). In two books, *La Classe ouvrière et les niveaux de vie* (1913) and *L'Evolution des besoins dans les classes ouvrières* (1933), Halbwachs offered a sociological method to determine what a social class is, using wider criteria than those of the economist. Here, too, we find an attempt at reaching "total facts," in the manner shown by Mauss in his early essay in social morphology: "Les Variations saisonnières dans les sociétés eskimo."

From the above summary of the main trends in French sociology, it may be seen that the approach established by Durkheim and Mauss still exerts a considerable influence at the present time. Therefore, an appraisal of French sociology cannot be made without a closer analysis of their principles and methods. The second part of this article is devoted to this task.

II

All that comprises the greatness and the weakness of Durkheim's work can be found in *The Elementary Forms of Religious Life*. First, the fundamental principle of his method, which is, at the same time, the fundamental principle of all sociological method: "When a law has been proved by a single well-made experiment, this proof is universally valid."[31] All the pitfalls of the comparative method are thereby eliminated. But there are also the contradictions:

> However simple the system I have studied may be, I have nonetheless found within it all the great ideas and all the principal forms of ritual conduct on which even the most advanced religions are based: the distinction between sacred and profane things, the ideas of soul, spirit, mythical personality, national and even international divinity; a negative cult with the ascetic practices that are its extreme form; rites of sacrifice and communion; mimetic, commemorative and piacular rites. Nothing essential is absent.[32]

Henceforth, precisely, this religion (i.e. the Australian one) may be a simple religion; it is not an elementary one. This may be inferred from the opening sentence of *The Elementary Forms*: "I propose in this book to study the simplest and most primitive religion that is known at present ... found in societies the simplicity of whose organization is nowhere exceeded," a religion which may be explained "without the introduction of any element from a predecessor religion."[33] Obviously we find here a confusion between historical and logical points of view, between the quest for origins and the discovery of functions. If, as Durkheim himself says, in a somewhat ambiguous way, every religion, while being "a species of delirium,"[34] cannot be "pure illusion"[35] – if, although the objects of religious thought are "imaginary,"[36] "no human institution can rest upon error and falsehood"[37] – then the direct study and analysis of any religion should suffice to bring forth its explanation – i.e. the function it fulfills in the society in which it is found. If, on the other hand, the study of "anterior" forms is called for, it can only be because the considered phenomenon can no longer be explained on a functional basis, a point which Durkheim – although called by Malinowski the father of functionalism – could well have accepted: "a fact can exist without serving any purpose, either because it has never been used to further any vital goal or because, having once been of use, it has lost all utility but continues to exist merely through force of custom. There are even more instances of such survivals in society than in the human organism."[38]

If this were true, the historical method should be predominant in sociology: "all societies are born of other societies."[39] However, it is an entirely different principle of explanation which Durkheim ultimately accepts: "The primary origin of social processes of any importance must be sought in the constitution of the inner social environment."[40] This oscillation between what would today be called functional and historical approaches is particularly striking in Durkheim's important article "La Prohibition de l'inceste," in which anthropologists may find a remarkably clear interpretation of the genesis of the Australian eight-class systems through the cross-cutting of a matrilineal dichotomy based on filiation and a patrilineal fourfold division based on residence.[41] From a sociological point of view, however, the general thesis is less satisfactory. It is well known that Durkheim, while formulating a devastating criticism of the theory which was later to become Malinowski's, explains the incest taboo through the horror for menstrual blood, itself based on totemic beliefs. If this theory were to be accepted, the only possible conclusion would be that incest taboos among us are mere survivals and void of any current sociological significance. But Durkheim cannot accept this conclusion. It then becomes easy to understand how he was led to the fundamental principles of *The Rules*: "the organ is independent of its function; ... the causes which give rise to its existence are independent of the ends it serves."[42] The historical and functional approaches are equally important but must be used independently. At least this is the first conclusion which comes to mind. But before inquiring as to how Durkheim attempts to reestablish the unity of his system, it is worth looking into the underlying structure of this dualism.

No social phenomenon can be explained, and the existence of culture itself is rendered unintelligible, if symbolism is not set up as an a priori condition of sociological thought. Durkheim was highly aware of the importance of symbolism, but perhaps not enough so: "Without symbols, social feelings could have only an unstable existence."[43] He could have said: no existence at all. But his hesitation, however slight, is highly revealing. It shows that this Kantian (for no other philosophical influence on him was stronger) was reluctant to think dialectically on the very occasion when an a priori form was inescapably necessary: sociology cannot explain the genesis of symbolic thought but must take it as a given in man. On the contrary, when the functional method is called for, Durkheim suddenly shifts to the genetic: he tries to deduce symbol from representation and emblem from experience. For him, the objectivity of the symbol is only a translation or an expression of this "externality" which is an inherent property of social facts.[44] Society cannot exist without symbolism, but, instead of showing how the appearance of symbolic thought makes social life both possible and necessary, Durkheim attempts the reverse – i.e. to make symbolism emerge out of society. He does this with an ingenious theory about the origins of tattooing, in which he discovers the missing link between nature and culture. In fact, he sees it as almost instinctive, as shown by the large part it plays among the lower classes of our society.[45] But either tattooing must be considered as a genuine instinct in man, and the whole argument breaks down, or it is a product of culture and we fall into a vicious circle.

Modern sociologists and psychologists resolve such problems by calling upon the activity of the unconscious mind; but, at the time when Durkheim was writing, the major insights of modern psychology and linguistics were unavailable. This explains why Durkheim struggled with what he conceived – and this was already a considerable advance over late nineteenth-century thinking as illustrated, for instance, by Spencer – as an irreducible antinomy: the blindness of history and the finalism of consciousness. Between the two, there is of course the unconscious teleology of the mind. Strangely enough, Durkheim, who saw with the utmost clarity the necessity of intermediary levels of collective reality to provide the specific object of sociological inquiry, refused to take the same step with respect to individual reality. Yet it is at those intermediary levels that the apparent opposition between individuals and society disappears and that it becomes possible to pass from the one to the other. Here lies perhaps the explanation for the stubbornness of this opposition throughout his system. On the first point, and when defining the principles of classification in sociology, he writes: "between the confused multitude of historical societies and the unique, although ideal, concept of humanity, there are intermediate entities: these are the social species."[46] He adds that the laws of social processes should be drawn not from the study of "historical societies," as Comte and Spencer wrongly attempted, but from that of "species" or types. This, he insists, shows the impossibility of any theory of the unilinear evolution of mankind.[47] One may criticize the methodological principles on which Durkheim built his social typology: "societies are made up of a number of parts added on to each other ... [which] are themselves societies of a simpler kind."[48] One may also doubt the validity of any genetic morphology making it possible to follow the way in which "these simple societies joined together and how these new composites also combined."[49] Even in the simplest society we may find each and every element of the more complex. But if Durkheim did not succeed in discovering the foundations of a sound social morphology, he was at least the first to undertake, with a clear conception of its paramount importance, the basic task of formulating one.

Thus, Durkheim fully acknowledged the existence of the intermediary levels which sociology claims as its specific object, in contradistinction with history, on the one hand, and social philosophy, on the other. However, he is quite unwilling to accept analogous levels for the individual, which could provide the link between psychological and sociological approaches. Beyond the meaningless diversity of historical processes, he sees nothing except "the tendencies, needs and desires of men."[50] Then, "unless we postulate a truly providential harmony established beforehand, we could not admit that from his origins man carried within him in potential all the tendencies whose opportuneness would be felt as evolution progressed, each one ready to be awakened when the circumstances called for it."[51] This is because "a tendency is also a thing; thus it cannot arise or be modified for the sole reason that we deem it useful."[52] And he concludes: "there are no ends – and even fewer means – which necessarily influence all men."[53] "If then it were true that historical development occurred because of ends felt either clearly or obscurely, social facts would have to present an infinite diversity and all comparison would almost be impossible."[54] This entire argument is based on the assumption that, in psychological and social life, there can be only one kind of finality, i.e. conscious finality. But the theoretical implications of Durkheim's position are nonetheless striking. According to these pages, social evolution, if teleological, could bring only disorder and an innumerable multiplicity of unconnected achievements. In contrast, it is based on the assumption of the purposelessness of social processes that he explains the "outstanding regularity" with which "[social phenomena] recur in similar circumstances."[55] He adds: "the widespread character of collective forms would be inexplicable if final causes held in sociology the preponderance attributed to them."[56] This argument is directed against Comte and Spencer, and the service that Durkheim thereby does to sociology can hardly be overestimated: without ridding itself of finalistic interpretation, sociology could never pretend to be a science. If finalism is to be abandoned, however, it has to be replaced by something else that makes possible an understanding of how social phenomena present themselves as meaningful wholes, as structuralized ensembles. Durkheim felt strongly the paramount importance of this problem, and it can be said that all of his work is an attempt to discover a solution. He did not fail because of a lack of insight, but because the more advanced human sciences, psychology and linguistics, had not yet, at the time when he was thinking, succeeded in bringing forward, through Gestalt and phonemics, the methodological instruments which were indispensable for sociology to make its own way.

But he saw the direction in which to travel, and he showed it firmly to his fellow scholars when navigating his way through these two pitfalls of sociological thinking: social philosophy, on the one hand,

and cultural history, on the other. Cultural analysis never reaches the social species, but only historical phases.[57] And while the monographic method is useful for gathering facts, it should not cause us to forget that "the true experimental method tends rather to substitute for common facts, which only give rise to proofs when they are very numerous, ... decisive or crucial facts, ... which ... have scientific value and interest."[58]

We may now measure the distance traveled by French sociology from Emile Durkheim to Marcel Mauss. The latter, nephew of Durkheim, was at first associated with his work, contributing to the preparation of the book which – from a methodological point of view at least – may well be considered his masterpiece: *Suicide*. Curiously enough, it is precisely in *Suicide* that Durkheim answered in advance the criticism that Kroeber was to address, forty years later, to the French school as represented by Marcel Mauss.[59]

One can hardly disagree with Kroeber when he finds evidence of the "philosophical ancestry" of the "Année sociologique" group in their "reluctance ... to embark actively in field studies."[60] Two remarks should be made in this respect, however. First, the fact that, at the beginning of the twentieth century, the British and the American schools had already accumulated such a vast body of factual material, without attempting to use it for scientific purposes, that it was not illegitimate for the French school to undertake the task of understanding that material, instead of joining in the work of gathering more, which would have soon become blind and meaningless. Practical and theoretical work can never be dissociated; on the contrary, they nurture and enlighten each other. Proof can be found in the testimony of one of the finest specialists:

> Although Professor Warner does not blindly follow Durkheim, his work shows that the latter's original interpretation of aboriginal ceremonial life ... was sound. I have long been convinced of this, and ever since it has been my good fortune to get to understand native life in Australia, I have been amazed at the remarkable manner in which Durkheim was able to penetrate that life through the medium of Spencer and Gillen, Strehlow and a few others. Durkheim's position cannot be completely held, but his work is an inspiration.[61]

That *The Elementary Forms of Religious Life*, twenty-five years after it was written, by a man who never went into the field, should remain an inspiration to this distinguished Australian fieldworker is, one must admit, no mean achievement, and rare in the history of sociological science.

Besides, when dealing with French sociology, one must never forget that the first generation of Durkheim's disciples was decimated in World War I, and that the void has not yet been filled. No doubt men such as Robert Hertz,[62] had they lived, would have accomplished brilliant fieldwork. The next generation of French sociologists, who reached maturity around 1930, has, over the last fifteen years, almost entirely – but no doubt temporarily – given up theoretical work in order to make up for this shortcoming.[63]

Kroeber's appreciation of Mauss's work, properly speaking, is more surprising. He reproaches him for what he calls his "categorizing" – i.e. "the grouping of phenomena under such concepts as Gifts or Sacrifice."[64] This, he says, is not a productive approach, "because these concepts are derived from common, unscientific experience, and not specifically from the cultural data under investigation."[65] And he adds: "No physicist or biologist would approach his data from the angle of the categories 'long' and 'flat' and 'round,' useful and real enough as these concepts are in daily life."[66] This criticism implies so many misunderstandings, and raises questions so fundamental to any comprehension of the French point of view, that it merits careful examination.

No other sociological school has ever dedicated so much attention to the problem of definition, and to the distinction between scientific and unscientific facts, as the French school. In *The Rules*, Durkheim criticizes Spencer, precisely on the grounds that the latter had confused, under the general category of "monogamy," two institutions which are entirely distinct: *de facto* monogamy, such as is found at lower cultural levels, and *de jure* monogamy, featured in modern society. "A definition at the appropriate time," he says, "would have obviated this error."[67] The fundamental requirement of an objective definition, on the other hand, is that it should express phenomena through an integrative element belonging to their nature, not through their conformity with a more or less ideal notion. This is exactly the problem raised by Kroeber. And here is the answer: "When research is only just beginning and the facts have not yet been submitted to any analysis, their sole ascertainable characteristics are those sufficiently external to be immediately apparent."[68] These are not the most important; however, the deeper strata, endowed with a greater explanatory value, are still unknown, and these external characteristics must be used as a starting point.[69]

Have Durkheim and Mauss been unfaithful to their methodological program, as suggested by Kroeber? Indeed, if behind such broad categories as Sacrifice, or Gifts, or Suicide, there are not at least some characteristics which are common to all forms – among, of course, many others which are different – and if this does not allow for the use of those categories as starting points for analysis, then sociology may as well abandon any pretension to becoming scientific, and the sociologist must be resigned to piling up descriptions of individual groups, without any hope that the pile shall ever become of any use, except, perhaps, for cultural history.

But the real point lies elsewhere. For neither Durkheim nor Mauss have ever maintained that these categories express the ultimate nature of their data. Quite the contrary, they have attempted – and sometimes succeeded – in reaching behind them to those hidden, fundamental elements which are the true components of the phenomena. The conclusion of Durkheim's *Suicide* is well known: there is not one suicide, but suicides. The whole point of the book is to distinguish, within the broad, superficial category of suicide, several irreducible types: egoistic suicide, altruistic suicide and anomic suicide. These categories can no longer be considered definitively valid; since 1897, many new data have appeared, especially on suicide among primitive peoples, and we cannot, now, maintain the clear-cut distinction suggested by Durkheim between suicide in primitive and modern societies. The inadequacies of Durkheim's work, mostly due to a lack or insufficiency of data, have been acknowledged by his disciples to the extent that one of them, Maurice Halbwachs, wrote a new book on the same question (*Les Causes du suicide*). But Kroeber's criticisms are methodological, and here, obviously, they are without merit.

We could say the same with respect to Mauss. It is true that he wrote on sacrifice (Henri Hubert and Marcel Mauss, *Mélanges d'histoire des religions*, 1909). But to what end? Let us take a look at his own comments: "[sociology] grasps the true coalescences of social phenomena; for instance, the widespread notion of the sacrifice of the god may be explained through a kind of fusion that occurs between certain sacrificial rites and certain mythical ideas."[70] And also: "Serious research work leads us to unite what the unscientific mind distinguishes and to distinguish what it confuses."[71] For, as he said in the same article, sociology should not be satisfied with the discovery of correlations; the pointing out of the cases when the correlations do not take place is no less important than its positive counterpart. A good sociological explanation must "account for differences as well as similarities."[72] Indeed, one could say that the entire purpose of the French school lies in an attempt to break up the categories of the layman and to group the data into a deeper, sounder classification. As was emphasized by Durkheim, the true and only basis of sociology is social morphology – i.e. the part of sociology whose task is "to constitute and classify social types."[73]

Let us open a parenthesis. This analytical work of trying to reduce the concrete complexity of the data (and of which Lewis H. Morgan shall forever remain the great forerunner) into simpler and more elementary structures is still the fundamental task of sociology. Mauss's *The Gift* and *Seasonal Variations of the Eskimo* may be considered, in this respect, as models. It should be confessed however that, on account of its philosophical ancestry (behind Durkheim is Comte and, behind Comte, Condorcet), the French school has sometimes felt a strong temptation to follow its methodologically impeccable analytical work with a less satisfactory attempt at synthesis. After having reduced the concrete into simpler types, they have tried to rearrange these types into one or more series. Durkheim consistently fought against the theory of unilinear evolution, but not so much because it is unilinear or because it is an evolution as because he was not satisfied with the kind of data which Comte or Spencer had arranged serially. For the historical data they used, he substituted social types or species; but even a superficial reading of *The Rules* makes it clear that these are to be classified into one or several genetic series. This tendency, which Durkheim never succeeded in overcoming entirely, is especially apparent in Fauconnet's *La Responsabilité* and Davy's *La Foi jurée*. The important point is that it is far less conspicuous in recent works (such as Mauss's) than in earlier ones.

We may now return to Kroeber's argument. When Durkheim studies the division of labor, it is in order to reach such abstract, hidden categories as "organic solidarity" and "mechanical solidarity"; when he analyzes suicide, he formulates the notion of integration of the individual into the group; when Mauss undertakes a comparison between the different types of gifts, it is to discover, behind the more diversified types, the fundamental idea of reciprocity; when he follows the transformation of the psychological conceptions of the "Ego," it is in order to establish a relation between social forms and the concept of personality. These categories may be good or bad; they may prove useful or be wrongly chosen;[74] but if they do not belong to the kind of categories which it is the aim of sociology to define and to analyze, then let us say again that sociology must abandon every pretense of becoming a scientific study. They resemble not the categories of "long," "flat" or "round" but, rather, such categories as "dilatation," "undulation" or "viscosity," which the physicist has precisely made his objects of study.[75] Physics finds its object in the study of the abstract properties of gases, for instance – not in monographic descriptions of the smell of roses, violets, turpentine or methyl phenyl acetate and their historical relation in the process of differentiation of organic life.

In this respect, Mauss follows Durkheim. Mauss himself has always made clear that he considers himself as the keeper of the Durkheimian tradition. There are, however, many differences between them – not the outcome of any disagreement but due, rather, to the fact that ten or twenty years make a big difference in the development of a young science.

In the first place, the turns of mind of the two men were different. Durkheim always remained a teacher of the old school. His conclusions are laboriously arrived at and dogmatically asserted. He was trained as a philosopher; and, notwithstanding his broad sociological and anthropological erudition, he always approached it from the outside, as a man accustomed to different topics and different ways of thinking. Also, at the time when he gathered his material, the great efflorescence of anthropological fieldwork had not yet begun, and in many respects the data he had available to him now seems inadequate. While Mauss's intellectual training – as in the case of the great majority of French sociologists – was also in philosophy, he had the benefit of Durkheim's pioneering work; furthermore, he had access to newer, better and richer material. Durkheim belongs decidedly to the past, while Mauss remains, still today, at the level of the most modern anthropological thought and research. In addition, his extraordinary memory and untiring intellectual curiosity have allowed him to build up a worldwide – and, if one may say so, a timewide – erudition: "Mauss sait tout," his students used to say half-humorously, half-admiringly, but always respectfully. Not only does he "know everything," but a bold imagination and a brilliant feel for the social drove him to make a highly original use of his vast knowledge. In his work, and still more so in his teaching, unimagined comparisons abound. While he is often obscure – due to the constant use of antitheses, short-cuts and apparent paradoxes which later prove to be the result of a deeper insight – he gratifies his listener with sudden fulgurating intuitions, providing the grist for months of fruitful thinking. In such cases, one has the sense of reaching the core of social phenomena, of, as he says somewhere, "hitting the bed-rock." This constant striving toward the fundamental, this willingness to sift, over and over again, through a huge mass of data until only the purest material remains, explains Mauss's preference for the essay over the book, and hence the limited volume of his published work.

These intellectual differences – a more productive and systematic, if also more ponderous and pedantic, mind for Durkheim; a less "athletic" and organized but more intuitive and, one might even say, more aesthetic mind for Mauss – do not exhaust the comparison. In many respects, Mauss's method is more satisfactory than that of his master. We have already pointed out that he escapes almost completely the temptation for synthetic reconstruction. When he follows Durkheim in refusing to dissociate sociology and anthropology, it is not because he sees in primitive societies early stages of social evolution. They are needed, not because they are earlier, but because they exhibit social phenomena in simpler forms. As he once told this writer, it is easier to study the digestive process in the oyster than in man; but this does not mean that the higher vertebrates were formerly shellfish. He also overcame another shortcoming of Durkheim's method. The latter had consistently criticized the comparative method such as it was used by the British school, especially Frazer and Westermarck,[76] but he was, in turn, severely attacked for having (in *The Elementary Forms*) drawn universal conclusions from the analysis of a privileged case. Mauss's method maintains an equal distance from these dangers. He always considers a small number of cases, judiciously chosen as representing clearly defined types. He studies each type as a whole, always considering it as an integrative cultural complex; the kind of relation he aims at discovering is never between two or more elements arbitrarily isolated from the culture, but between all the components. This is what he calls "total social facts," a particularly felicitous formulation for the type of study called elsewhere – and later – functionalist.

We saw how Durkheim struggled to navigate between his methodological attitude, which led him to consider social facts as "things," and his philosophical training, which made those "things" into a ground on which to base fundamental Kantian ideas. Hence, he oscillated between a dull empiricism and an aprioristic frenzy. This antinomy is obvious in the following quotation: "If sociological phenomena were mere objectivized systems of ideas, to explain them would consist of thinking them through again in their logical order and this explanation would be a proof in itself. At the most, there might be a need to confirm it by a few examples. On the contrary, only methodical experimentation can force things to yield up their secrets."[77] Durkheim consistently repeated, however, that these things, i.e. social facts, are "collective representations" – and what could this mean, if not "objectivized systems of ideas"? If, on the other hand, social facts are psychic in nature, nothing would preclude an attempt to "think them through again in their logical order," although this order would not be immediately given to the individual consciousness. The solution to Durkheim's factitious antinomy lies in the awareness that these objectivized systems of ideas are unconscious, or that unconscious psychic structures underlie them and make them possible. Hence their character as "things"; and, at the same time, the dialectical – by which I mean unmechanical – character of their explanation.

Mauss was more aware than Durkheim of this basic problem of the relationship between sociological and psychological phenomena. Although the former never wrote a word that was inconsistent with the latter's teaching,[78] he listened more carefully to the echoes of modern psychology and kept on the alert, such that the bridges between the two sciences would never be cut. In his early article "Sociology,"[79] Mauss states that, although sociology is a certain kind of psychology distinct from individual psychology, "it is nevertheless true that one may pass from the facts of individual consciousness to collective representations through a continuous series of intermediaries." More recently, he has insisted on the necessary cooperation between sociology, on the one hand, and psychoanalysis and the theory of symbolism, on the other. Durkheim's hesitations with respect to the theory of symbolism had decidedly disappeared: "The activity of the collective mind is still more symbolic than that of the individual mind, but in the same way."[80] And if he remains faithful to Durkheim when he writes that "the notion of symbol is entirely ours, an outcome of religion and law,"[81] he re-establishes contact with psychology by concluding his analysis with this remark about Pavlov: the musical sound which induces salivation in the dog is, at the same time, the condition and the symbol of its response.

Lévy-Bruhl's opposition to Durkheim represents a protest against the latter's thesis that social representations and social activities are syntheses which are more complex, and morally higher, than individual achievements. This conflict is not new in French sociology. The individualistic point of view of the eighteenth-century philosophers had been criticized by the theoreticians of reactionary thought, especially by de Bonald, on the grounds that social phenomena, having a *sui generis* reality, are not simply the combination of individual ones. There is a tradition linking individualism to humanism, while the assumption of the specificity of the collective in relation to the individual seems, also traditionally, to imply the higher value of the former over the latter. To what extent this dilemma should be considered irreducible cannot be discussed here. But the passage from the objective to the normative is almost as apparent in Durkheim as it is among his predecessors. Durkheim was undoubtedly a democrat, a liberal and a rationalist. However, the Preface to the second edition of *The Division of Labor and Society*, written in 1901, arouses disturbing echoes when one reads it today. Somewhere in *The Elementary Forms*, he identifies the social order, evil and unjust, with Satan.[82] However, in a system which finds in social life the aim and origin of every high spiritual activity, it is difficult to keep society, considered as the universal form of human life, constantly separated from the concrete cultures of each individual group, which are its only visible expressions. A group in which collective feelings are strong is "superior" to another in which individualism predominates: "We are going through a period of transition and moral mediocrity."[83] The tendency toward normative conclusions is still more obvious in *The Rules*: "Our method is by no means revolutionary. In one sense it is even essentially conservative, since it treats social facts as things whose nature, however flexible and malleable it may be, is still not modifiable at will."[84] The opposite method is "dangerous." The following passage of *The Elementary Forms* starts as a refutation of Lévy-Bruhl and ends with a glorification of the social group: "Society is by no means the illogical or alogical, inconsistent, and changeable being that people too often like to imagine. Quite the contrary, the collective consciousness is the highest form of psychic life, for it is a consciousness of consciousnesses. ... It sees things only in their permanent and fundamental aspect. ... It sees from above, it sees far ahead. ... It embraces all known reality."[85] Obviously, any social order could take such a doctrine as a pretext for crushing individual thought and spontaneity. All moral, social and intellectual progress has made its first appearance as a revolt of the individual against the group.

Lévy-Bruhl's conception of the primitive mind as "pre-logical" may now appear queer and outmoded; but it cannot be rightly understood without placing it in this context. Durkheim describes social life as the mother and eternal nursemaid of moral thought and logical thinking, of science as well as faith. On the contrary, Lévy-Bruhl believes that whatever has been achieved by man was done not with but against the group; that the individual mind can only be in advance of the group mind. But, while he is fundamentally opposed to Durkheim, he commits the same methodological mistake – i.e. to "hypostasize" a function. His society – illogical, mystical, dominated by the "participation" principle – is the counterpart of that society conceived by Durkheim as the eternal spring of science and morality. The only difference is that the individual goes from being society's obedient pupil in one conception to its rebellious son in the other. The analysis of the pre-logical mind of the primitive, wholly dominated by the group, allows us to measure the paramount importance of the advance realized when the individual started to think independently from the group: this advance, says Lévy-Bruhl, is rational thought.

Thus Lévy-Bruhl – while missing what was really important in Durkheim's teaching, i.e. his methodology – was fascinated by its weaker part: the philosophical residues. The first half of his work is dedicated almost entirely to building a different interpretation; but it is equally residual. He certainly intended to work in the opposite direction to a Bonald–Comte–Durkheim type of synthesis; he succeeded only in reversing the synthesis. But it is no more acceptable as the starting point for the evolution of human thought than as its point of arrival. Against Lévy-Bruhl, Mauss has rightly pointed out that, if the study of "participations" (not only in the primitive mind but also the modern) is important, the study of "oppositions" is no less so.[86] There is no such thing as a primitive state of syncretism and confusion.

During the later part of his life, however, Lévy-Bruhl became more and more aware of the inadequacies of his theory. He gradually relinquished his first attempts to describe the primitive mind as specifically and objectively different from the civilized (*How Natives Think*, 1926 [1910]; *Primitive Mentality*, 1923 [1922]) and came to adopt a more prudent position: that the categories of the civilized mind cannot be used in the study of the primitive.

In this respect, his belated fight against Tylor and Frazer would have been more successful if, by that time, field anthropologists had not already abandoned the intellectual prejudices of the old school. However, his later books (from *The Soul of the Primitive*, 1928 [1927], to *The Mystic Experience and Primitive Symbols*, 1938) still make for challenging and fruitful reading. They contain a broad range of information, and the way it is put to use reveals a subtle feel for the suggestive and the significant. An exceptionally clear mind and a delightful style make it easy to digest the material. Rarely has the reading of compilations been so pleasurable an experience. The integrity, charm and generosity of the author's own soul may still be felt in his work, even after his early conclusions have been criticized and discarded.

It is difficult to pass definitive judgment on the work of Georges Gurvitch, since this author is still in full swing, and there is no doubt that many of the problems raised in his previous books will be resolved by him in future ones. Like Lévy-Bruhl, he belongs to the group of independent thinkers who, while working in close cooperation with the "Année sociologique" group, made no mystery of their dissent from Durkheimian orthodoxy. In Gurvitch, we find a meeting point for two different currents: on the one hand, a philosophical heritage coming directly from Bergson and phenomenology; on the other hand, a keen feel for certain aspects of sociological experience in modern society, sharpened by a broad familiarity with Proudhon, as well as with the daily life and struggles of labor unions. On the one hand, an intuitionist philosophy; on the other, the intuitive apprehension of determinate aspects of social reality. In Gurvitch's system, theory and practice always support each other and converge toward the same interpretation. This interpretation, in turn, is at once ontological and methodological: we have, first, the assertion that the division of human reality – between the individual, on the one hand, and society, on the other – is entirely fictitious; and, next, the idea that the traditional debate between sociologists with regard to the ultimate nature of social phenomena is meaningless, since every type of approach is but a specific point of view on reality, itself complex and diversified.

The inspiration for Gurvitch's sociology is juridical; his material comes mainly from the analysis of transformations of law – especially the status of property and labor – in modern society. These transformations show that the eighteenth- and early nineteenth-century conception of an abstract state, the depositary of all right and power superseding the isolated citizen, could not withstand the impact of concrete needs and tendencies. Instead of the jurist's tendency to systematize abstractions, he offers a fluid picture of what has actually taken place: the formation of a multiplicity of groups, each generating its own law, and the gradual establishment of an antagonistic equilibrium between them. Thus, according to Gurvitch, social life should be considered as the gushing forth of a constantly renewed multiplicity of social forms. This is the basis of his ontological pluralism.

But this pluralism is also methodological; it does not consist only in the thesis that society is ultimately reduced to groups that never yield to dissociation into the collective and the individual. It insists also on the fact that the nature of these groups is expressed, phenomenologically, on a multiplicity of levels: the geographic and demographic basis of social life, the social system of symbols, organizations, behavior – both fixed and non-crystallized – the world of ideas and values, and, finally, the collective consciousness. Between all these levels of reality there is no opposition, still less exclusion. Therefore, Gurvitch's method aims at integrating into a structuralized whole all these approaches that sociologists have usually considered incompatible. His pluralist realism supports a resulting relativism which, in turn, serves as the basis of a positive empiricism.

Whether Gurvitch's many-sided construction will prove durable and resistant to fissures is difficult to say in advance, not knowing how he intends to complete the structure. But his attempt is significant: while the "Année sociologique" group has felt more and more the urge to move away from its philosophical origins and to maintain an increasing interest in anthropology, it is, on the contrary, in an open confrontation between a clear-cut philosophical position and lived sociological experience that Gurvitch finds an opportunity to overcome the traditional conflicts of sociological thought. One tends to believe that this concrete experience represents the true foundation of his contribution and what gives it its original value, together with its deep significance. It is to be hoped that the novel and rich notions that Gurvitch has thus far applied primarily to the history of ideas will soon find their expression in the analysis of some concrete aspects of social reality.[87]

III

What future can be foreseen for French sociology? Over the last forty years, its progress has come mainly from the shift which has taken place, under Mauss's influence, from the method of concomitant variations to that of residues. For Durkheim, the former constituted the fundamental method of the social sciences.[88] He overlooked the fact that, since all the components of a given culture are necessarily connected, the method of concomitant variations will always give a positive answer: between two given series of variations, some kind of correlation will appear. Thus, Durkheim discovered, in Western societies, a correlation between progress in the division of labor and an increase in population, in terms of both volume and density. Bouglé worked along the same lines in his book on *Les Idées égalitaires* (1899). Correlations of this type undoubtedly exist, but they do not provide – as Durkheim thought – an explanation for the phenomenon under consideration. Should the series be chosen differently, other correlations would appear, probably ad infinitum.

Mauss's use of the method of concomitant variations is quite different. He needs it less to achieve an integrative synthesis, as was the case with Durkheim, than to dissociate the series under consideration according to the requirements of a critical analysis. But when this analysis is achieved, there is something that remains, which furnishes the true nature of the phenomenon: "The various explanations which can be brought forward as motives for beliefs in magical acts leave a residue, which we must now try to describe ... . It will be here that we shall find the real basis of these beliefs."[89] This method does not contradict Durkheim's but limits and deepens it. From now on, the focus will be on analysis, not synthesis.

There is another landmark which should help continue to orient French sociology in the right direction. We saw how Durkheim hesitated between an external, empiricist approach to social facts considered as "things," mechanically and atomistically conceived, and a method which, while equally experimental, paid more attention to the dialectical character of social processes. This confused attitude may be held responsible, at least partly, for Malinowski's misinterpretation of Durkheim's teaching, when he tries to align it with behaviorism: "the whole substance of my theory of culture ... consists in reducing Durkheimian theory to terms of behavioristic psychology."[90] Nothing could be further from a true understanding of the core French point of view. But French sociology must guard against the opposite danger – i.e. to try to save rational thought at the price of creating an external mysticism, which later turns against rational thought itself. This is the story of Lévy-Bruhl. We saw how, from a systematic theory of the "pre-logical" character of primitive thought, he progressively came to a purely critical point of view, avoiding any hypothesis about how primitives actually think. But one does not accumulate "pre-logisms" with impunity. From his original dogmatism, Lévy-Bruhl turned toward a complete agnosticism: nothing can be known of primitive thought except that it is wholly and utterly different, that it belongs to the realm of another "experience," totally heterogeneous to our own. But this mystery which surrounds primitive thought surreptitiously contaminates modern thought: "What needs explanation is not that many more or less primitive societies show a frank belief in the truth of these tales [he is referring to folktales] but, rather, that in our society this belief disappeared long ago."[91] Thus, in his early work, we find civilized thought studying and appraising, from its safe position on high, the heterogeneous character of primitive thought. But, then, modern thought discovers in itself the same mystery which was supposed to differentiate the primitive mind from the civilized. First a dogmatic interpretation then an agnostic attitude, in relation to the primitive mind, were supposedly required to save rational thought and individual freedom. Finally, it is the modern mind which appears altogether incapable of understanding the primitive mind, even while reducing itself to a mere extension of it.

Lévy-Bruhl's setback will undoubtedly serve as a cautionary tale for French sociology against the dangers of general theories. In fact, the time for theorizing seems to be decidedly past. In one of his last publications before the outbreak of the war, Mauss presented French sociology with the most elaborate and illuminating agenda for concrete research ever devised in his country.[92] And its conclusions leave no doubt as to the clear understanding, on the part of French sociologists, of the causes of some of their predecessors' misadventures:

The supreme achievement of all those observations – biological, psychological and sociological – of the life of individuals inside the social group is the seldom made observation of what must be the principle and end of all sociological observation: the birth, life and death of a given society from three perspectives: the purely sociological, the socio-psychological and the bio-sociological ... It would be useless to philosophize about general sociology when there is so much to be made aware of, then known, and finally understood.[93]

Elsewhere he says: "There is no need for discussion; just observe, and measure the importance."[94]

Faced with these new tasks, modern French sociologists will undoubtedly continue to hold Durkheim up as an important example. Durkheim, who was well trained in philosophy and the history of religions, but was not a field anthropologist, wrote a book in which he developed a new theory of the origin of religion on the ground provided by contemporary fieldwork. It is generally acknowledged that, as a theory of religion, his book is inadequate, while the best Australian fieldworkers hailed it as the forerunner of the discoveries they made only several years later. Why this apparent paradox? First, the time was not ripe for drawing up general hypotheses about the origin of human institutions; second, that it is precisely because Durkheim was well acquainted with the principles and classifications of the religious sciences that he was able to perceive, in data gathered by others, significant traits and hidden meanings that the fieldworker could not grasp without this theoretical training. And, now, what are the conclusions to be drawn? The first is obviously that sociology should renounce any attempt at discovering origins and laws of evolution. This is what we learn from Durkheim's failures. But his successes teach us something different: sociologists cannot content themselves with being craftsmen, exclusively trained in the study of a particular group or of a particular type of social phenomenon. They need, even for the most limited study, to be familiar with the principles, methods and results of other branches of the study of man: philosophy, psychology, history, etc. They must, indeed, turn more and more toward concrete studies; but they cannot hope to be successful if they are not constantly assisted and supported by a general, humanist culture. The philosophical heritage of French sociology has played some tricks on it in the past; but it may well prove, in the end, to be its greatest asset.

Selected Bibliography

Durkheim, Emile, *The Elementary Forms of Religious Life* (New York: Free Press, 1995).
—— *The Rules of Sociological Method* (New York: Free Press, 1982).
—— *Suicide: A Study in Sociology* (New York: Free Press, 1951).
Granet, Marcel, *La Civilisation chinoise* (Paris: 1929).
—— *La Pensée chinoise* (Paris: 1934).
Gurvitch, Georges, *Essais de sociologie* (Paris: 1938).
—— *Sociology of Law* (New York: Philosophical Library, 1942).
Halbwachs, Maurice, *Les Causes du suicide* (Paris: 1930).
—— *L'Evolution des besoins dans les classes ouvrières* (Paris: 1933).
Hubert, Henri, *The Greatness and Decline of the Celts* (London: Routledge, 1934).
Lévy-Bruhl, Lucien, *L'Expérience mystique et les symboles chez les primitifs* (Paris: 1938).
—— *Morceaux choisis* (Paris: 1936).
Maunier, René, *Essai sur les groupements sociaux* (Paris: 1929).
Mauss, Marcel, "Une catégorie de l'esprit humain, la notion de celle de personne," *Journal of the Royal Anthropological Institute*, 68 (1938).
—— *The Gift: Forms and Functions of Exchange in Archaic Society* (London: 1966).
—— *Seasonal Variations of the Eskimo: A Study in Social Morphology* (London: Routledge, 1979).
Simiand, François, *Le Salaire, l'évolution sociale et la monnaie* (3 vols, Paris: 1932).
Tarde, Gabriel, *The Laws of Imitation* (New York: 1903).

II

In Memory of Malinowski

A great ethnologist and great sociologist has just died. His work, of a prodigious diversity, though founded on the exclusive study of a limited province of Melanesia, cannot fail to impress any of those who, in any field, have devoted themselves to truly free research. In the social sciences, he has taken steps of the greatest importance. In a sense, it is no exaggeration to say that Malinowski has set ethnology on the path of freedom. He was the first anthropologist, after the prophetic but unfortunate attempts of Freud and his disciples, who undertook to connect the two most revolutionary disciplines of our time: ethnology and psychoanalysis. In facts and interpretations, he no doubt departed from an ill-informed orthodoxy. But the Freudians themselves will one day realize that, in subordinating the psychological history of the individual to the cultural frame in which he developed, instead of deducing an imaginary evolution from one knows not what universal psyche, Malinowski has extended psychoanalysis into a domain where psychoanalysts themselves are not competent and in a direction faithful to its origins. He was also the first to approach primitive societies in a spirit not only of formal interest and scientific curiosity but, above all, with a strong human sympathy. He accepted the natives whose guest he was without any reservations, sacrificing to them all the prohibitions and all the taboos of a society whose emissary he, more than anyone else, refused to be. From Malinowski's time onward, ethnology ceases to be a mere profession or technique and becomes a true calling. To be an ethnologist will demand strong independence and great love. It cannot be denied that both a certain affectation and the desire to shock an academic public which is not worth the trouble form part of his attitude. His influence will nevertheless remain so fertile and so deep that, in the future, ethnological works will probably be classified as "pre-Malinowskian" or "post-Malinowskian," according to the degree to which the author shall have committed himself personally.

The theoretical part of Malinowski's work raises more serious doubts. This admirably concrete mind has evinced an inexplicable disdain for history and the most absolute contempt for material culture. His refusal to see in a culture anything but actual or virtual psychological states has led him to develop a system of interpretation – functionalism – which makes it dangerously possible to justify any regime whatsoever. In the presence of this ever-soaring mind, whose ingenuity and vivacity never flag, one is tempted to overlook dialectical imperfections, or even contradictions. Even when agreement with him seems least likely, Malinowski retains an admirable capacity to stimulate sociological reflection. His work no doubt will suffer periods of criticism and oblivion. Yet for those who rediscover it after those intervals in the shadows, from which no living thought is spared, it will without question offer the same vibrant freshness.

Translated by Patricia Leblanc

III
The Work of Edward Westermarck

The passing of Edward Westermarck has been received with particular sadness by sociologists. The event awakened memories and triggered reflections that have considerably broadened the extent of the very real grief caused by the disappearance of a master, one who was among the greatest of his times.

For, indeed, it is not only an illustrious scholar that we have lost but an entire moment in sociological thought that has now come to an end. And this on two counts: Westermarck was the last and most famous representative of the British school of anthropology – he embodied, with an exceptional militant fervor, a school of thought that has renewed our social and moral understanding, and within which the earliest attempts to develop a comprehensive representation of humanity were made. However, this filiation was not manifest only in Westermarck's doctrine; it was also, in a more intimate and moving manner, manifest in his person. The advanced age at which he passed away made him less of a continuator than a survivor. The seventy-four-year-old man who, in 1936, still engaged in polemics with those he considered to be audacious innovators – Lowie, Radcliffe-Brown, etc. – had known Tylor. He had engaged in discussion over many years with Frazer and, on our side of the channel, with Durkheim. He was the last one standing among a group of men of truly phenomenal temperament, diligence, erudition and productivity, who played the same role for the nineteenth-century social sciences as the Renaissance masters had done for modern thought.

Westermarck was born in Helsinki in 1862. He completed his studies in 1889 with a doctoral dissertation on *The Origin of Marriage*, which was to form the core of his first major work, the *History of Human Marriage*.[1] It was immediately distinguished as much for the easy and agreeable manner with which the author's considerable erudition was brought to bear on rather austere subjects as for two important innovations: one methodological, which consisted in situating sociological analysis within the framework of biological evolutionism, and the other a brilliant repudiation of the theory of primitive promiscuity, which enjoyed authoritative status at the time.

Between 1906 and 1908, Westermarck published *The Origin and Development of the Moral Ideas*,[2] in which he offered a systematic interpretation of the nature and origin of moral judgments, followed by a large-scale investigation to verify his theory by putting it to the test of concrete reality. The eclecticism that presided over this double endeavor was to ensure the book's lasting success, as evidenced by the fact that it was deemed worthy of a first French translation twenty years after its original publication.[3] His last book, *Ethical Relativity*, extends the conclusions of the earlier work to the field of theoretical morality.

In 1906, Westermarck was appointed professor in practical philosophy at the University of Helsinki. The University of London had hired him to teach on the same topic in 1904, and in 1907 it appointed him to its chair of sociology. He was to teach in both London and Helsinki, alternating semesters in each city, until the founding of the first Swedish-language university in Finland, called Abo Academi University. He then left Helsinki in 1918 to serve as rector of the new university until 1921 and taught there through his final years.

These considerable teaching commitments did not keep him from fieldwork, however. He made several trips to Morocco, and a large portion of his publications is devoted to monographs of a folkloric nature, mostly focusing on the relationship between moral ideas and magical beliefs. These works include, most notably, "The Magic Origin of Moorish Designs,"[4] "Midsummer Customs in Morocco,"[5] *Marriage Ceremonies in Morocco*[6] and, finally, a general work in two volumes, *Ritual and Belief in Morocco*.[7]

These works are of considerable interest, and not just for Africanists. They shed special light on Westermarck's conceptions of the relationship between anthropology and folklore, on the one hand, and between theory and empirical research, on the other. It was indeed Westermarck the fieldworker that the Royal Anthropological Institute had in mind when it awarded him the Rivers Memorial Medal in 1928. Several years earlier, Rivers had already honoured Westermarck by dedicating to him his famous article on "The Disappearance of Useful Arts."[8]

* * *

In his 1891 review of *The History of Human Marriage*, Tylor wrote: "The distinctive character of the entirety of Dr. Westermarck's work lies in his vigorous attempt to consider the biological and the cultural sides of anthropology as the elements of a single linked system." Westermarck himself saw in his critique of the theory of promiscuity not just the historical starting point for his work but the foundation of his later methodological orientation. In 1890, it was generally believed that "primitive man lived in a state of promiscuity, where individual marriage did not exist, where all the men in a horde or tribe had indiscriminately access to all the women, and in which the children born of these unions belonged to the community at large." In the article "Methods in Social Anthropology,"[9] from which these lines are excerpted, and which constitutes his philosophical legacy, Westermarck immediately added: "I commenced my work as a faithful adherent of that hypothesis."

What was to lead him away from it – and this is fundamental to understanding the development of his thinking – were not the social facts in themselves but the difficulties that resulted from the theory of promiscuity once one tried to fit phenomena of social evolution into the larger process of biological evolution. It was by becoming "acquainted with the doctrine of organic evolution" that he drew the "conclusion that the social habits of the anthropoids might throw some light on those of primitive man."[10] At the very dawn of his scientific career, a fundamental tendency was already taking shape that was immediately to pit him against Durkheim and his school, as well as against Frazer and, later, against both the "cultural anthropologists" in the United States and the "pure sociologists" such as Radcliffe-Brown: i.e., for Westermarck, the sociological explanation is never in itself satisfactory. To grasp the phenomenon in an intelligible form, the social must be transcended to reach the psychological dimension behind it, and, whenever possible, the biological as well.

In this respect, his critique of promiscuity is revealing. According to Westermarck, the facts prove that the social unit among gorillas and chimpanzees is the family; orang-utans and gibbons also live as monogamous family units. In addition, ethnographic studies have shown that the family is a universal human institution. Based on this double observation, "an evolutionist ... is therefore naturally inclined to believe that it existed among primitive man as well."[11]

This conclusion is further supported by a number of arguments of Darwinian inspiration: natural selection must have favored couples in which family life was spontaneously adopted; among great apes, indeed, the small number of offspring, together with the extended period of childhood, required the male, through acquired instinct, to care for the female and young ones. All these considerations also apply to the human species.

Westermarck was thus the first to reject the theory of promiscuity, a good twenty years ahead of the consensus that would later form among specialists. But objections to his arguments, and to the assumptions on which they are based, can still be raised. If promiscuity had existed in certain human societies, it would have been as a cultural innovation, and not as a legacy of nature. The example of anthropoids would then be irrelevant. Above all, it was a rather risky attempt to try to settle uncertainties regarding the early stages of human life by calling on hypotheses that were even more fragile still, concerning the mode of life of primates in the wild. On that subject, we are still reduced to conjecture – and were even more so fifty years ago.[12]

But Westermarck's theory of marriage forms part of a broader ambition. The connection it establishes between sociology and biology does not end there; if well founded, it confers on sociology a scientific status as eminent as that of biology, and perhaps even more so. For if social institutions are, as Westermarck thinks, based on instinct, they become explainable insofar as we can connect the former to the latter. Yet the sociologist is better placed than the biologist to do so, for the latter is entirely ignorant of the causes of organic variations presupposed by natural selection. On the contrary, the causes of social phenomena are accessible. The sociological method is thus the appropriate method for discovering the causes of social phenomena.

* * *

In his insistence on a sociology that could furnish a comprehensive explanation and his conviction that only the fundamental characteristics of human nature were capable of supplying such an explanation, Westermarck can be considered among the defenders of a comparative approach. In his view, the social sciences proceeded through revealing similarities between beliefs and institutions, classifying these similarities, and explaining them through the psychological or biological laws that govern them. He did not reject out of hand interpretations that conceived of phenomena as borrowed and acquired through cultural contact, but he systematically limited their field of application. Indeed, how else could we understand the identical behavior of animals of the same species if not as informed by an identical nature? "From seeds of the same sort grow very similar plants." Turning the diffusionist thesis upside down, Westermarck went so far as to argue that not only did geographical proximity and historical intimacy between various peoples fail to support the idea that similarities in their institutions could be accounted for through reciprocal borrowings, but that, on the contrary, it reinforced the likelihood of independent evolution for each of them. For the more similar they were, the more likely they were to give rise to the same social and moral manifestations. This dissatisfaction with historical and local explanation also informed his African monographs. The eyespot pattern found on Moroccan ceramics and in the Ionian columns of the Greeks did not necessarily share a common geographical origin; rather, they should be interpreted as resulting from the magical belief that eyes ward off the evil eye.[13] For Westermarck, the diffusionist theory relied exclusively on exterior analogies; it was the method of a museologist, not that of a sociologist.

Indeed, the most universal traits – property rights, punishment, blood kinship, marriage, the incest prohibition, exogamy, slavery, etc. – may be considered, a priori, as falling outside the realm of explanation by cultural contact. Yet, even when a historical connection is established, it does not mean progress has been made with regard to their explanation. How did the phenomenon appear in the first place? For there must be a beginning. It is through comparison that the ultimate origin is to be found, in the residue that is common to all analogous institutions. A psychological explanation might even be established in the absence of points of comparison: "Very frequently the knowledge of the cause of a certain custom found among one people is suggestive of the meaning of the same or similar customs among other peoples."[14] Such an extrapolation is justified, in Westermarck's view, by the recognition of a link of "common humanity" between all men.

His intransigent evolutionism, which he maintained to the end of his life, allowed for only two reservations. He conceded that the British school had been imprudent on two counts. The first was an excessive interpretation of obscure phenomena as "survivals" of other and better-known phenomena. But a custom cannot be the survival of another custom which cannot also be identified as its logical origin. Briffault thus interprets the sharing of wives as a survival of promiscuity, through the assimilation of the guest to the clan brother, but why would the survival have applied to the exceptional case of the guest and not to the regular and more common case of the clan brother? Aside from their "extravagant and uncritical" use of the survival principle, evolutionists were guilty of another excess: their tendency to "infer, without sufficient reason, from the prevalence of a custom or institution among some savage peoples, ... that this custom or institution was a relic from a stage of development which the whole human race once went through."[15] Westermarck thus rebutted Lewis Morgan and his famous fifteen stages which would have universally preceded monogamous marriage. Yet, while he rejected unilinear sequences, he consigned himself to delineating rather basic evolutionary schemas, since, in his view, institutions always had the same origin and tended to the same end.

* * *

In Westermarck, the evolutionist interpretation is indeed always bounded, and sometimes contradicted, by the search for ultimate causes in the field of psychology. This other tendency in his thinking is particularly salient in his major work, *The Origin and Development of the Moral Ideas*. In the first part of this work, the author proposes to relate various moral maxims to a few dispositions constitutive of human nature in general, which already exist among the most inferior societies known to us. Indeed, he thought that there were no qualitative differences among types of morality, but a single Morality, of which the various forms were only progressive approximations. In short, he adopted the perspective of classical natural philosophy. To this was added, as with eighteenth-century thinkers, the sentiment – in contradiction with the previously stated theory – that morality was a complex thing, and that it was necessary to study it through its historical manifestations. The latter can, however, always be reduced to a few elementary sentiments.

In an apparent paradox, a book that is presented first and foremost as an empirical study thus begins by pronouncing a moral system that is fully formed before any reference to the social is made or suggested. All moral judgment, according to Westermarck, originates in a special category of emotion that he called retributive emotions; faced with the actions of others, we sometimes manifest anger and indignation, sometimes good will and sympathy. This very simple emotional process may be discovered through introspection. Is it sufficient to constitute the field of morality? Probably not, since it can be found in both animals and humans. But once it is given tentative systematization – offering "a certain flavour of generality," supplying the basis for a priori deduction of the fundamental categories of duty, law, fairness, injustice, merit and virtue – the general framework of morality, with its permanent and universal character, has been provided. It is still Kantian philosophy, albeit in diluted form.

Social observation thus cannot make any claim to explaining morality; it cannot even reveal the general orientation of morality, since determining its framework also entails, in large part, determining its content. At most, it can provide a demonstration, an illustration of the psychological theory, and enable a precise determination of the gaps, lapses, confusions and progress in relation to a direction that is given in advance. The flaws in the theory are glaring. As Rivers put it: "It leaves us at the end just where we were at the beginning."[16] But, what is worse, the flaw affects the very way in which social facts are treated, the rigor with which they are introduced, critiqued and compared. Durkheim had strongly reproached him for this immediately upon the work's publication. He had also pointed out how the initial psychological premise (which is characteristic of the entire British school of anthropology) had led the author to content himself with what Durkheim called "a rapid and disorderly review." If one is convinced that the causes of morality must be sought among the most permanent dispositions of human nature, "rather than limiting and circumscribing the field to see what is specific about it ..., one should expand it ad infinitum to reveal, ... through heterogeneity itself, the most general principles that are to be attained."[17] One is thus led to accumulate facts rather than selecting ones that are clear and demonstrative. The rigor of philosophical reflection is weakened by the shifting of attention onto positive studies, while the seriousness of positive studies is diminished by subordination to the justification of preestablished philosophical theses.

This is why every chapter of *The Origin and Development of the Moral Ideas* – despite the liveliness of its style, the lightness of its tone and its richness of information – leaves the reader with a vague sense of dissatisfaction and the idea that the result was not quite commensurate with the effort. The famous argument between Frazer and Westermarck about *The History of Human Marriage* is a good case in point.[18]

When Frazer concluded his analysis of the incest prohibition by turning, as an ultimate explanation, to certain magical beliefs regarding female infertility, he was himself aware this recourse was flawed: on the one hand, the beliefs in question presupposed the existence of the prohibition that they were said to have induced; on the other hand, they were of such a special and limited kind that they could not account in any convincing manner for a quasi-universal custom. But at least Frazer tried to account for a cultural fact through another cultural fact. By contrast, Westermarck, following the critiques that we just mentioned, declared that "the home is kept pure from incestuous defilement neither by laws, nor by customs, nor by education, but by an instinct which ... makes sexual love between the nearest kin a psychical impossibility."[19] This impossibility would derive from habituation, itself the result of the proximity of the parents' lives. The psychological approach is defeated here: not only does this "impossibility" admit exceptions, but society does not prohibit two individuals who share an intimate proximity from maintaining sexual relations (and, among them, brothers and sisters), but it does forbid close kin from indulging in such relations, not because of their proximity but because of their familial ties. This ban includes all individuals that may be considered to be kin, even if there is no physical proximity between them. In other words, at the root of the prohibition of incest lies neither the physiological link of kinship, nor the psychological link of proximity, but the fraternal or paternal link, in its exclusively institutional dimension.

However, Westermarck could not admit that the origin of a moral rule should be found elsewhere than in the deepest recesses of human nature. "All the theories [on incest prohibition] assume that men avoid incestuous marriages only because they are taught to do so."[20] Indeed, can a social rule originate elsewhere? But a theory that makes morality an autonomous reality cannot recognize either education or disuse as factors: "Even when the meaning of a custom is obscure or lost, [the researcher's] knowledge of the native mind and its modes of thinking and feeling may enable him to make valuable conjectures."[21] But to turn the native mind, as he does, into a microcosm of the culture of the group is to run the risk of replacing the concrete history of the society in question not with, as imagined, the underlying universal psychological foundations but with the by-products deposited by folklore in credulous minds. Against Radcliffe-Brown and Rivers, considering fieldwork as the essential basis for any legitimate sociological speculation, Westermarck invoked his seven years of work in Morocco. It is not to detract from the high value of his monographic work to say that it is more folklore than anthropology. But, on the theoretical front as well, he explicitly confused the two disciplines.[22] If he was disposed, as we have seen above, to reconstitute the psychological history of customs by forcing individual minds beyond the limits of forgetting, the "immediate data" of the native mind seemed to him just as likely to supply institutions in their entirety. In his "Midsummer Customs in Morocco," he had no qualms in rejecting Frazer's interpretation of the midsummer games as survivals of solar and pluvial rites, on the sole grounds that the Berbers he had interviewed did not have any recollection of this significance. Yet individual forgetting does not prove that the institution never had any such meaning.

* * *

These abuses of psychology have led polemically inclined theorists to pass very severe judgments. Radcliffe-Brown thus went so far as to declare that "in England we have very little of anything that can be called sociology," and that "any explanation of a particular sociological phenomenon in terms of psychology ... is invalid."[23] Westermarck had picked up these attacks with much bitterness and considered them quite unfair. In the midst of a discussion on the relationship between psychology and sociology, he interrupted Rivers to ask him how he purported to account for blood quarrels except through a desire for vengeance. Rivers replied that, on the contrary, it was the psychology of vengeance that could not be made sense of without the blood quarrel. Reducing customs and social rules to historical expressions of inner, psychical and organic tendencies is indeed to reduce culture to the temporal and ghostly transposition of an autonomous psychological development, one that could be grasped prior to any objective experience. Real events, migrations, wars, contacts, borrowings, inventions and destructions were (*de jure* if not *de facto*) ruled out as causes of the appearance or disappearance of an institution among a given people at a specific time and place. The history and geography of human groups is effectively abolished.

Yet, as distant as Westermarck might have been from the direction taken by the social sciences in the last years of his life, it was in his work that the largest number of intuitions, and sometimes prophetic intimations, of now common conceptions are to be found. And, through a curious paradox, if his psychological approach constantly limited the scholarly reach of his work, it was his vigorous sense of psychological reality that allowed his thinking to be, in many respects, so ahead of the theories of his time. It also accounts for the fresh and vivid tone that makes Westermarck the most current of the great masters of the British school.

It is perhaps the monumental character of the body of work that remains its most salient trait. Not only have we not seen elsewhere in the field of the social sciences such a vast attempt to achieve comprehensive scope, but this attempt is consistently supported by a truly prodigious erudition. The compilation of authors is made with constant care to include only reliable sources. Nowhere else – except in Frazer – do we find such a considerable collection of information on human opinion.

But, above all, we cannot overstate the importance of the step Westermarck took for sociology when he dispatched the theory of promiscuity. It was standing like a distorting screen between primitive psychology and our own. It afflicted the former with what appeared, depending on the beholder, as a scandal, an absurdity or an enigma. It forced theorists to desperately generate ever more intermediary institutions, since they had to account for the hypothetical transition between the most radically opposite forms of union: promiscuity and monogamous marriage. An ever-deeper gulf was thus being formed between the primitives and ourselves. Westermarck's critique was surely insufficient, as best evidenced by the fact that his refutation of the promiscuity theory, which dealt a final blow to sociological evolutionism, was grounded primarily on evolutionist arguments. Not only, however. Beyond the litany of evidence and discussions looms the sound and durable cornerstone of his work: a sympathy for the human and a solid sense of psychology, which always and everywhere saved him from the excesses of the theorist. Morocco aside, he had never had direct contact with actual primitive peoples, but a kind of secret intuition kept him from attributing to their institutions motivations or explanations that were entirely incompatible with this norm of "common humanity" to which he so often referred.

His "psychologism" thus had two consequences – one negative and the other positive, but both fertile. In the first place, the manifest contradiction that characterizes his work, between the diversity of the collected facts and the simplicity of the explanations provided, helped his successors understand that psychological elements, precisely because they are universal and permanent, cannot account for social phenomena that are diverse, particular and contingent. Through an almost kneejerk reaction to the theses of the English school, the distinction between *nature* and *culture* became clearer, paving the way for a cultural and historical interpretation of social phenomena.

However, if cultures must be considered as specific and sometimes heterogeneous realities, we should henceforth remember that the individuals who participate in these cultures are united in a kind of psychological fraternity and that, despite the variety of their techniques, beliefs and customs, the African or the American savage and the civilized European are, as individuals, fellow human beings who are permeable in relation to one another and are subject to the same mechanisms, albeit within different contexts.

This notion of "permanent humanity" and belief in a psychological constant form the core as well as the great originality of Westermarck's work. They obtain at all times and at every turn. It was on these notions in particular that his critique of the unilinear evolutionism of Spencer and Lewis Morgan was based. For, in his view, human evolution consisted not in a progression through increasingly heterogeneous stages but in a haphazard and gradual verification of fundamental notions and trends. The evolutionary schema that forms the general framework both of *The History of Human Marriage* and of each chapter of *The Origin and Development of the Moral Ideas* is, in short, the following: a primitive humanity in which various confused approximations of the great psychological and moral imperatives of man begin to appear; then, with the middle cultures of Antiquity and the Middle Ages – Egypt, Greece, Rome, Christian Europe, India, China, Mexico – a series of distortions and specializations around these primitive trends emerge; and, finally, from the Renaissance onward, with the development of critical thought, there is a gradual rationalization that brings humanity to a refined consciousness and application of the fundamental imperatives. He had thus anticipated one of the most original manifestations of contemporary sociological thought. His interpretation of middle cultures as being located outside the general evolutionary process heralded the diffusionist theory of Rivers and Elliot Smith, which conceives of Mediterranean civilization not as a necessary transition but as a historical event, at once exceptional, sensational and formidable.

In addition, Westermarck's constant concern to highlight the similarities between the moral customs of cultures that were seemingly most removed from one another, and to reestablish the responsibility of the great civilizations, the heirs of which we consider ourselves to be, in the development of norms and customs that are often deemed "savage," confers on his work a critical and politically engaged quality of which he was fully aware. In his view, moral evolution had a meaning: it was going to bring humanity closer to an ideal of liberalism and rationalism, to free it from its errors and prejudices. He was the first to grasp the sterile conservatism of unilinear evolutionism, which justified all institutions by showing them to be inevitable modes of a necessary development. But, for Westermarck, the role of sociology was not to justify what has been, or what is, but to prepare for what must be. He considered the relativist critique to be an instrument of spiritual emancipation.

Further evidence of this can be found in one of his last polemics, toward the end of his life, against a disciple of Briffault who had taken up, against him, the defence of promiscuity. What most upset him about the critics of his work was not when they misinterpreted his arguments or when they ignored all the evidence that had since piled up in his favor; what he found most intolerable was when they accused him of having sought to provide, through his critique of promiscuity, a transcendental moral basis for the superiority of monogamous marriage. And, in an attempt to capture the significance of a half century of scholarly work, he concluded with a forceful sentence that

I shall quote in its original tongue: "Both in my book *The Origin and Development of the Moral Ideas* which appeared before the war, and in my recent book *Ethical Relativity*, I have emphatically refuted the objectivity and absoluteness of all moral values."[24]

IV

The Name of the Nambikwara

In a joint communication published in a recent issue of this journal,[1] Messrs. Emilo Willems and Egon Schaden have taken exception to some transcriptions of tribal names, the location of tribes and the linguistic affiliations proposed by Dr. Steggerda.[2] While some of their comments are relevant and others not, as pointed out by the editor, the entire note displays a pedantic approach to the problem of tribal names which should be dismissed once and for all, especially in relation to South America. The best example is provided by the name of the Nambikwara.

The authors blame Dr. Steggerda for spelling it *Nambiquara* or *Nambikuara*; they punctiliously emphasize that it is not a Spanish word, but Tupi, and that it ought to be written *Nhambikwara*. Since it is only a nickname of foreign origin and entirely unfamiliar to the natives, one might think that the question of spelling is not of the utmost importance. But there is more to the point.

The name Nambikwara was mentioned for the first time, and only as hearsay, by Antonio Pires de Campos at the beginning of the eighteenth century. Since then it has appeared several times with reference to an unknown tribe located at the headwaters of the Tapajós. There is a great discrepancy between the different spellings. When General (then Colonel) Cândido Mariano da Silva Rondon began to explore the land between the Tapajós and the Ji-Paraná, in 1907, he met with an unknown group speaking several dialects of an unknown language, and he did not hesitate to identify them with the tribe often mentioned in the early documents. It was at that time that the name *Nhambikwara* was definitely adopted, its spelling fixed, and it was recognized as a Tupi nickname the meaning of which is "big ears."

Some anthropologists remained vaguely disturbed, however, as the ears of the Nambikwara are not particularly big, and they do not use any of the ornaments worn in some other parts of Brazil with the result of enlarging the earlobe. The Tupi nickname would suggest, of course, some conspicuous custom of the kind.

Such was the state of things when, during my 1938–9 expedition to the Nambikwara, my attention was called to a tribe never mentioned before but of which the few dwellers of these otherwise uninhabited regions were well aware, as they raided and partly destroyed the telegraphic post of Paressi a few years previously; other clashes with gold-diggers and rubber-tappers venturing too far inland have also occurred. I did not have a chance to see the natives, but their campfires were getting closer and closer while I was there, and the Brazilian dwellers at the border were becoming increasingly worried. I was shown the weapons they had abandoned on retiring from their recent raid, together with a few other items, none of which could be attributed to the Nambikwara culture.

Besides, there are two interesting facts: the tribe's territory is close to the Nambikwara but it is situated more to the east. This means that any expedition coming from the Cuiabá region (as was the case for eighteenth-century travelers) should have approached them before reaching the Nambikwara. Furthermore, present-day adventurers in search of gold, diamonds or rubber who happened to see these much dreaded natives call them *beiços de pau*, a Portuguese expression which means "wooden mouths." They all agree that the natives wear wooden discs in the earlobes as well as in the lower lip, whence the designation now commonly used in the *sertão* northwest of Cuiabá. Therefore, I submit that this tribe is the "big ears" of the Tupi and of the older literature, whose nickname was mistakenly transferred to the Nambikwara at the beginning of the twentieth century because, at that time, no other tribe was known to dwell in that particular region. The name Nambikwara is not only a nickname of foreign origin; it was not even intended for the people who will probably be labeled as such forever.

To rename the modern Nambikwara would only bring more confusion, since they have now been called that for almost forty years. A new name would be artificially created, for they have names only for their different bands and do not use any general appellation for the linguistic group taken as a whole. Thus, the reasonable solution points to retaining the present name of the Nambikwara; at the same time, one should be aware that, under these circumstances, the word is absolutely meaningless, a code word of which only the phonetic spelling can give an adequate treatment.

I have related this story because it teaches us a lesson, for many similar cases exist in South America and elsewhere. Tribal names should not be approached with an overly dogmatic mind. There are other topics which are more deserving of a scholar's care and attention.

Individual and Society

V

Five Book Reviews

SIMMONS (Leo W.), ed., *Sun Chief: The Autobiography of a Hopi Indian*, published for the Institute of Human Relations, New Haven, Yale University Press, 1942.

As we know, American anthropology has been increasingly preoccupied with the question of the relationship between the individual and the group. This interest has given rise to many native autobiographies, in which the role of the anthropologist is generally limited to initiating the project and discreetly organizing the material produced by the informant. This kind of research – practiced in the US from the early nineteenth century, producing narratives of an anecdotal nature (*The Autobiography of Black Hawk*, 1834; *Lives of Illustrious Indians*, 1843; *Life of Tecumseh*, 1841; etc.) – took a scientific turn with three successive publications by Paul Radin: *Personal Reminiscences of a Winnebago Indian* (1913); *The Autobiography of a Winnebago Indian* (1920); and *Crashing Thunder: The Autobiography of an American Indian* (1926). Over the past few years, other first-rate works have been published, among the most remarkable of which were *Son of Old Man Hat: A Navajo Autobiography*, by Walter Dyk (1938), *Smoke from Their Fires: The Life of a Kwakiutl Chief*, by Clellan S. Ford (1941), and the work being reviewed here, which represents a document of exceptional value for anthropologists and psychologists alike. The first meeting between Mr. Leo Simmons and Hopi Indian Don Talayesva took place in the indigenous village of Oraibi in 1938. The latter was roughly fifty years old, and his life experience had made him a particularly sensitive witness to the conflict between native traditions and the path of civilization. Deemed from the start to be ill-adapted to his original milieu, Don was sent to an American school at age ten, and he came to think of himself as definitively assimilated into the modern world. Yet, in his twentieth year, he fell gravely ill and, while lying in his hospital bed, was assailed by the gods and myths of his childhood. His guardian spirit berated him, presenting his physical ailment as punishment for his betrayal. When he came out of hospital, he was a new man, returning to his native village and meticulously following all Hopi customs and rites. What this enlightened conservative, this deliberate and conscious reactionary, provides is not so much a description of his people as a persistent plea, obsessed as he is to justify his return to his native land and to account for the inner transformation that brought him to a highly formalistic respect of tradition, which had become for him vibrant and venerable.

From a psychological and literary perspective, his testimony is unique, and of no less value to the anthropologist. First, because of the trove of details and the volume of new information it contains on Hopi society, which was already rather well known. But above all because it achieves what the fieldworker desperately tries and most often fails to do: to narrate a native culture "from within," so to speak, as a living whole governed by an inner harmony, and not as a random assortment of customs and institutions whose existence can only be observed. We thus understand how the objective situations in which the child is placed from birth may make the supernatural world appear more real than daily appearances; and that the subtleties of the kinship system are no easier for the native to master than for the theorist – i.e. what appears as a contradiction to the latter also appears as such to the former, and both manage, through a similar effort of reflection, to make sense of the system; a sense that, in the end, is the same for both.

In our view, it is this "cathartic" function that constitutes the primary merit of works based on native autobiographies. The author of *Sun Chief* probably grants them a more important function: he expects them to solve problems that had gone hitherto unheeded. But this is true only in a negative sense. The customs and institutions which, from an outside perspective, appeared as utter enigmas are explained by psychological experience, which is readily universalizable because it is psychological, and the mystery is thus dissolved in a situation in which the same behavior appears reasonable to us too. We are thus not introduced to new problems, but we manage to eliminate several old ones which were artificially given the appearance of reality by our external perspective.

KLUCKHOHN (Clyde), "The Personal Document in Anthropological Science," in *The Use of Personal Documents in History, Anthropology and Sociology*, New York, Social Science Research Council, bulletin 53, 1945.

This remarkable study, complete with an invaluable bibliography of nearly two hundred titles, develops rather different perspectives from those presented in the previous review. The author classifies and analyses the major indigenous autobiographies published to date in the US and beyond, assessing their methodological and informational value. In a more theoretical chapter (pp. 133–49), he then proceeds to show how personal life stories serve not only to eliminate false problems but also to raise new ones, as well as to discover novel methods for dealing with those already identified. His penetrating analysis showing how documents of this sort constitute a precious resource is readily convincing. They provide a means of checking and moving beyond ethnographic studies; a more direct and intuitive access to the "style" of each culture; a means of defining individual status and establishing a more concrete picture of the social hierarchy; an introduction to the life of a given native community; a study of the processes and mechanisms by which individuals acquire the culture of their group; a means of substituting lived events for the schematic history of anthropologists; a refinement of the technique of studying one personality by another personality; a sense of the role of orthodoxy and heterodoxy within a given social group; etc. Yet his suggestion, in conclusion, that the systematic and comparative study of personal documents might open a new era in anthropological research leaves us somewhat perplexed. For it is the uniqueness of the documents that constitutes their exceptional value: they bring to life more than they teach. The elements for a theoretical systematization, whatever form it might take, are no more apparent to the subject observing himself than to the researcher observing him. For all a foreigner can tell us about his experience as a speaking subject, it will not teach us much about the phonological structure of his language, which is the only scientific truth. For our part, we remain convinced that social facts must be studied as things. In reducing some of these "things" to experiences, personal documents do not demonstrate that scientific study should be conducted at the level of experience, but, rather, that the so-called things with which we had imprudently contented ourselves are always only part of the phenomenon and that the true object is located further still. These documents allow for a critique of the object, but they do not constitute it.

LLEWELLYN (Karl N.) and ADAMSON HOEBEL (Edward), *The Cheyenne Way: Conflict and Case Law in Primitive Jurisprudence*, Norman, University of Oklahoma Press, 1941.

Few and far between are the works dedicated to the law and jurisprudence of primitive societies. This favorably disposes us to the one at hand, born of the collaboration between a theorist and a fieldworker whose earlier works had prepared him for research of this kind. Indeed, a year earlier, Mr. Hoebel had published a monograph, *The Political Organization and Law-Ways of the Comanche Indians* (Memoirs of the American Anthropological Association, no. 54, 1940), which followed a rather traditional model but contained a wealth of keen and precise observations. Would we go so far as to say that we prefer the more classical approach of the earlier work to the rampant intellectual excesses of *The Cheyenne Way*? The later book is not without merit. It is constructed around the study of fifty-three legal cases – analyzing them, classifying the principles that shaped their resolution, and studying their impact on public consciousness with an astuteness that is worthy of praise. From a theoretical perspective, the authors succeed in highlighting some fundamental dimensions of primitive law, especially the compensation mechanisms which consider both the crime and the punishment as disruptions of the social order – and as identical in this respect – and which attempt to restore balance after punishment for the guilty party, just as the punishment itself had originally restored balance for the society. Crime thus calls for punishment, and punishment in turn requires measures of redemption that the guilty party must legitimize through ritual trials. The initial blow is gradually absorbed by a series of diminishing oscillations, some of which target the criminal while others work to his benefit.

This makes it all the more regrettable that the book should be characterized by such a simplistic form of thought and expression. In an effort at popularization, which is fraught with danger when dealing with such technical matters, the authors frame their discussion through a parallel between Cheyenne law and contemporary American law. They might as well have compared a palomino and an oyster, which would have led them to observe that one had legs and the other did not; one was hairy, the other slimy; that the horse was yellow and the oyster green, etc., without getting much further. They can compare vertebrates and invertebrates, mammals and molluscs. But there is not the slightest attempt to classify the concrete forms offered up to the observer into types and families. Description never prevails over empirical phenomena but gives way to enthusiastic commentaries on the profound and elevated culture of the native Solomons. We thus imperceptibly slip into apologetics, which detracts considerably from the scientific value of the work and recalls, in a rather embarrassing way, celebrations of the "noble savage," the golden age and primitive simplicity.

This defect cannot be overlooked given its direct link to the modern revival of providentialism commonly known as functionalism. Malinowski and his disciples have the great merit of demonstrating, against a sterile form of historical empiricism, that cultures form wholes whose elements function each in relation to the others. Yet, if the basic premise for the definition of any social system is that it functions, there is no reason to celebrate when we observe that the law punishes crime, or families raise children. This explanation is condemned to a certain circularity, left only to observe that institutions and customs indeed serve the functions that they were designed to serve, with the effect of reducing social science to phenomenological description, which sacrifices history without replacing it with anything else. However, institutions do not necessarily – and in fact rarely – serve the function they proclaim to serve, and the mechanisms through which they operate are not always those that are immediately apparent to the observer. In sociology, as in any other sciences, explanation does not flow directly from description.

OPLER (Morris E.), *An Apache Life-Way: The Economic, Social and Religious Institutions of the Chiricahua Indians*, Chicago, University of Chicago Press, 1941.
GOODWIN (Grenville), *The Social Organization of the Western Apache*, Chicago, University of Chicago Press, 1942.

Much can be learned from comparing these two works, on two neighboring sections of the same linguistic group, by two of the most brilliant American anthropologists of the new generation: Opler and Goodwin – the latter sadly passed away immediately after finishing writing the book, even before it was published. For, if the subject is nearly the same, the method and concerns of the two authors are quite different. Goodwin has produced a systematic monograph that attempts, along the lines of the great classical models, to restore a still recent past, despite the cultural and demographic collapse of the tribe; whereas Opler, more sensitive to the current state of a social group in the process of rapid assimilation, has described the Apache of today. This divergence is apparent right from the start, in the table of contents: Goodwin deals, in turn, with questions of morphology, historical evolution, the clan, the family, kinship and marriage, social rules, the individual life cycle, representations and customs; Opler, by contrast, follows the successive stages of individual existence: childhood, maturation, adult life, beliefs, political and economic activities, sexual and conjugal life, and, finally, the milestones of native life. The one has sought to re-create a picture of Apache society, the other to describe the Apache as individuals in what today serves as their society.

Goodwin's work draws on observations collected over a period of ten years. One cannot help but admire the talent on display in the resulting seven hundred pages of analysis and discussion based, for the most part, on the accounts of thirty-four elderly informants. Despite the difficulties posed by research under such conditions, the material is of rare quality, and it probably represents our best source on the social organization of a North American tribe.

The theory of the clan (pp. 97–122) is of particular interest. Apache society is subdivided into a hierarchy of unilinear groupings consisting of clans, groups of closely related clans, and still vaster clan formations that acknowledge distant kinship. This situation has an impact on the system of kinship (pp. 193–283) and results in a conflict between two sets of terminology – one based on blood kinship and one used to define clan kinship – as well as a very interesting precedence of kinship ties from parallel cousinship in the paternal lineage over all others.

Even more than Goodwin, Opler relies on the accounts of his informants. His book provides a kind of tapestry into which their remarks, comments and reflections are woven. Great patience and skill are necessary to make a whole out of so many fragments, and the disappointing aspects of the result are to be attributed less to the talent of the author, which is considerable, than to the intrinsic nature of the object of study. This particularly brilliant example serves to raise the question of so-called acculturation studies, which are somewhat in fashion in the United States today.

Acculturation studies take their inspiration from one of two equally valid concerns: either from the rapid extinction of the majority of primitive societies, which compels young researchers to focus their work on degraded groups which are, practically speaking, the only accessible subjects; or from concerns about the economic and spiritual destitution of such and such a society which has collapsed through contact with a more powerful civilisation, leading to a search for remedies to relieve its particular ills. The two recent books by Clyde Kluckhohn and Dorothea C. Leighton, *The Navajo* and *Children of the People* (Cambridge, Harvard University Press, 1946 and 1947), provide a particularly endearing example of what two excellent observers and theorists, having a long familiarity with a social group in a state of decomposition – with its past, its language and its traditional institutions – may do to make its problems intelligible to public opinion, as well as to local educators and authorities. They thus pave the way for practical and urgent solutions and facilitate the assimilation of a long-suffering and disdained community.

But one suspects that specialists of acculturation have something quite different in mind than adapting training methods for young anthropologists to twentieth-century conditions or a secularization of the missionary project. Their work is based on theoretical positions that consider the debased group as equivalent, from the perspective of anthropological research, to the best-preserved society. And, indeed, is this distinction not purely subjective? Are not all societies undergoing perpetual transformation? The debased group is defined as such in relation to a situation to which we have ourselves contributed – the group has collapsed upon contact with our civilization. But what about the native society that has remained most removed from any contact with Whites? What do we know of the shocks it might have experienced, in a more or less remote past, from other native societies that are as remote from it, perhaps, as we are, and whose impact we cannot identify, whose influence we cannot trace, ignorant as we are of its history? From another point of view, we could also argue that all human community is a sociological object, simply by virtue of the fact that it exists and must function, from the moment that it exists. Each would then form an experience, probably a unique experience in its specific modes, but which, as experience, is as valuable as any other.

These implicit assumptions appear all the more dangerous now that a more general impression is emerging from the large number of monographs on "acculturated" peoples. This impression is particularly distressing: far from each adding something to the landscape provided by the previous ones, they all seem to repeat the same illustration of a monstrous destitution. Indeed, whereas there is an infinite variety of social forms, there is only one way of radically losing those we possess and adopting others that have been imposed from the outside. And this process does not amount to a form of sociability; it is a sickness that is common to all, or, rather, to which all are equally prone.

The approach of the monograph thus seems the least appropriate for acculturation studies. For they are dealing not with *systems* (which hypothetically no longer exist, or which, insofar as they have subsisted, are precisely not the object of the investigation) but with *symptoms*. And these symptoms are very few in number. In the process of coming undone, all of these societies, however different they may have been in their original states, converge. There are Melanesian, African and American cultures; but debasement has only one face.

A monograph that resolutely adopts, as Opler's does, the perspective of the individual fails to offer much for the anthropologist. And certainly not any description of techniques, beliefs or customs since, in an "acculturated" society, all of these have by definition collapsed, without having been replaced by anything that would qualify as a new and living culture. All that is left are attitudes. Yet, however interesting they might be to the psychologist, the local civil servant or the colonial administrator, these attitudes are strikingly similar across all societies placed in the same position: a combination of humility and arrogance, of a meagre dogmatism that fails to conceal an eagerness to conform with the new models, and a conciliation of these opposing attitudes in the rationalizations of an elementary syncretism. This is all rather poignant, but it raises the question of whether anthropology, whose object is the study of cultures and Culture, may pass with impunity to the study of individuals who find themselves deprived of any. This research is surely legitimate and may well produce results, but it springs from radically different concerns and methods. It is also questionable whether it may be expected to yield significant theoretical insights. When, as early as 1895, Boas suggested that the study of phenomena of acculturation might form one of two methods on which anthropology as a historical science could be based (the other being the study of phenomena of distribution), what he meant by "acculturation," as he would himself later explain, was the way "in which foreign elements are remodelled according to the patterns prevalent in their new environment" ("The Methods of Ethnology," *American Anthropologist*, vol. 22, 1920, p. 315). This is exactly the opposite of what is meant by the same term today – i.e. the way autochthonous elements disintegrate following an invasion by a foreign culture. The focus is thus no longer on the way cultures are made but on how they come undone; no longer on genesis but on pathology. But, then, we need to be aware of it.

NIMUENDAJÚ (Curt), *The Apinayé*, Washington, Catholic University of America, Anthropological Series, no. 8, 1939; *The Šerente*, Los Angeles, Publications of the Frederick Webb Hodge Anniversary Publication Fund, volume IV, 1942; *The Eastern Timbira*, Berkeley and Los Angeles, University of California Publications in American Archaeology and Ethnology, volume 41, 1946. All three volumes translated by Robert H. Lowie.

The great researcher, who passed away suddenly on 10 December 1945, surrounded by the Indians whom he had loved so much, will probably take with him the poignant secret that hovers over his entire anthropological oeuvre. Forty years of uninterrupted work and more than thirty publications – the numbers cannot do justice to a body of work that is the very definition, if ever there was one, of a "committed" anthropology. No one will have contributed more than Nimuendajú to our understanding of the Brazilian natives, and particularly of the primitive levels of Central and Eastern Brazil, about which he was to provide so many striking illuminations, the most important of which are collected in these three works, carefully translated and published by Mr. Robert Lowie.

The Apinayé, Šerente and Timbira share the same very rudimentary material culture, but their social organization is arrestingly complex. Among the Apinayé, we find a division into moieties together with a distribution into four "sides," or *kiyé*, which preside over marriage. This curious social structure only appears to be exogamic, since *kiyé* are passed on through matrilineal lines for males and through patrilineal lines for females; the *kiyé* that share the same *connubium* are thus dissociated into as many truly endogamous sections. The men are also organized by age groups, of which there are four, each with their initiation ceremonies, remarkably described by the author. The social organization of the Šerente comprises exogamic moieties (unlike those of the Apinayé), each divided into three primitive clans, plus one formed by adopted foreign tribes; to this must be added sports teams and male and female associations, which play a fundamental social role.

The monograph on the Timbira, by far the most developed, covers the full extent of their material life and social organization. The latter offers the most surprising compilation of classes and moieties: exogamic matrilineal moieties; so-called rainy season non-exogamic moieties; so-called town square groups; age groups; age group moieties; and male societies, of which there are six. About each of these organizational categories, Nimuendajú provides invaluable information. Yet none of the three studies could claim to exhaust the prodigious sociological trove offered by these long spurned tribes, whose rapid rate of extinction will probably never allow another researcher to devote to them the years of devout and patient friendship that had made Nimuendajú one of their own and given him access to their institutions. It is in light of the great monument that his work represents, and the number of lacunae that only he could have filled, that we shall measure the value of the man and the magnitude of the irreparable loss that his passing has visited on American anthropology, as well as on sociology as a whole.

VI

Techniques for Happiness

No other human group is as strongly committed to the existence of social laws as the Americans. The often striking results of surveys conducted by the Gallup Institute are less a feat of science – of a new science whose methods are in fact incredibly unsophisticated – than the natural consequence of a social environment. During the presidential election in November,[1] two major daily papers – the *Times* and the *Tribune*, which supported Mr. Roosevelt and Mr. Dewey, respectively – published identical first editions announcing the reelection of the incumbent president, whereas only 10 percent of the votes had been counted; and the Republican candidate himself conceded defeat when about a quarter of the results were in. In the United States, it appears that what is valid for part of society is also valid for the whole. The superficiality of such hasty conclusions aside, it is true that the life of the group there seems to obey a particular determinism that surpasses individual minds, and that the individual can grasp more easily from the outside than by searching inwardly, through analysis and reflection.

The primacy of the group, and of group activity, is probably not a distinctive characteristic of American society. It defines all social life. Yet cultural developments sediment in different ways and at a different pace, depending on whether the society in question is recently formed or of older vintage. In the latter case, the individual always offers richer ground than that of his environment; and social movement tends to operate through the constant readjustment of the group to the level of the individual, who is ahead of it and who casts judgment upon it. New societies present the opposite characteristic: the layers of culture settle more rapidly and thickly around group institutions and activities. These take shape first, and the frameworks of social life have already solidified by the time the cycle of individual development begins to unfold.

Yet we would be gravely mistaken if we were to consider the United States as a young society only. Young it is, insofar as it re-creates itself daily as an original reality. But the remote province of Europe that it was initially inclined to being has not yet completely disappeared. Certain traditions, certain archaic lifestyles have been preserved there, sometimes with more obstinacy and more faithfulness than in the very regions from which they were originally transplanted. American civilization lies at the crossroads of two folklores: one ancient, of European origin or locally created in the first centuries of colonization, of song – hymns, spirituals, laments from the Far West – of celebrations – Thanksgiving, Christmas, Halloween – and of rural life – hillbillies and cowboys, the people of the bayou; and the other the folklore of urban cataclysm, always in ferment, with its slang, which is much more than just an argot, and the authentically popular ways of the American underworld – Damon Runyon, Raymond Chandler, Dashiell Hammett – its beliefs and superstitions – sects, the rites of the California modern – and, finally, its pleasures – swing and hot jazz, jitterbug and boogie-woogie, movies, burlesques, crooners. Extending ever more deeply into this double gray area, American civilization remains no less subject to the fatalism of exteriority: alternately amazed and appalled, it discovers itself every day from the outside.

It is only from this perspective that we can make sense of the opposition – probably not specific to the United States, but which stands out particularly sharply there – between the plasticity and often indeterminate character of individual reactions, on the one hand, and the coherence and firmness of collective articulations, on the other. The skeletal structure of American society is still external, accounting for several of the apparent paradoxes of American life, which can be seen in a wide range of areas: in agricultural life, the farmer is more likely to eat canned food than the bounty of his own land, since, even before he started producing food, the system of processing and distribution that returns it to him was already in place; in industrial and commercial life, the big companies seem less in the service of individual desire than in charge of shaping and steering it, assuming even a general educational role; and, finally, in political life, the government is in advance of public opinion. American liberalism, which appears so audacious, must be interpreted along the same lines: didactic rather than revolutionary, it expresses a desire to discipline the unformed responses of individuals in the name of an existing community ideal, rather than a rebellion of the individual against an outdated social order.

The United States today thus still lives as a stranger to itself. One might even say that this condition is only intensifying, since an awareness of the phenomenon has only recently developed, and it must first be perceived before its full potential can be explored. One of the best-selling books of the past two or three years is an analysis of contemporary American society by an anthropologist, Mrs. Margaret Mead, who was originally trained to study Melanesian tribes rather than a great modern civilization.[2] The scholarly world did not embrace Mrs. Mead, but the wider public has done so enthusiastically. Moreover, in public administration, ethnographers and anthropologists are being given a greater role. And the most heeded among them are those who have dedicated themselves to the study of social types that are most remote from our own, as well as the most difficult to access and analyze. This is because the American mind has become more and more convinced that all societies, including (and perhaps first and foremost) the American society itself, present themselves to the individual mind as an irreducible whole, just like the strange customs of Oceanian savages. The average man unconsciously submits to this group heterogeneity. The cultivated and optimistic American sees the courageous recognition of this phenomenon as the prerequisite to any search for solutions.

Taking off from premises so very different from those to which we are traditionally accustomed, American social philosophy could not have adopted the same perspective as ours. Indeed, if it is the social group that constitutes an objective and durable reality, and the individual that acts as the plastic and unstable intermediary, then it is on the individual and not on the group that an intelligent effort at social improvement must concentrate – in the language of modern American psychology, the "conditioning" must begin "from within." When all social systems appear equally irreducible and heterogeneous, it would be vain to attempt to identify which is best: all will be equally bad if the individual cannot manage to create a familiar atmosphere within it. Mercifully, the individual can always be altered to adapt to the group in which he was born, whatever form it might take. In the broadest sense of the term, we might say that American thought is conservative. It wants to maintain first and foremost those elements of American social life that the individual has managed to make his own and to which he has successfully fastened himself, so to speak: i.e. the American way of life, which forms a whole down to its most intimate details, Saturday night movies and huckleberry pie ... However, the American reality overflows this island of clarity and security on all sides. A mystery to itself, it aspires to understand and master itself much more than to transform itself. When confronted with Europe's social concerns, the American sees only his own society and is inclined to think it would be foolish to set out to rebuild the house when one has neither the plans nor an inventory of the furniture. It is thus not surprising, then, that the United States should have regarded the question of the political reconstruction of Europe as one of restoration.

The individual does not wait; to integrate him into the group, to have him accept it, to give him at least the illusion that he understands it, in short to make him happy, one has to be quick about it – and any means will do so long as it proves effective. We therefore deal with the child first, or, rather, the eternal child that every man inevitably carries within himself. Indeed, in all societies, from the most primitive to the most complex, the individual bears within himself, in his heart of hearts, like an unknown and still open wound, the frustrations of his infantile sensibility, compelled to comply – at an age that will vary with each culture but will always be premature – with the rigid discipline of the group. Everywhere and at all times, it is the thinking of the adult, the sensibility of the adult, the activities of the adult that are posited as the ideal; yet how many adults ever actually achieve the social model of the adult? Experimental psychology reveals that the mental age of the vast majority of individuals remains much lower than their physical age. How could societies that ignore this most important fact not foster unhappiness by asking from their members always more than they can give, and by giving them, in other respects, far less than they unconsciously would like to receive? It would be too much to say that America has formulated this problem clearly. But, as so often over the past few centuries, it has intuited it long before it was raised in scientific terms and, in a confused and empirical way, it has begun to work out solutions.

Recognizing, legitimizing and meeting the demands of this inner child that lives on within each and every one of us – that is what is obscurely manifest in the United States in the social types on which both private and public life model themselves. The American woman is and will always remain above all a "mom," a permanent feature of mainstream American sensibility, and in whose growing prestige some American sociologists – probably more sensitive to superficial analogies than to the actual substance of social phenomena – identify the advent of a modern matriarchy. Respect for the government in power, even on the part of the political opposition, is one aspect of American life from which all democracies would do well to learn; but it is hard not to suspect that this almost sacred deference of the citizen for the president of the United States, or of the employee for his boss, is the direct consequence, in the end, of the reverence for "grown-ups" that has remained vivid in the adult's heart, and in which American society has found an effective instrument of collective discipline. The great national pastime, baseball, with its finicky rituals, its complexities and its quarrelsome rivalries, is less a sport than the apotheosis of a child's game. To all of America, from childhood until old age, the drugstore and its "soda fountain," with a thousand spigots, offers the concrete realization of the gingerbread house, with its praline walls, its caramel furniture, its ponds of syrup and its rivers of marmalade. And it is to all ages that the comics are addressed – the illustrated Sunday newspaper supplements and their amazing adventures of *Dick Tracy*, *Superman*, *Buck Rogers*, or else their initiation into the problems and conflicts of American life, between husband and wife, with *Mr. and Mrs*, *Homer Hopee* or *Polly and her Pals*, between parent and child, with *Teena*, *Our Jim* or *Bringing Up Father*, or of the young woman and the single woman, in *Little Orphan Annie, Dixie Dogan, Debbie Dean*, etc. Finally, it would be difficult to understand the place of the radio and the car in American life – the passionate interest (indeed simply the passion) that suddenly draws the attention of Americans to new models and away from those of the previous year – if we failed to see them as toys for adults. Just as the official recognition, and often the collective organization, of hobbies and amateur pastimes supports, at all ages of life, the right – and even the obligation, or at the very least the legitimate claim – to play.

Let us hope that adults whose eternal inner child has never been and never will be wronged shall be able to live together with greater ease and good will than if their youth had been filled with bitterness. Indeed, in the United States, the question of establishing harmonious relations between one another and of turning social life into a well-oiled mechanism is presented in remarkably simple terms. Here, again, technical know-how is called upon to do away with clashes and even minor frictions. First, it is in the domain of material life that constant ingenuity is applied, to eliminate effort and superfluous gestures through the proliferation of gadgets and small inventions. Physical beauty can be attained through a diet that is often disheartening but whose efficacy is made clear in American teenagers. For those whom nature itself would seem to have given up on, there are "finishing schools" from which the fat girl comes out skinny, the hunched emerges upright, and the homely full of grace. Body care is taught as an element of success in the world, in the same way as the art of conversation. "To be a good conversationalist" is taught through naïve recipes, and even correspondence courses. Conversely, a new employee, or even a university professor, will not be hired on the sole basis of their professional qualifications; in addition to their competence, they are expected to be "a nice guy" – i.e. never to jeopardize, through any personal instability, singularity or problem of private life the smooth functioning of the small community that is preparing to welcome them. This concern to avoid anything that might clash, shock or threaten the harmony of the group is not without its drawbacks. Indeed, it is very tempting to attribute to it the utter dullness that pervades many group relations. To a European academic marveling at the lack of spiritedness of university meetings, an American colleague responded: "But you Europeans, you argue too much." And when asked how one could possibly argue "too much": "You might hurt somebody."

It is a question of avoiding not only conflict between individuals but also conflict with oneself, which is no less fatal to one's peace of mind. The thousands of ways in which American life provides its members with opportunities for relaxation and exerts its control over them form a nuanced hierarchy. Few injunctions are heard as often – at school, in advertisements, in daily conversation – as that to "relax." The habit of chewing gum would probably not be as firmly established if it did not achieve the same social function, beyond its mechanical and physiological effects. The same goes for sports, and even more so for religion, whose social role seems to extend increasingly beyond the satisfaction of strictly spiritual needs. Finally, the extraordinary popularity of psychoanalysis (a hairdresser on unassuming 23rd street offers their clients the combined services of manicure, pedicure and psychology while their hair is drying!) should not blind us to the extensive modifications made to Freud's method and principles. For the point is no longer to unveil the inner conflicts of the subject who remains free, once enlightened about himself, to choose which direction he wishes to take. American psychoanalysis is increasingly focused on readjusting the individual to the norms of the group: less an awakening of the patient into freedom than a reconnection with happiness.

This optimistic sociology has already accomplished quite a few feats. Material happiness, which results from both the systematic simplification of everyday life and high living standards (which is, it must be said, the privilege of a minority), represents a theme already familiar enough to the French reader not to warrant further elaboration here. Rather, we would like to insist on the contrast between the European and American childhood experience. The latter is so free, so full of comforts, so blissfully unaware of any barrier between child and adult; and, in high school and at university, so keen to learn that the American upper class has managed, in the end, to do away with the concept of the "dunce." As far as adults are concerned, we should first highlight their professionalism, especially among civil servants and scientists, which guarantees that all problems will be carefully considered and methodically studied until solutions are found. Then there's the American civic-mindedness, which is but the application to collective life of the care taken in all things: from the "paper salvage" to the "tin can salvage" – i.e. the recycling of old newspapers and empty cans – to the sale of Treasury bonds, which is always the pretext for an avid and friendly competition between neighboring villages. Where else but in America do business enterprises invite the public to give priority to the purchase of war bonds over that of their own products? A watch, some flour, a tie – "Yes, but buy a War Bond first." Finally, while the fact that group antagonisms often take a violent turn in the United States should not be ignored, what is most striking is how smooth relations between individuals are. On all these fronts, the techniques for happiness have met with unquestionable success. Its most moving symbol might be the thousands of squirrels that roam American public parks, whose delightful sense of security among visitors might tip the balance, pending Judgment Day, in favor of a childhood without malice, an adolescence without hatred and a humanity without rancor.

And yet techniques, even techniques for happiness, cannot consume the individual as its raw material with impunity. American civilization, as passionately intent as it has been to free society of all drama, now has quite a few reasons for concern. Methods that have been so effective with individuals have proven powerless with groups. In fact, American society operates according to a double dynamic of the permeability of the individual and the impermeability of the group. Nothing is smoother or more spontaneous and fluid than the relations between individual child and individual adult, individual man and individual woman, individual boss and individual worker. But generations, sexes, classes could not be more estranged from one another. An American child will be easier to engage with than a thousand of his European peers, yet the American childhood experience also produces major pathological accidents, such as "Sinatra fans," "hoodlums" and "victory girls,"[3] which parents are stunned to discover and collective mechanisms are powerless to control. The frankness that characterizes social relations between men and women cannot dispel the latent antagonisms of American life that turn women not only into guardians of the home and the stable element in an otherwise insecure life, as in the days of the pioneer, but increasingly into the ruthless propagator of norms that this form of transmission has failed either to enrich or to humanize. Finally, the brutality of strikes and lockouts is well known; and yet it is considerably less than that of the tragic racial conflicts.

Even at the individual level the problem is still far from finding any solution. Indeed, if there is no other country where it is as easy to be happy like everyone else, there is no other country either where those who cannot, or will not, be content with collective solutions meet with a more uncertain fate. And this is where the true drama arises, the fundamental drama of American civilization, the drama that the techniques for happiness have successfully ascertained but not resolved, and which, from the perspective of the individual conscience, may be identified as the fear of loneliness. For American happiness forms a whole in a double sense: first, because society offers only a single model; then, because all its elements are interconnected and leave no room for choice. American civilization comes in a single block – it must be embraced in its entirety or abandoned altogether.

This is why the American soul, from childhood onward, feels an anxiety rising within itself that is truly its own: that of being alone, of being left behind. It tries to elude this sensation through what we might call relentless sociability. In primary and secondary school, the main objective is to be popular – to have as many friends, dates and letters as possible. Later it will be memberships in clubs and more or less obscure associations, parties – group visits and excursions – and even those American holidays, so disconcerting to the European sensibility, where everything seems to have been organized to preclude the solitude of nature and intimacy with oneself. And, finally, the skyscraper – the symbol of American civilization in the eyes of the world – is far less a technical feat than a pathetic expression of that need to huddle together, that anxious desire for communion.

Will the techniques for happiness manage to overcome these obstacles, or will they continue to meet, in the always receding yet desperately irreducible resistance of the individual, its absolute limit, in which European thought will find its traditional values confirmed? What is at stake here, ultimately, is whether there can be a civilization in which both masses and elites find satisfaction. Outside of a few radicals who declare their readiness to rid themselves of the latter, contemporary America's answer is a vigorously optimistic affirmative. A suffering Europe, now painfully emerging from a crisis that could easily convince it of the sterility of its destiny, would do well to closely monitor this experiment, whose originality and fertility should not obscure the fact that it has developed on a spiritual and moral ground that forms the everlasting common heritage of the Old and the New Worlds.

Reciprocity and Hierarchy

VII

War and Trade among the Indians of South America

Few aspects of the culture of South American Indians have struck the imagination of early travelers more than those having to do with the preparation, conduct and consequences of war. It seems that the contrast between the primitive lifestyle of the native populations of Brazil, for instance, and the degree of refinement of their techniques of war, as well as the size and frequency of military operations between the various groups, allowed the chroniclers of old to find their bearings, in a certain sense, enabling them to rediscover – in this remote land and among peoples that were, indeed, rather strange – the turbulent atmosphere of sixteenth-century Europe.

Authors such as Jean de Léry, Hans Staden, André Thevet, Yves d'Evreux and many others devoted considerable attention to these sorts of endeavors. It must be said that the study of intertribal relations among the Brazilian coastal populations was of the utmost political importance to the early explorers. No sooner had the Portuguese forged friendly relations with one tribe than its hostile neighbors would extend a warm welcome to the French, rivals of the former, and support them in their feuds. Moreover, the spectacular warring expeditions of the Tupinamba, as recounted by Jean de Léry in particular, are enough to excite the imagination. From the warriors' attire – simultaneously sumptuous and terrifying, with their feather headdresses and bodies painted red and black with *urucu* and *genipa* dyes – to the skillful use of incendiary arrows and the asphyxiating smoke of chilli plants, every detail of the war preparations gave cause for horror and admiration. The depiction of Brazil's international life thus reconstructed offered a picture in which a multitude of groups were essentially occupied in bloody combat, sometimes between neighboring tribes speaking the same language and whose separation into distinct groups dated back only a few years.

These representations no doubt corresponded for the most part to reality. How else could one account for the fragmentation of the primitive peoples of South America, their dispersal into a multiplicity of small social units that often belonged to the same linguistic families, and yet were isolated from one another at opposite ends of the Brazilian forest and plateau? It seems undeniable that, in pre-Columbian tropical America, the forces driving them apart were much stronger than those of unity and cohesion. There is little doubt that, in ancient times, as indeed still nowadays, neighboring groups were more likely to treat one another as enemies than as allies, that they feared and avoided one another, and that they had very solid grounds for adopting such an attitude. Yet it also seems clear that, even in the narratives of our early modern authors, this attitude of indigenous groups had its limits, and that their relationships were not entirely determined by negative motivations. We might mention the frequent use of objects and raw materials that must have been of foreign origin – such as the green gemstones, described by Yves d'Evreux and Jean de Léry, worn by coastal tribes as insets in their lips, cheeks and ears, which they considered as their most precious goods – testifying to the existence of trade relations between distant groups.

A close reading of Jean de Léry reveals that, among the Tupinamba of Rio de Janeiro, war was not at all the result of disorder, nor was it the expression of a purely anarchical state of affairs. War had a clear objective, one which left a deep impression on the explorers: the procurement of prisoners to be consumed, according to a carefully elaborated ritual, in the course of cannibalistic meals. These meals, which filled European explorers with such horror, – especially Léry, who witnessed them, and even more so Staden, who on several occasions narrowly escaped being a victim of one himself – served multiple functions for the Tupinamba, which explains why these ceremonies occupied such an essential place in the native culture. Anthropophagous rites are linked to both magic and religion, as well as to social organization. They challenge metaphysical beliefs and guarantee the longevity of the group, and it is through them that the social status of individuals is defined and transformed. That the wars in which Amerindians engaged were intended primarily to ensure the regular performance of this ritual is made amply clear by their despondent response when Villegaignon forced them to sell him their prisoners: "What is the point of war, then, if we can no longer keep our prisoners to eat them?" A radically different image of the practice of war thus emerges from the reading of the classical works: not only negative but also positive; not just the expression of an imbalance and a crisis in relations between groups but, quite the opposite, a regular mechanism for ensuring the functioning of institutions. To be sure, war pitted the various tribes against one another, both psychologically and physically, but it also served to establish unconscious relations of exchange, perhaps inadvertent but surely inevitable, of reciprocal services, which were essential to the maintenance of the culture.

But it was not until the end of the nineteenth century and the major expeditions of Karl von den Steinen that this fact was fully established, rather than just suspected by the explorers of earlier centuries – the presence, alongside conflict and opposition, of multiple factors of cohesion between the small social units of which native America was composed. The conditions of social life in the regions that von den Steinen was the first to explore, in 1884 and 1887, seemed fully to confirm such observations, and so it might be helpful to sketch a morphology of them.

The upper course of the Xingu, a tributary on the right bank of the Amazon, forks out into several branches that run for the most part parallel to one another. On this vast river network, clinging to the banks as if to the teeth of an enormous comb, von den Steinen discovered a dozen small tribes belonging to different groups, representing the major linguistic families of Brazil. These tribes lived short distances away from one another, their geographical proximity having little to do with any cultural or linguistic affinities. Quite the opposite: villages that spoke the same language were often separated from one another by different tribes which themselves constituted enclaves of remote groups. Since von den Steinen's explorations, the Xingu was visited on several occasions by other ethnographers and travelers: Hermann Meyer, Max Schmidt, Fawcett, Hintermann, Dyott, Petrullo and, more recently, Buell Quain. The surveys of the distribution of groups made by these various observers vary sometimes widely from that of von den Steinen, demonstrating that the location of tribes is only temporary, at least in the details. But the essential traits of the Xingu morphology have remained unchanged to this day. We are still dealing with the relative concentration, over a limited territory, of a large number of heterogeneous groups that either belong to different families or consider themselves as such, even if they speak the same language.

If Petrullo insists on a homogeneity of material culture across the entire geographical area, it is also certain that a high degree of specialization once distinguished the various tribes. The homogeneity is a mere semblance, resulting from trade between the groups. This phenomenon is particularly apparent with regard to ceramics, which, in von den Steinen's day, were supplied to the Bakairi and Nahukuá by the Kustenau and the Mehinaku, and to the Trumai and the other Tupi-speaking tribes by the Waura. This system of exchange persists to the present day, at least in its essential aspects. In 1887, the Bakairi specialized in the production of *urucu* and cotton and in the making of hammocks, rectangular beads and other kinds of shell beads. Their neighbors considered the Nahukuá as the best makers of gourd containers, walnut shell beads and pink mother-of-pearl beads. The Trumai and the Suya held a monopoly on the making of stone weapons and tools, and they were highly advanced in the growing of tobacco. In similar fashion, the making of salt from water lilies and palm tree ashes was, and still is, the province of the Trumai and Mehinaku. The Arawak-speaking tribes traded their pottery for gourd containers from the Nahukuá and, still in 1938, Quain confirmed von den Steinen's observation regarding the bows of the Trumai, which were fabricated by the Kamayura.

This artisanal specialization corresponded to differences in living standards. Von den Steinen was struck by the poverty of the Yawalapiti: among these Indians, foodstuffs were meagre and manufactured objects scarce. Their situation may have been the result of a bad harvest or an unexpected attack, since international relations on the upper Xingu were not terribly peaceable.

Each tribe has its own territory, delineated by well-known borders, generally defined by riverbanks. These rivers are considered routes of free passage, even though the fishing weirs that cut across them are tribal property and accepted as such. Despite these simple rules, there is little mutual trust among neighboring groups – an attitude that is illustrated in the custom of lighting a warning fire several hours, or even several days, before reaching a village one sets out to visit. Tribes are designated "good" or "bad" based on expectations regarding either the relative degree of generosity of their welcome or the extent of the conciliation or aggression anticipated in the attitude of a feared neighbor. When von den Steinen explored the Kuliseu, one of the branches of the Xingu, the Trumai had just been attacked by the Suya, who had previously taken many prisoners from the Manitsaua. The Bakairi, for their part, feared the Trumai, whom they accuse of drowning their prisoners of war after tying them up. In 1938, just as in 1887, the Trumai would flee before the Suya, of whom they were terrified. Conflicts of this kind often erupt between groups speaking the same language, as for instance between the various villages of the Nahukuá group.

Yet, even though visiting strangers are often prey to theft, the ties that bind these tribes together are probably stronger than their antipathies. Quain highlights the general multilingualism that prevailed over the entire geographical area and points out that most villages hosted a contingent of visitors from neighboring groups. Most often, these visits had their origins in intertribal customs or else were necessary for the normal functioning of institutions. We have already noted the commercial exchanges between tribes, which often took the form of games, such as the "barter auction." Members of different groups engage in wrestling matches, and villages invite one another to their festive celebrations. These invitations may serve as more than polite gestures or calls for the opening of trade negotiations, and they may originate in a real ritual necessity. Indeed, some important ceremonies, such as initiation rituals, can only take place with the cooperation of a neighboring group.

These relations – half-bellicose, half-amicable – often result in marriages between members of different groups. At the time of von den Steinen, such marriage alliances would occur between the Mehinaku and the Nahukuá, as well as between the Bakairi, on the one hand, and the Kustenau and Nahukuá, on the other. When such intermarriages are systematically practiced between two groups, they can also give rise to a new social unit, such as the Arauiti village, which was constituted from Auetö and Yawalapiti couples.

It is thus clear that, in the Xingu region, warlike clashes are just the counterpart of positive relations, and that these have both economic and social dimensions. The same observation can be made with regard to the Tupi-Kawahib Indians who live on the Rio Machado, a tributary on the right bank of the Rio Madeira.

When they were discovered in 1914 by General (then Colonel) Cândido Mariano da Silva Rondon, these Indians, even though they spoke the same language and were aware of their linguistic and social homogeneity, were scattered across a rather vast area and divided into approximately twenty clans, which were sometimes allies, sometimes enemies of one another. At the instigation of a particularly dynamic chief, one of these clans was in the process of gaining hegemonic control over the entire group through a series of successful wars. This ambition was never fully achieved, however, and the Tupi-Kawahib fell into a rather complete state of physiological and social decrepitude immediately upon their first contacts with Whites. But, still in 1938, it was possible to observe among their last survivors that the policy of intermarriage was the counterpart of war and that, in many cases, there was a resort to war only when prior efforts to impose an alliance through intermarriage had failed.

* * *

Yet there is no better example to highlight the intimate correlation between the activities of war and other kinds of relations than that of the Nambikwara, whom we studied in 1938–9. The facts we collected demonstrate in such clear fashion the abiding character of the different kinds of intertribal relations that it is impossible to begin analyzing them without first providing a quick sketch of the major characteristics of the cultural context of which they are a part.

The Nambikwara Indians live in one of the least known and most impoverished regions of Brazil. The plateau, an ancient formation, covers the entire eastern and central part of the South American continent and ends to the west in the vast loop formed by the confluence of the Rio Guaporé and the Rio Madeira. On these highlands, at an altitude ranging between 300 and 800 meters, the sandy soil of decomposed sandstone offers scant support for vegetation. These conditions are made even harsher by the irregular distribution of rainfall over the course of the year: torrential from October to March and then ceasing almost entirely for the rest of the year. The only vegetation that can survive in such conditions is the tall grass that is burnt by the sun over the dry season and the shrubs that grow at wide intervals, with thick bark and gnarly trunks. The rare animal takes refuge in the gallery forests that have sprung up along riverbanks and in the copses that form around springs. The Nambikwara live in the southern part of this region, and their semi-nomadic bands roam the plateau, for the most part between the valleys of the rivers that feed the Tapajós and the Rio Roosevelt. General Rondon discovered them in 1907, during the construction of the strategic telegraph line from the Mato Grosso to the Amazon.

The cultural level of the Nambikwara is one of the most elementary in contemporary South America. During the rainy season, they settle in villages made of primitive huts, which sometimes amount to simple shelters, located near streams. In the circular, burnt clearings they create within the gallery forests, they grow a few crops, primarily manioc. These crops sustain them during the sedentary period and partly into the dry season, since they are able to preserve the manioc by burying large cakes of it underground. When the dry season comes, the village is abandoned and its inhabitants scatter into small nomadic bands of thirty to forty people, rarely more. Each family carries one or several sacks that contain all of their earthly possessions – manioc cakes, calabash gourds, cotton threads, blocks of wax or sap, and a few instruments made of stone, and now sometimes of metal. For seven months a year, these bands roam across the savanna in search of small animals, lizards, spiders, snakes and other reptiles, wild berries and seeds, edible roots and, more generally, anything that might keep them from starving to death. Their camps – set up for one or several days, sometimes as long as a few weeks – consist of coarse shelters made of palm leaves and branches stuck in the sand in a semicircular formation. Each family builds its own shelter and fire.

Life in these encampments, in whose intimacies we shared, merits brief description. The Nambikwara wake with the daylight, rekindle the fire to warm up as best they can from the night's chill, then have a light meal of the manioc cakes left over from the previous day. A bit later, the men leave on a hunting expedition, either together or separately. The women remain at the camp, where they tend to the cooking. The first bathing session takes place when the sun begins to heat up. The women and children often bathe together for fun, and sometimes a fire is lit, around which they squat to warm up once they have come out of the water, jokingly exaggerating their natural shivers. The daytime chores vary little. Food preparation takes the most time and care. When they feel the need, the women and children go picking or gathering. Otherwise, the women spin cotton while squatting on the ground, or they carve beads out of walnuts and shells, delouse one another, laze about or sleep.

During the hottest hours of the day, the camp falls silent; the inhabitants lie quietly or sleep, enjoy the precarious shade of the shelters. The rest of the time, daily life unfolds amidst animated conversations. Nearly always gay and laughing, the natives maintain a steady joking banter, sometimes obscene or scatological, with unambiguous gestures that send everyone into fits of laughter. Work is often interrupted by visits or questions. The children laze about for much of the day, with the girls sometimes engaging in the same chores as their elders and the boys remaining idle or fishing in the streams. The men who have remained at the camp spend their time in basketwork or manufacturing arrows or musical instruments, or sometimes doing small household chores. A great harmony prevails within the household. At around three or four, the other men return from hunting and the camp livens up, the conversations become livelier, groups form along other than family lines. They dine on manioc cakes and anything that has been procured during the course of the day: fish, roots, wild honey, bats, captured creatures, and the small, sweet nuts of the "bacaiuva" palm tree. Sometimes a child starts to cry, to be quickly consoled by an elder. When night falls, a few women, newly appointed each day, go in search of wood for the night, to be gathered or felled from nearby bushes. The branches are piled up in one corner of the camp and everyone can then draw from it as needed. Family groups form around their respective fires as they begin to flicker. The evening is then spent conversing, or else singing and dancing. Sometimes these distractions go on well into the night, but generally, after a bit of caressing and friendly fighting games, couples come together in more intimate ways, mothers press their already sleeping children tighter, everything turns silent, and the cold night is punctuated only by the crackling of logs, the light tread of the fire tender, the barking of dogs or the cries of a child.

Among the many bands like the one I have just described, we must distinguish, on the one hand, those that are related through family ties and who together often comprise a village – or group of villages – that have "split up" for the purposes of nomadic life. These bands usually maintain peaceful relations, even though the contrary may sometimes result from trade or amorous disputes. Other bands, however, are unrelated to one another, are comprised of individuals that are neither kin nor allies; they come from widely dispersed territories and can sometimes even be separated by differences of dialect, as Nambikwara is not a homogeneous language. These bands adopt an ambiguous attitude toward one another. They fear one another and at the same time they feel a certain reciprocal need. It is indeed through encounter with one another that they will be able to come by certain desired articles, which only one of them owns or can produce or fabricate. These articles can be organized into essentially three categories: first come women, whose procurement can come only as the result of victorious war expeditions; then seeds, and especially bean seeds; and finally ceramics, or even fragments of ceramics that are used to make spindle whorls. The eastern Nambikwara, who are ignorant of pottery and whose cultural level is far inferior to that of their western and southern neighbors, had thus recently launched several war campaigns with the sole objective, according to their chief, of procuring for themselves bean seeds and pottery fragments.

The behavior of two bands who know themselves to be neighbors is particularly remarkable. The natives dread encounter even as they desire it. It is impossible that any such encounter might occur by chance: for several weeks, the two bands will have been on the lookout for the vertical smoke billowing from their respective campfires, visible for miles in the clear skies of the cold season. It is indeed one of the most impressive spectacles of the Nambikwara territory, those troubling billows of smoke that suddenly appear in the evening on a seemingly deserted horizon. The natives cast anxious glances at the clear evening sky: "There are Indians camping ..." But which Indians? Is the approaching band friendly or hostile? The attitude to be adopted is discussed at length around the fire. Contact sometimes seems inevitable, in which case it might be best to initiate it. If the band feels strong enough, or if it is lacking in certain products deemed indispensable, contact is, on the contrary, desired and sought after. For weeks, the groups avoid one another and maintain a prudent distance between their respective campfires. Then one day the decision is made, the women and children are told to spread out in the bush, and the men go out to confront the unknown.

We have ourselves participated in one of these encounters, which constitute the most memorable event in a Nambikwara's life. The two bands, reduced to their male elements, cautiously converge and immediately engage in an extended conversation. Or, more accurately, each in their own turn, the leaders of each band deliver a long monologue interjected with exclamations and delivered in a plaintive and tearful tone, a nasal and drawling voice that stretches out the end of each word. A group with bellicose intentions catalogues its grievances, while a peaceful one professes its good intentions. It is unfortunately impossible to reconstitute *post facto* the exact words of these parliamentary discourses, pronounced on the spur of the moment. But here is a fragment of one, which gives a sense of their structure and tone: "We are not angry! We are your brothers! We are well disposed! Friends! Good friends! We understand you! We come with amicable intentions!," etc. The same oratory style might also be used for preliminary invocations prior to declarations of war.

Following this exchange of peaceable appeals, the women and children are summoned, groups re-form and a camp is organized. Yet each group maintains its own individuality even while making its campfire close to others. The signal to begin singing and dancing is often given (the two activities being in fact inseparable; they are designated by the same word in the native language). Each group will then, following etiquette, deprecate its own performance and laud that of the other: "The Tamandé sing well! *Our* singing days are over …" In the same way, upon finishing a song or dance, each team exclaims in a piercing tone of voice, affecting sadness, "What horrible singing that was!," while the other warmly protests, "No! No! It was lovely!"

In the case we witnessed, the protocols of courtesy were not observed for very long. On the contrary, the mood quickly became more animated in the overall excitement of the encounter, and it was not long into the evening before the discussions, mingled together with chants, began to make an extraordinary racket, whose meaning at first completely escaped us. Menacing gestures were made tentatively, erupting into the occasional brawl, which prompted others to intervene as mediators. However, these expressions of hostility did not quite convey an impression of disorder, enfolding as they did at a leisurely pace and with a sense of propriety, the ambient din notwithstanding. Nambikwara anger expresses itself through stylized gestures, most often involving the sexual parts. The man thus seizes his own "sex" in both hands and points it at his opponent, sticking out his belly and bending his knees. A second stage involves assaulting the enemy in order to pull out the tuft of hay hanging from the bead belt just above his lower abdomen. The hay "covers the sex," and "pulling out the hay" becomes the object of the combat. Yet, even if the operation succeeds, it is only of a symbolic nature, the loincloth (that is often not even worn) being of such flimsy material that it could not ensure the protection, and indeed not even the concealment, of the organs. Finally, the utmost insult is when the bow and arrows are seized and thrown into the surrounding bushes. In such circumstances the natives maintain the appearance of calm, yet their attitude is tense, as if they were (and clearly they are) in a state of violent but contained anger. These fights probably sometimes degenerate into full-fledged conflict, but in this case they calmed down as dawn approached. Still in the same state of manifest irritation, they proceeded to inspect one another, not at all in a gentle manner, brusquely feeling each other's drop earrings, cotton bracelets, and small feather ornaments while rapidly mumbling the words: "This ... this ... see ... that's pretty ... ."

This *reconciliation inspection* indeed marks the conclusion of the conflict. It introduces a new dimension into the relations between the two groups: that of commercial exchange. As coarse as the Nambikwara's material culture might be, the products of other groups' industry are highly prized by their neighbors: the eastern tribes need pottery and seeds; the northern and central tribes consider the necklaces of their southern neighbors to be especially precious. Thus, a meeting of two tribes, when it can unfold peacefully, inevitably leads to a series of mutual gifting: the ever-present possibility of conflict gives way to the market – but a market of a very special kind. If we consider the transactions as a series of gifts, it must be said that reception of the gifts does not involve any expressions of thanks or satisfaction; and if we consider them as trade, the trade is carried out without any bargaining, without any attempt by the seller to enhance the value of the item, or to lower it on the part of the buyer, or any manner of disagreement whatsoever between the two parties. In truth, one is reluctant to admit that any form of trade is occurring at all: each native tends to his usual occupations; as the objects or products quietly move from one to another, the giver does not draw attention to his giving of the gift, nor does the receiver seem to pay any attention whatsoever to his new possession. In this way, cottonseeds and balls of thread, blocks of wax or resin, bars of *urucu* dye, shells, pendant earrings, bracelets and necklaces, tobacco and seeds, feathers and bamboo shards for the making of arrowheads, yarns of palm fibre, hedgehog spikes, whole pots and ceramic fragments, and calabash containers are all exchanged.

This mysterious circulation of goods takes place at a leisurely pace over the course of half a day or even a whole day, after which the groups go their separate ways. Then, at a subsequent stage, each takes inventory of what he has received and recalls what he has given away. As regards the fairness of the exchanges, the Nambikwara thus trust in the good faith and generosity of their trading partners. The idea of evaluating, negotiating, bargaining, demanding or collecting is totally foreign to them. We once sent a native on a mission to a neighboring tribe and promised him our forest knife in exchange. When our messenger returned, thinking he would come and claim his reward of his own accord, we failed to bring it to him immediately. He never came and, on the following day, we could not find him. He had left in a most annoyed state, his friends told us, and we never saw him again. Under these conditions, it is hardly surprising that, once the exchanges are completed, one of the groups should leave feeling unhappy with its lot and, upon taking stock of what it had acquired and what it had given away, should develop feelings of bitterness that take an increasingly aggressive turn over the weeks or months to follow. It seems that the wars between the bands often found their origins here. There are also entirely different causes: avenging murder or the abduction of women, either by taking the initiative or avenging a previous attack. However, as a general rule, bands do not feel any sense of collective responsibility to avenge a wrong done to one or several of its individual members. Much more often, given the acute and abiding animosity between groups, these serve as pretexts to arouse the spirits, in which case they are most welcome, especially when the group feels it has the upper hand. The proposal for war is made by an especially excited individual, or one that presents to his companions the particular grievances he harbors. His speech is couched in the same style, and delivered in the same tone as the direct appeals between foreign groups encountering one another: "Hey! Come here! Listen! I am angry! Very angry! I want arrows! Long arrows!"

But before embarking on a war expedition, the omens must be read by the chief or, in groups where the chief and the sorcerer are distinct roles, by the sorcerer. Adorned in the proper attire, tufts of hay daubed with red and jaguar-skin caps, the men perform war chants and dances while shooting arrows into a symbolic pole. The presiding member then solemnly hides an arrow somewhere in the bushes, which has to be found the next day stained in blood for the auspices to be considered favorable. Many a war expedition thus decided will come to an end after a few kilometres' march – the excitement and enthusiasm having waned – and the small army will return to camp. Sometimes, however, war parties do see their mission through, with potentially very deadly effect. The Nambikwara usually attack at dawn and spread out in the bushes to await the time of assault. The signal for the attack is sounded using the small double whistle that the natives wear on a string around their necks, which is called a "cricket" because the sound it produces is similar to that of the insect. The war arrows are the same as those used for hunting large animals but, before they are used against humans, the edges of their wide lance-like tips are serrated. Poisonous arrows dipped in curare, commonly used for hunting, are never employed in war.

Many of the details of these techniques of war recall the descriptions of the early travelers, as well as more recent accounts involving different tribes, such that we now feel licenced to generalize, to a certain extent, some of the facts that we have related and that have been less frequently observed. For the Nambikwara, as probably for many of the peoples of pre-Columbian America, war and trade are activities that cannot be studied separately. Commercial exchanges are but potential wars that have been peacefully resolved, and war is the outcome of unhappy transactions. In the sixteenth century, objects of Inca origin were found in the hands of the most primitive inhabitants of the Brazilian forest and coast. In the other direction, iron introduced by early colonizers preceded their advance into the more remote regions of the continent by several decades. These facts demonstrate that positive relations between groups – such as collaboration in the field of social life to ensure the smooth functioning of institutions, as well as economic exchanges – have fully outweighed conflict, which at first captured exclusive attention due to its more spectacular nature. The profoundly heterogeneous dimension of the South American dialects – whose vocabularies reflect such diverse origins that, in many instances, they can only be grouped into linguistic families through an uncertain play of percentages – offers further evidence still of the multiple contacts and exchanges that must have occurred in a distant or not so distant past.

* * *

Other clues are supplied by the study of the complex systems of social organization of these tribes, which contrast so strikingly with their low economic level and very rudimentary technical capability. We are only beginning to discover systems in South America that are every bit as sociologically refined as Australian societies.[1] Tribes with small populations, whose structure was not expected to hold much mystery, have suddenly revealed themselves, upon closer examination, to be an extraordinary combination of clans, age cohorts, societies and phratries into which individuals are distributed, thus naturally accumulating multiple titles. Almost all of these societies are divided into two moieties whose role is alternately to perform ceremonies, and sometimes to deal with weddings as well. But in South America, this institution, which is so widespread in other parts of the world, presents an additional characteristic: asymmetry. At least in the names they bear, these moieties have an unequal status in a large number of tribes. Thus, we find coupled together the "Strong" and the "Weak," the "Good" and the "Bad," the "Upstream Ones" and the "Downstream Ones," etc. The terminology is so close to that used by different tribes to designate one another and the system itself is so directly reminiscent of the dual organization of the Inca empire – with its dichotomy between "Those from Above" and "Those from Below," whose historical origins are well documented – that we should not hesitate to recognize in these divisions the vestiges of a stage where the fundamental groups formed isolated units. We lived among the Nambikwara, sharing the daily lives of two bands that spoke different dialects and who had decided, by common agreement, to merge with each other. They established between their respective members an artificial kinship system that resulted in identical relations to those which might exist between the members of two exogamic moieties of a single society.[2] It is indeed unquestionably the case, since the discovery of the West Indies – which were inhabited in the sixteenth century by Carib natives whose women still bore, in their special language, traces of their Arawak ancestry – that processes of social assimilation and dissimilation are not incompatible with the functioning of Central and South American societies. More recently, as we have seen, von den Steinen witnessed the same phenomenon in the Arauiti village of the upper Xingu. But, as with the relationship between war and trade, the concrete mechanisms of these articulations have long been overlooked.

We have tried to show, in this article, how conflict and economic exchange in South America represent not only two types of coexisting relations but also two opposite and indissoluble dimensions of a single social process. The example of the Nambikwara Indians shows how hostility may give way to cordiality, aggression to cooperation, and vice-versa. But the continuity between these elements of the social whole does not end there. The facts outlined in the paragraph above show that primitive institutions possess the technical means to move hostile relations beyond the stage of peace and know how to use the latter to integrate new elements into the group, even while profoundly altering its structure.

We are of course not suggesting that all dual social organizations in South America result from the fusion of groups. Reverse processes – of dissimilation this time, rather than assimilation – can also occur within an already formed group. One of these processes could, for instance, result from the coexistence, within many South American tribes, of avuncular unions (maternal uncle and niece) and unions between cross-cousins (born respectively of a brother and a sister). Thus, from the fact that two individuals belonging to different generations can be competing for the same woman, a dichotomy may arise within the group between "Elders" and "Youngers." These are, in fact, the names by which the Tupi-Kawahib designate their moieties, without necessarily confirming that the hypothesis we have just formulated as a theoretical possibility is borne out in that example. But if such were the case, it should be pointed out that the dual system mentioned above differs considerably from other known systems. Whatever reservations we may have about any exclusive interpretation of the origins of dual organizations, it is nonetheless highly probable that, in certain cases, the integration explanation is appropriate. War, trade, the kinship system and the social structure must thus be studied in their intimate correlations. Just how far the study of these correlations can take us is another question. An overly systematic attempt at synthesis would fall prey to the unacceptable excesses of the functionalist interpretation. If we would not hesitate, for instance, to read some dual structures as the happy result of the dynamic integration of a former alliance system, it is much less certain that the differentiation of clans based on technical prowess – such as what we have shown among the Bororo[3] – can be interpreted as the legacy of the industrial specialization of tribes, as still exists today among the Xingu tribes. The sociologist should always keep in mind that primitive institutions are capable not only of conserving what is, and of provisionally retaining vestiges of a past that is coming undone, but also of hatching audacious innovations, even when that means profoundly transforming traditional structures.

VIII

The Theory of Power in a Primitive Society

Few anthropologists would admit today that human groups displaying an extreme primitiveness in either the field of material culture or that of social organization can teach us anything about the early stages of the evolution of mankind. Primitiveness in one field is often accompanied by great sophistication in another, as shown by the Australian refinements concerning kinship. Since these primitive peoples have their own history, it would be a serious mistake to think that it may be discounted because we know nothing of it. The partial similarities which archaeological remains allow us to infer between primitive societies and those of prehistoric man, while they remain sheer hypotheses, do not preclude the tremendous differences which may have existed in fields outside of the archaeologist's reach. The above considerations, which are only a few among many others, have led most anthropologists in recent years to consider each human group as a particular case which should be studied, analyzed and described from the point of view of its uniqueness, without any attempt to use the results for a better understanding of human nature.

However desirable this attitude may have been after the evolutionist orgies, and however fruitful the results obtained, there are many dangers in it which should raise increasing concern. Are we condemned, like new Danaids, endlessly to fill the sieve-like basket of anthropological science, vainly pouring monograph after monograph, without ever being able to collect a substance with a richer and denser value? Fortunately, primitive societies do not have to be considered as illusory stages in the evolution of mankind to teach us a truth endowed with general validity. The fact that they are (at least some of them, and all of them in some respect) simpler societies than our own does not need to be taken as a proof of their archaism. They still throw light, if not on the history of mankind, at least on some basic forms of activity which are to be found, always and everywhere, as prerequisites for the existence of human society.

Simpler organisms may provide a better field for the study of organic functions than those which exhibit the same functions, although in a more complex form. Simple human groups render the anthropologist the same kind of service without any need of surmising that they represent survivals of older types of organization. Now, to call upon the notion of function in the field of anthropological science is no discovery. This notion, first introduced by Durkheim in 1894,[1] has been exploited only too often since then, sometimes in the most abusive way. There are indeed functions of social life as well as functions of organic life. But neither in one domain nor in the other does everything correspond to, nor may it be justified by, its functional value. To state the opposite view can lead to only two results: either an anthropological return to eighteenth-century Providentialism, where culture would play in relation to man the same utopian tutelary role which was attributed to nature by the author of *Paul et Virginie*;[2] or the reduction of the notion of function to a mere tautology – to say, for instance, that the function of the notched lapel on our coats is to gratify our aesthetic feeling would be meaningless, since, here, obviously, the feeling results from the custom, and not the contrary. The custom has a history which explains its existence. It does not, under present circumstances, possess any function.

The preceding may appear to be a very ponderous introduction to an address dedicated by its title to the psychological aspects of political power in a small tribe of the Brazilian interior. But I do not believe that the data which I am going to present, if considered only as descriptions of forms of leadership/command among a hitherto little known group, would honestly warrant much attention. Similar facts have been recorded many times, either together or separately. The particular interest of the Nambikwara is that they confront us with one of the simplest conceivable forms of social and political organization. Political power exists, among all human groups, in very different forms, but it would be vain to assign a special functional value to each of the modalities down to their smallest details. Power, undoubtedly, has a function. It can, however, be reached only through analysis bearing on the underlying principle of the institution. In other words, the differing structure of the digestive organs in man, ox, fish and clam do not point toward different functions of the digestive system. The function is always and everywhere the same and can be better studied, and more fully understood, where it exists under a simple form – for instance, in a mollusc. Similarly, and as Professor Lowie once wrote, if anthropology is to be considered as a scientific study, its subject matter cannot be individual cultures, but culture taken as a whole; the role of individual cultures being to offer, according to their own characteristics, special angles from which the basic functions of culture, although universal in application, can be more easily reached.

This will perhaps help us to eliminate preliminary questions which otherwise could have proved very difficult. Anthropologists in South America and elsewhere have been eagerly debating the question of whether these South American tribes – nomadic, relying mostly on collecting and gathering, with little or no agriculture, little or no pottery, and, in some cases, with no dwelling other than crude shelters – should be considered as truly primitive and as having preserved their exceptionally low cultural level through tarriance, or whether they did not previously possess a higher type of social and material organization and have regressed to a pseudo-archaism under unfavorable circumstances. The Nambikwara are one of those tribes which – along with the Siriono, on the other side of the Guaporé valley, the Cayapo, Bororo, Karaja of central Brazil, the so-called Gê of Central and Eastern Brazil, and some others – together form a kernel of primitiveness surrounded, in the west, by the higher tribes of the upper Amazon, the Bolivian plain and the Chaco, and from the Orinoco to the La Plata estuaries, by a coastal strip inhabited mostly by the Arawak, Carib and tribes of the Tupi-Guarani linguistic families. An independent linguistic stock divided into several dialects, the Nambikwara seem to display one of the more backward cultures in South America. Some of their bands do not build huts and are wholly ignorant of pottery, and even among others these two arts are exceedingly poor. There is no weaving, except for the narrow arm and leg bands which are made of cotton; no clothing whatsoever, either for the men or for the women; and no hammocks or platforms for sleeping, the natives being used to sleeping on the bare ground without the protection of blankets, mats or hides. Gardening exists only during the rainy season and does not spare the Nambikwara from wandering during the seven months of the dry season, looking for wild roots, fruits and seeds, small animals such as lizards, snakes, bats, spiders and grasshoppers and, generally speaking, anything which may prevent them from starving. As a matter of fact, their geographical surroundings, located in the northwestern part of the state of Mato Grosso and including the headwaters of the Tapajós, Rio Roosevelt and Rio Ji-Paraná, consist of a desolate savanna with little vegetation and still less game.

Had I approached my subject from a point of view other than the one outlined above, I would not have been able to avoid a long discussion of South American cultural history, aimed at establishing whether this apparent primitiveness constituted the survival of early conditions of life in South America or as a more recent – although undoubtedly pre-Columbian – regression resulting from culture clashes and processes of acculturation. Whichever may be the case, it does not substantially alter our problem: whether conserving ancient institutions or regressing to pseudo-primitive conditions, Nambikwara society functions, in the present, as one of the simplest conceivable forms of human society. We shall not seek to understand the particular history which kept them in their exceptionally crude organization or brought them back to it. We shall look only at the experiment in social anthropology which now unfolds under our very eyes.

This holds especially true in respect to their social and political life. For if we do not know what the material culture of the Nambikwara was forty years ago (they were discovered only in 1907), we do know that their numbers were tremendously reduced after their contact with white civilization. General (then Colonel) Cândido Mariano da Silva Rondon, who discovered and studied them, initially estimated their number at about 20,000. That was around 1915. I take this figure to be greatly exaggerated, but, even if reduced by one half, it considerably exceeds the present number, which is hardly more than 2,000. Epidemics have taken care of the difference. What does this mean from the point of view of our study? During the dry season, the Nambikwara live in nomadic bands, each one under the leadership of a chief, who, during the sedentary life of the rainy months, may be either a village chief or a person of position. General Rondon wrote that, at the time he was exploring the country, it was not rare to see bands averaging two or three hundred individuals. Now, sixty or seventy people are seldom encountered together, with the average size of bands being twenty individuals, women and children included. This demographic collapse cannot possibly have taken place without affecting the structure of the band. But here, too, we do not need to concern ourselves with questions about the type of political organization in earlier times. It is perhaps more difficult to understand Nambikwara sociology now than it was thirty years ago. Or, on the contrary, the much reduced Nambikwara bands might offer, more so than in the past, a privileged field for a study in social anthropology. My contention is that, precisely on account of its extreme impoverishment, the Nambikwara political structure lays bare some basic functions which may remain hidden in more complex and elaborate systems of government.

Each year, at the end of the rainy season – that is, in April or in early May – the semi-permanent dwellings placed in the vicinity of the gallery forest where gardens are cleared and tilled are abandoned and the population splits into several bands formed on the basis of free choice. Each band includes from two to ten families usually tied by kinship. This can be misleading when encountering a band, for one easily gets the impression that it is formed by an extended family. It does not take long to discover, however, that the kinship tie between two families belonging to separate bands may be as close as, and possibly closer than, those between two families within the same band. The Nambikwara have a simple kinship system based on cross-cousin marriage and the subsequent dichotomy between "cross" and "parallel" in every generation. Therefore, all the men in one generation are either "brothers" or "brothers-in-law," and men and women are to one another either siblings (true or classificatory) or spouses (true or classificatory). Similarly, children are, in relation to the adults, either sons and daughters (true or classificatory) or nephews and nieces, which is the same as actual or potential children-in-law.[3] As a result, there is a limited choice of terms to express kinship, and this explains why kinship within the band may appear closer than it actually is and kinship between people belonging to different bands more remote than shown by genealogies. Furthermore, a bilateral cross-cousin marriage system functioning in a relatively small tribe must produce a progressive narrowing, and even a multiplication, of the kinship ties between any two individuals. This is a supplementary reason preventing family relationship from becoming really operative in the constitution of the band. It could be said that, within a band as well as between different bands coming from the same temporary village, everybody is everybody else's kin and in pretty much the same fashion.

How then to explain the division into bands? From an economic point of view, the scarcity of wild food resources and the subsequently large area needed to feed one individual during the nomadic period make the division into small bands almost compulsory. The real question is not why there is a division but, rather, on what basis it takes place. I have said that this is done by free choice, but this freedom is not arbitrary. There are, in the initial group, several men acknowledged as leaders (who likely acquired this reputation from their behavior during the nomadic life) and who comprise the relatively stable nuclei around which the different aggregates form. The importance, as well as the permanence, of the aggregate through successive years depends largely upon the ability of each of these leaders to maintain his rank and possibly to improve it. Thus, it may be said that leadership does not exist as a result of the band's needs, but, instead, that the band receives its shape, size, and even origin, from the potential leader who pre-dates it.

There is, however, a continuous function of leadership, although not permanently assumed by the same individual. Among the Nambikwara, chieftainship is not hereditary. When a chief grows old, or is taken ill, and does not feel able to fulfill his heavy duty anymore, he himself designates his successor. "This one will be the chief ...," he says. It seems likely that this autocratic power to ensure one's own succession is more apparent than real. We shall emphasize later the small amount of authority enjoyed by the chief, and, in this case as in many others, the final decision is probably preceded by a careful survey of public opinion, the designated heir being, at the same time, the one with the greatest support from the members of the band. The appointment of the new chief is not only limited by the wishes or disapproval of the band; it needs also to correspond to the plans of the individual to be chosen. It is not rare for the offer of leadership to meet with a vehement refusal: "I don't want to be the chief." Then a new choice must be made. As a matter of fact, leadership does not seem to be coveted by many, and the general attitude of the different chiefs I happened to know was less to brag about their importance and authority than to complain of their many duties and heavy responsibilities. What, then, are the privileges of the chief, and what are his obligations?

When, in about 1560, the great French moralist of the sixteenth century, Montaigne, met in Rouen with three Brazilian Indians brought there by some explorer, he asked one of them what the privileges of the chief (Montaigne said, "the King") were in his country; and the native, himself a chief, answered: "To walk ahead on the warpath." Montaigne related this story in a famous chapter of the *Essays*, where he wondered a great deal about this proud definition;[4] but it was a greater wonder to me when, almost four centuries later, putting the same question to my informants, I was given the same answer. Civilized countries are certainly not accustomed to such constancy in the field of political philosophy! Striking as it may be, this answer is less significant than the name by which the chief is designated in the Nambikwara language. *Uilikande*, the native word for chief, seems to mean "the one who unites" or "the one who joins together." This etymology suggests that the native mind is fully conscious of the extremely important phenomenon which I have pointed out from the beginning, namely, that the leader appears as the cause of the group's desire to aggregate rather than as a result of the need for a central authority felt by a group already constituted.

Personal prestige and the ability to inspire confidence are thus the foundations of leadership in Nambikwara society. As a matter of fact, both are necessary in the man who will become the guide for the adventurous experiment that is the nomadic life of the dry season. For six or seven months, the chief will be entirely responsible for the management of his band. It is he who orders the start of the wandering period, selects the routes, chooses the stopping points and the duration of the stay at each of them, whether a few days or several weeks. He also orders and organizes the hunting, fishing, collecting and gathering expeditions and determines the conduct of the band in relation to neighboring groups. When the band's chief is, at the same time, a village chief (with the word "village" having the restricted meaning of the semi-permanent dwellings for the rainy season), his duties do not stop there. He will also determine the moment when, and the place where, the group will settle as well as direct the gardening and decide what plants are to be cultivated. Generally speaking, he will organize the occupations according to the seasons' needs and possibilities.

The performance of these rather versatile duties, it should be pointed out from the start, is not facilitated by any fixed power or recognized authority. Consent is at the origin of leadership, and consent, too, furnishes the only measure of its legitimacy. Disorderly conduct (according to native standards) or unwillingness to work on the part of one or two discontented individuals may seriously jeopardize the chief's program and the welfare of his small group. In this eventuality, however, the chief has no coercive power at his disposal. Ridding himself of the bad element can take place only insofar as the chief is able to bring public feeling in line with his own. Thus, he must continuously display a skill belonging more to that of the politician trying to hold on to his fluctuating majority than to an all-powerful ruler. Furthermore, it is not enough for him to keep his group together. Although the band lives practically on its own during the nomadic period, the existence of the other bands is not forgotten. It is not enough to do well; the chief must try – and his people count on him for it – to do better than the others.

No social structure is weaker or more fragile than that of the Nambikwara band. If the chief's authority appears too exacting, if he keeps too many women for himself (I shall later analyze the special features of the chief's polygamy), or if he does not satisfactorily solve the food problem in times of scarcity, discontent will very likely appear. Then, individuals, or families, will separate from the group and join another band believed to be better managed. For instance, this band may have better fare due to the discovery of new hunting or gathering grounds, or it may have become richer in ornaments or implements through trade with neighboring groups, or more powerful as a result of a successful war expedition. The day may come when a chief finds himself heading a group too small to face the problems of daily life and to protect his women from the covetousness of other bands. In such cases, he will have no alternative but to give up his command and join, together with his last followers, a more successful group. Thus, Nambikwara social structure is in a continuously fluid state. Bands come together, then break up; they increase in size and they disappear. Within a few months, sometimes, their composition, number and distribution become unrecognizable. Political intrigues within the same band and conflicts between bands impose their rhythm upon these fluctuations, and the ascent or decline of individuals and groups follow each other in an often surprising manner.

How can the chief overcome these difficulties? His first and main instrument of power lies in his generosity. Generosity – an all-important feature of leadership among most primitive peoples, especially in America – plays an essential role even at those crude cultural levels where worldly goods are limited to the most primitive weapons and tools, coarse ornaments made of feathers, shells and bones, and raw materials, such as lumps of resin and wax, hanks of fiber and splinters of bamboo for arrow-making. In truth, great economic distinctions between families, each of which must pack all of its belongings in the baskets carried by the women during the long travels of the dry season, are impossible. But, although the chief does not seem to fare better, in this respect, than any other, he must always have at hand surpluses of food, tools, weapons and ornaments which, however meager, acquire great value relative to the general condition of scarcity. When an individual, a family or the band itself needs or covets something, the chief is called upon to secure the desired article. Thus, generosity is the essential quality expected of a new chief. It is the note constantly struck which lends the general consent to leadership a harmonious or discordant sound. There is little doubt that the chief's ability to give is exploited to the utmost. Band chiefs were my best informants and, well aware of their difficult position, I liked to reward them liberally; but I seldom saw one of my many gifts remain in their hands for more than a few days. Each time I took leave of a band, after a few weeks or a few months, its members had had time to become the happy hoarders of axes, knives, beads, and so on. As a rule, however, the chief was just as poor as he was when I first arrived. Everything he had received from me (and this was considerably more than the average) had already been squeezed out of him. This collective greed often drives the chief to a position of desperation. Then the refusal to give plays roughly the same role, in this primitive democracy, as a vote of confidence in a modern parliament. When a chief reaches the point where he must say "No more giving! No more being generous! Let another be generous in my place!," he must, indeed, be sure of his power and prestige, for his rule is undergoing its severest test.

Ingenuity is but the intellectual form of generosity. A great deal of skill and initiative are the prerequisites of a good leader. It is he who makes the arrow poison, although the preparation of curare among the Nambikwara is a purely profane activity surrounded by no ceremonial taboos or magic prescriptions. It is he, also, who makes the rubber ball used in the head-ball games which are played occasionally. The chief must be a good singer and dancer, a merrymaker always ready to cheer up the band and brighten the dullness of daily life. This could easily lead to shamanism; and, in some cases, I have met chiefs who were at the same time healers and sorcerers. Mystical life, however, is kept in the background among the Nambikwara, and, wherever they exist, magical functions are only secondary attributes of the leader. More often chieftainship and sorcery are divided between two different individuals. In this respect, there is a strong difference between the Nambikwara and their northwestern neighbors the Tupi-Kawahib, among whom the chief is, first of all, a shaman, generally a psychopath given to dreams, visions, trances and impersonations.

But although they are oriented in a more positive direction, the Nambikwara chief's skill and ingenuity are nonetheless amazing. He must have a perfect knowledge of the territories traversed by his and other groups, be familiar with the hunting grounds and the location of fruit-bearing trees and the time of their ripening, and have some idea of the itineraries followed by other bands, whether hostile or friendly. Therefore, he must travel more, and more quickly, than his people, have a good memory, and sometimes gamble his prestige on risky contact with foreign and dangerous groups. He is constantly engaged in some form of reconnaissance or exploration and seems to flutter about his band rather than lead it.

Except for one or two men without actual power, but eager to cooperate and to receive occasional rewards, the passivity of the band makes for a strong contrast with its dynamic leader. It seems as if the band, having relinquished certain advantages to the chief, were in exchange relying entirely upon him to provide for its interests and safety. I witnessed a particularly striking demonstration of this under rather strange circumstances. After several weeks' discussion, I had obtained from a chief the favor of taking me, together with a few companions and some animals loaded with presents, to the semi-permanent dwellings of his band, which were uninhabited at that time. This was a chance for me to penetrate more deeply into the unexplored Nambikwara territory and to meet groups too shy to venture forth on the outer fringe. The native band and my own group set out together on a journey that was supposed to be short; but, because of the animals I had taken, the chief had decided that the usual route through a dense forest could not be used. He led us through the open country, lost his way several times, and we did not reach our destination on the scheduled day. Supplies were exhausted and no game was in sight. The not unfamiliar prospect of a foodless day fell gloomily upon the natives. But, this time, it was the chief's responsibility. The whole enterprise was his own, as well as the attempt to find an easier route. So, instead of trying to discover food, the hungry natives simply lay down in the shadow of the brush and waited for their leader to see them out of this most unpleasant situation. He did not wait or discuss but, taking the incident as a matter of course, simply left the camp accompanied by one of his wives. At the camp, the day was spent sleeping, gossiping and complaining. There was no lunch or dinner. But, at dusk, the chief and his wife reappeared, both heavily laden with baskets filled to the brim. They had hunted grasshoppers the entire day, and, although the expression "to eat grasshoppers" has approximately the same meaning in Nambikwara as the French *manger de la vache enragée*,[5] this food was enthusiastically received, shared and consumed, amidst restored good humor. The following morning, everybody armed himself or herself with a leafless twig and went grasshopper-hunting.

 I have several times referred to the chief's wives. Polygamy, which is practically the chief's privilege, brings him a moral and sentimental reward for his heavy duties together with the practical means of fulfilling them. In the Nambikwara band, apart from rare exceptions, only the chief and the sorcerer (when these functions are divided between two individuals) may have several wives. The chief's polygamy, however, presents special features. It constitutes not a plural marriage but, rather, a monogamous marriage to which relations of a different nature are added. I have already mentioned the fact that cross-cousin marriage is the usual pattern among the Nambikwara. Another type of marriage also exists between a man and a woman belonging to the generation following his own, either a wife's "daughter" (true or classificatory) or a sister's "niece." Both forms are not uncommon in South America and, together or separately, have been recorded among many tribes. Now, what do we find in the chief's case? There is first a monogamous marriage of the cross-cousin type – that is, where the wife belongs to the same generation as her husband. This first wife plays the same part as the monogamous wife in ordinary marriages. She follows the pattern of the division of labor between the sexes, taking care of the children, doing the cooking, and collecting and gathering wild food. To this marriage are added one or several unions, which, technically, are true marriages, but of a different type. Usually, the secondary wives belong to a younger generation. The first wife calls them daughters or nieces. Besides, they do not follow the pattern of the sexual division of labor but share indifferently in men's or women's activities. At the camp, they disdain domestic tasks and remain idle, either playing with the children to whose generation they belong or flirting with their husband, while the first wife keeps busy with the food and the fire. On the contrary, when the chief leaves on an exploration, a hunt, or some other manly task, they will accompany him and provide him with moral and physical help. These somewhat "tomboy" girls, chosen by the chief from among the prettiest and healthiest of the group, are to him "girlfriends" rather than spouses. They live on the basis of an amorous friendship which contrasts strongly with the more conjugal atmosphere of the first marriage.

This system has tremendous consequences for the whole life of the group. The periodic withdrawal by the chief of young women from the regular cycle of marriages creates a permanent imbalance within the group between the number of boys and girls of marriageable age. Young men are the chief victims of that situation and must either remain bachelors for several years or marry widows or old women discarded by their husbands. Thus, the right to plural marriages represents a concession of considerable importance made by the group to its leader. What does it mean from the latter's point of view? There is little doubt that access to young and pretty girls brings him much appreciated gratification, not so much on the physical side (as the Nambikwara share in the quiet dispositions of most South American tribes) as on the psychological and sentimental one. But, above all, plural marriage, together with its distinctive features, constitutes the technical means and the functional device placed at the chief's disposal by the group to enable him to carry out his exacting duties. By himself, he could hardly do more than the others. His secondary wives, freed by their special status from the customary constraints of their sex, are his helpers, comforters and assistants. They are simultaneously the prize and the instrument of power. Can it be said, from the native point of view, that the prize is worth the trouble? To answer that question, I shall now have to consider the problem from a broader angle, namely, what does this elementary social structure, the Nambikwara band, teach us about leadership, its basis and function?

There is a first point which does not require great elaboration. Nambikwara data confirm those from many other sources in debunking the theory originated by early anthropologists, and temporarily revived by psychoanalysis, that the primitive chief could find his prototype in a symbolical father, and that the simpler forms of the state could have grown gradually out of the family. We have found at the root of the crudest forms of political power a decisive step which introduced something entirely new with respect to biological relations, and this step consists of consent. Consent, we have seen, is at the same time the origin and the limit of leadership. Unilateral relations such as gerontocracy, autocracy or other forms of government may appear in groups having an already complex structure. In simple forms of social organization, such as the one I have tried to describe, they are inconceivable. Here, on the contrary, the relationship between the chief and the group can be seen as a perpetual process of arbitration where the chief's talents and authority, on the one hand, and the group's size, cohesion and willingness, on the other, constantly interact and influence each other. If I had the time, and if it were not so far removed from my topic, I would have liked to show what considerable support modern anthropological observations lend, in this respect, to the ideas of the eighteenth-century social philosophers. I am well aware of the fact that Rousseau's "social contract," which is the step by which individuals renounce their autonomy in favor of the General Will, is profoundly different from the quasi-contractual relations existing between the chief and his followers. It remains true, however, that Rousseau and his contemporaries displayed a keen sociological intuition when they understood that cultural attitudes and elements such as "contract" and "consent" are not the result of secondary processes, as claimed by their opponents, particularly Hume; they are culture's raw materials, and it is impossible to conceive of a political or social organization in which they would not already be present. If I understand correctly, the recent analysis by modern American anthropologists of the military societies among the Plains Indians leads to exactly the same conclusion.[6]

My second point follows directly from the first: consent is the psychological basis of leadership, but in daily life it expresses itself in, and is measured by, a game of give-and-take played by the chief and his followers, and which brings forth, as a basic attribute of leadership, the notion of reciprocity. The chief has power, but he must be generous. He has duties, but he is entitled to several wives. Between him and the group, there is a perpetual balance of prestations, privileges, services and obligations. The notion of reciprocity, originated by Marcel Mauss, was brilliantly analyzed by Malinowski in his *Crime and Custom in Savage Society*. With respect to leadership, he says: "The claims of chief over commoners, husband over wife, parent over child and vice versa are not exercised arbitrarily and onesidedly, but according to definite rules, and arranged into well-balanced chains of reciprocal services."[7] This statement is somewhat in need of correction. Malinowski is right when he points out that the chief–commoner relationship, as every relationship in primitive society, is based on reciprocity. In the first case, however, the reciprocity is not of the same type as in the others. In any human society, whether primitive or civilized, two different cycles of reciprocity are constantly at work: first, the chain of individual prestations linking the isolated members of the group; and, next, a relation of reciprocity binding the group taken as a group (not as a collection of individuals) and its ruler. In the case we have studied, this is well illustrated by the rules of marriage. Taken in its broadest sense, the incest prohibition means that everybody in the group is obliged to deliver his sister or daughter to another man and, conversely, is entitled to receive his wife from the latter (whether from the same man, as in exchange marriage, or from a different one). Thus, a continuous chain of reciprocal prestations is directly or indirectly set up between all the collective or individual members of the group.[8] This type may be called qualitative reciprocity. However, the incest prohibition also provides the basis for a quantitative reciprocity. We may consider it as a "freezing" measure, which, while it forbids the appropriation of women who are at one's natural disposal, prepares the formulation of marriage rules allowing every man to get a wife. Therefore, a close relationship exists in a given society between the degrees of prohibition and the extent to which polygamy is allowed. How does the preceding apply to the Nambikwara? If they had cross-cousin marriage associated exclusively with monogamy, there would be a perfectly simple system of reciprocity (from the individual's point of view), both qualitative and quantitative. This theoretical formula is, however, upset by the chief's privilege of polygamy. The withholding of the simpler rule, in favor of the chief, creates for each individual an element of insecurity which would otherwise not exist. Let us state this in other terms: the granting of polygamous privilege to the chief means that the group has exchanged *individual* elements of security resulting from the monogamous rule for the *collective* security provided by leadership. Each man receives a wife from another man, but the chief receives several wives from the group. In exchange, he offers guarantees against want and danger – not to the individuals whose sisters or daughters he marries, not to those who will be deprived of a spouse by his polygamous right, but to the group, taken as a whole. For it is the group, taken as a whole, which has suspended the common law in his favor. The preceding considerations may have some bearing upon the theory of plural marriage. But, most of all, they remind us that the interpretation of the State conceived as a security system, recently revived by discussions of a national insurance scheme (such as the Beveridge plan and others), is not a modern development. It is a return to the fundamental nature of social and political organization.

Such is the group's point of view on leadership. What about the chief's own attitude in relation to his function? What is his incentive in assuming duties of which I have given a none too favorable account? We saw that the Nambikwara leader has a difficult and exacting role; he must exert himself without respite to maintain his position. What is more, if he does not constantly improve, he runs the risk of losing what he has taken months or years to achieve. This explains why many men, as I have already said, shun leadership. But why do others accept and even seek it? It is always difficult to appraise psychological motives; and the task is almost impossible when a culture totally alien to our own is considered. I venture to say, however, that the polygamous privilege, highly valued as it may be from the point of view of sexual gratification, sentimental appeal and social prestige, would not suffice to determine a leader's vocation. Plural marriage is but a technical prerequisite of chieftainship; its individual value can only be residual. There must be something more. Going over the moral and psychological features of the Nambikwara chiefs I came to know, and trying to take into account those fleeting and irreplaceable glimpses into their intimate selves (of which no scientific approach may certify the accuracy, but which gain, from a deep feeling of friendship and human communication, some sort of intuitive value), I feel irresistibly led to this answer: there are chiefs because there are, in any human group, men who, unlike most of their companions, enjoy prestige for its own sake, feel a strong sense of responsibility, and for whom the burden of public affairs brings its own reward. These individual differences are certainly emphasized and "played up" by different cultures, and to unequal degrees. But their clear-cut existence in a society with as little spirit of competition as the Nambikwara strongly suggests to my mind that their origin itself is not cultural. They are, rather, part of those psychological raw materials out of which any given culture is made. Men are not all alike; and, in primitive societies, believed by early anthropologists to be overwhelmed by the crushing power of custom, these individual differences are as keenly perceived and worked out as in our so-called individualistic civilization.

It is remarkable how far the practical experience of colonial administrators has surpassed, in relation to the previous considerations, the theoretical studies of anthropologists. Over the past twenty years, Lowie's pessimistic appraisal of anthropological work in the field of political institutions[9] has certainly not lost its pertinence. We have much to learn from the scientifically untrained who deal with native institutions. I shall not record here Lyautey's testimony without reservation: "In every society, there is a leadership class born to lead and without which nothing can be accomplished."[10] What may be true for the simpler structures cannot be considered equally valid when considering complex ones, where the function of leadership is no longer manifested in a "pure" state. But let us hear from Eboué, who passed away a few months ago. He wrote the following when he was governor-general of French Equatorial Africa in reference to those nomadic tribes which, as he put it, "live under a regime of organized anarchy." I quote: "Who is to be chief? I shall not answer, as was the custom in Athens, 'the best.' There is no best chief, there is just a chief"; and further: "The chief is not interchangeable ... the chief pre-exists."[11] This is precisely what was suggested to us from the start by our analysis of Nambikwara society.

In conclusion, I submit that, in developing the study of political institutions, anthropologists will have to pay increasing attention to the idea of "natural leadership." I am well aware that this expression appears almost contradictory. There is no possible form of leadership which does not receive its shape and specification inside a given cultural context. But this expression can be taken as a borderline case, or as a limit, as the mathematicians say. While the limit can never be reached, simple social structures give us, by virtue of their simplicity, an ever closer approximation of it. In such studies, we may thus see rich opportunities for close collaborative work between anthropology and individual psychology.

IX

Reciprocity and Hierarchy

The 89th volume (March–April 1943) of the excellent Brazilian review *Revista do Arquivo Municipal de São Paulo* contains new and important information on the structure of the dual system of the Bororo, which I wish to discuss briefly. This information appears in an article, "O exorcismo da caça, do peixe e das frutas entre os Bororo," by Senhor Manuel Cruz. Senhor Cruz is not an anthropologist, but, as a resident for many years of Lageado and the surrounding region, he may be considered as one of our most reliable informants on Bororo life and customs.

Senhor Cruz's account of the food ritual of the Bororo does not add much to what we already knew from Frič and Colbacchini,[1] but it sheds new light on some specific features of the moiety system. Senhor Cruz tells us that the Bororo shaman (*bari*) offers food to the evil spirit (*maeréboe*) on behalf of the spirit's son if the food was brought by a member of the Tugare moiety; and on behalf of the spirit's son-in-law (or grandson, since the kinship term *ouagédu* (*waguedo* according to Colbacchini) means both) if the food was brought by a member of the Cera moiety. He points out, however, that "the Cerae are treated as sons by the *bari* and the Tugaregue as sons-in-law" (p. 154, n. 1). Thus the *bari* stands in the opposite relation to the members of both moieties to that of the *maeréboe*. Senhor Cruz does not comment on this fact, which can only be explained if the *bari* himself stands to the *maeréboe* in the relation of son to father. This interpretation is confirmed by Colbacchini, who, in his own description of the food ritual, says that the *bari* calls the *bope* (the alternate name of the *maeréboe*) *i oga*, "my father."[2] In both cases, then, the *bari* would belong to the Tugare moiety.

Now this is explicitly refuted by Colbacchini, who says in another chapter: "A *bari exeraeddo*, when addressing the sun, who is *exeraedo*, will say *i eddoga*, 'my grand father,' while a *tugaregueddo* will say *i ogwa*, 'my father.'"[3] He adds elsewhere: "Any man ... may become a *bari*."[4] On the other hand, the equivalence of the sun and of the *maeréboe* – i.e. the souls of the dead *baire* – seems a well-established fact: "they are the *baire* themselves (or else *maeréboe*) who, carrying an incandescent piece of metal on their head (*aro-meriurugo*), use it to heat men by looking down to the earth."[5] Thus we have several pieces of corroborating evidence: the sun is Cera, the *maeréboe* is Cera, the *bari* calls the *maeréboe* "father," and the *maeréboe* and the *bari* stand accordingly in the opposite relationships of "father" and "grandfather" (or "father-in-law") toward the members of one and the other moieties respectively. Against this evidence there is the only discordant statement of Colbacchini that a *bari* may be either Cera or Tugare. If the latter is true, the whole picture becomes unintelligible (at least on the basis of the available information): for the *bope* – i.e. the souls of the dead *baire* collectively designated as *maeréboe* – should belong to the two moieties, and then what of the sun and of the moon who, as we know, are the *maeréboe* themselves, while undoubtedly belonging to the Cera moiety?[6] If, on the contrary, the *baire* were always Tugaregue, the whole system of appellations would become much clearer.

The interesting article by Senhor Cruz calls for another comment. From what we know of the moiety system of the Bororo, it is clear that the moieties are bound to exchange reciprocal services in feasts, funerals, initiation rituals, etc. But, at the same time, as occurs in Assam[7] and elsewhere, there is a definite relation of subordination between the moieties: the Cerae, to whom the two chiefs of the Bororo village always belong, and who possess the best ornaments, are "superior" to the Tugaregue. Colbacchini's informant emphatically denied that the usual meaning of those words – "strong" and "weak" – could be attached to the names of the moieties.[8] However, the Bororo of the Rio Vermelho were positive of the fact that Cera meant "weak" when I visited them in 1936.[9] This fits well with the "unequal" names of the moieties among other South American tribes: "Younger" and "Elder" among the Tupi-Kawahib, "Good" and "Bad" among the Tereno, etc. ... Among the Bororo, however, an apparent contradiction results from the fact that the "Superior" moiety would be at the same time the "Weak," and the "Inferior" the "Strong." This can perhaps be explained through the use of the kinship terms reported by Cruz and Colbacchini: if an exogamous moiety claims as its own the cultural heroes and the supernatural beings of the tribe, and thus achieves political and cultural supremacy over the other moiety, the immediate result, in a matrilineal system where patrilineal filiation follows the pattern of alternate generations, is that the members of this moiety will become removed from their male ancestors one degree further than the members of the opposite moiety. If the sun and the moon, and the heroes Bakororo and Itubore, belong to the Cera moiety, they can only be the "grandfathers" of the Cerae men, while becoming the "fathers" of the dethroned Tugaregue. These, in turn, become the "elders" of the ruling Cerae. A perhaps one-sided analysis of the dual organization has too often put the emphasis on the principle of reciprocity as simultaneously its main cause and result. We would do well to remember that the moiety system can express not only mechanisms of reciprocity but also relations of subordination. But, even in these relations of subordination, the principle of reciprocity is at work, for the subordination itself is reciprocal: the priority which is gained by one moiety on one level is lost to the opposite moiety on the other. Political primacy has to be purchased at the cost of a subordinate place in the system of generations.

It is possible that the system of multiple pairs of cross-cutting moieties, typical of the dual organization in South America (and not at all comparable to the Australian systems, since in the first case never more than one pair of moieties act as marriage classes), should be explained as an attempt to surmount the contradiction resulting from these opposite consequences. There are numerous indications that the present relations between the Cera and Tugare moieties of the Bororo are not very ancient.[10] Whatever the case may be, it is not this system but the secondary pattern of the "Upstream" and "Downstream" moieties of the São Lourenço,[11] probably corresponding to something similar on the Rio das Garças,[12] which seems to have the more numerous equivalents inside and outside the cultural area. I am referring to the many "Upper" and "Lower" systems connected with east and west, which, among the Bororo, correspond more closely to metaphysical ideas, and of which new evidence has just been brought to light by Lowie.[13] Therein should be sought the core of dual organization in South America.

X

The Foreign Policy of a Primitive Society

In its very formulation, the subject of this article presents a paradox. Indeed, one would not naturally think of primitive societies – or, rather, the incredibly diverse grouping that we have somewhat haphazardly lumped together under this label, which ultimately does not mean much at all – as having a foreign policy. The reason for this is that we think of so-called primitive societies as a kind of conservancy, as living museums. More or less consciously, we tend to imagine that they could never have preserved such archaic lifestyles, so far from our own, if they had not remained enclosed worlds, completely shut off from any contact with the outside. And it is only insofar as they represent experiences isolated from the rest of the social world that they may claim the title of "primitive societies."

Such thinking leads to a major methodological error. For if it is true that, vis-à-vis us, so-called primitive societies are heterogeneous, this does not by any means entail that they should also be so in relation to others.

It is quite obvious that these societies have a history; that their representatives have lived on this globe for as long as any others; that, for them too, *something has happened*. Their history may not be the same as ours. But it is no less real for the fact that it is not defined within the same system of references. I am reminded of a small village in the center of Borneo, located in one of the most remote parts of the island, which, for centuries, developed and maintained itself without much contact with the outside world, and in which a rather extraordinary event transpired a few years ago: a film crew arrived to shoot a documentary. One would have expected this total disruption of indigenous life – trucks, sound recording machines, electrical generators, spotlights – to have left an indelible mark on the indigenous mind. And yet, three years after this extraordinary incident, when an ethnographer[1] visited that village and asked members of the tribe whether they remembered it, the only response she received was: "It is said that it happened at a time long ago ..." – i.e. the standard formulation used by the tribe at the start of their mythical narratives.

Thus, an event that would for us have been eminently historical is processed by indigenous thought in a manner entirely lacking in historicity, because it does not insert itself into the sequence of events and the circumstances that affect the core of one's life and existence.

However, this is not the part of the world I had in mind to discuss. I will rather take as a starting point a small group in central Brazil, among whom I had the opportunity to live and work for the better part of a year, in 1938–9, and which, in this respect, is probably not an exemplary case. Indeed, I would like to avoid reproducing the very mistake I evoked earlier, by suggesting that it is possible to contrast primitive societies, taken as a single bloc, with our civilized societies, considered as another bloc. We must keep in mind that two so-called primitive societies may present as deep and perhaps even deeper differences between them as either of them with ours.

Yet the group on which we will focus is perhaps of particular interest in that it represents one of the most elementary forms of social life that can now be found on the surface of the earth. I do not mean to suggest in any way that, through some extraordinary and truly miraculous historical privilege, this group has managed to preserve until now vestiges of the social organization of Palaeolithic or Neolithic times. I very much doubt there exists on earth any people we might consider as the faithful representatives of a lifestyle that is tens of thousands of years old. For them, as for us, over the course of these thousands of years things have happened, events have occurred. In this particular case, I think there are solid reasons to believe that this apparent "primitive character" is a regressive phenomenon rather than an archaic vestige, but this is of little importance for the matter at hand.

It is a small indigenous community – small, that is, in the number of its population but not in the territory it inhabits, which is vast at roughly half the size of France. The Nambikwara of central Mato Grosso, whose very name was still unknown as of the late nineteenth century, came into contact with civilization for the first time only in 1907; since then, their contact with Whites has been only intermittent.

The natural environment in which they live largely accounts for their cultural bareness. These regions of central Brazil differ in every respect from the equatorial and tropical regions that Brazil is likely to conjure up in one's mind, even though the Nambikwara's territory is in fact equidistant between the tropic and the equator. They are comprised of savannas, and sometimes even isolated steppes, where the very ancient soil, covered with sandstone sediments, crumbles into infertile sand, and where the highly uneven pattern of rainfall (daily torrential downpours from November to March, followed by total drought from April to September or October) further combines with the character of the soil to produce the general poverty of the landscape: tall grasses that grow rapidly during the rainy season and then quickly dry up in the drought season, leaving the naked sand exposed, covered only by scattered vegetation of thorny bushes. On such poor soil, farming is difficult if not outright impossible. The Nambikwara do a bit of gardening in the gallery forests that run along the banks of rivers. In the dry season, game animals that are generally scarce throughout the year also take refuge, sometimes from very great distances, in the impenetrable thickets that have grown up around these rivers, which contain small pastures.

This contrast between dry and wet seasons has had considerable impact on indigenous life and what one might be tempted to call their "double social organization," if this is not too strong a term to describe such crude phenomena. During the rainy season, the Nambikwara settle in semi-permanent villages, not far from waterways and near the gallery forests, where they burn land to create clearings and farm a bit of manioc and maize to get them through the six months of sedentary life and even a bit beyond. They bury manioc cakes, which slowly decompose but can be extracted and consumed after a few weeks or even months, if need be.

Then, in the dry season, the village breaks up, so to speak, into several small nomadic bands which – under the leadership of a non-hereditary chief chosen for his spiritedness, initiative and audacity – roam the savanna in stretches of 40, 50 or even 60 kilometers, foraging for seeds and berries, small mammals, lizards, snakes, bats, and even spiders, indeed anything and everything that might keep them from starving to death.

It is difficult to estimate Nambikwara population numbers, for nomadic life leads them to range from one end of their territory to the other. Over a short period of time, and at different points, a traveler may encounter bands that he might mistake for distinct populations but that in fact belong to one and the same group.

How many of them were there when they were first discovered? Five thousand, perhaps ten thousand. Decimated by the epidemics that broke out immediately after their first contact with civilization, they currently number around two thousand – two thousand people over a territory the scale of which I have described above.

These two thousand individuals are widely scattered. They speak dialects that are sometimes closely related, but sometimes also distinct enough that they require the help of an interpreter to be understood. Further north, toward the fringes of the great Amazonian forest, their borders are inhabited by other peoples that are radically different – ethnically, linguistically and culturally. These are more powerful peoples that have contained the Nambikwara within their desolate habitat.

On these unforgiving lands, the Nambikwara lead a meager existence, not only with regard to the natural resources at their disposal but also in terms of their level of technical development, which is on a par with their economy. They do not know how to build huts and instead make do with frail shelters made of branches that are grouped together to form the semi-permanent villages of the rainy season, but that, most often, are not expected to last longer than a few days. Made out of branches planted in the ground, these shelters are moved to provide protection against the sun, wind or rain, based on their direction at different times of the day and in different seasons.

The Nambikwara are ignorant of weaving techniques, except for the making of very thin strips of wild cotton that they wear around their arms and legs, and, with the exception of a few groups, they know nothing of pottery either. The sum total of their material goods amount to their bows and arrows, a few sharp tools made of flintstone and sometimes pieces of metal mounted between two wooden sticks, and raw materials such as feathers, fiber skeins, and blocks of wax and resin, which they use to fabricate their weapons and tools.

And yet this most destitute of human groups has an intense political life.

The main point is that, for these indigenous groups, as for so many others, the sharp distinction between compatriot and foreigner, so clear-cut in our minds, does not exist; instead, a whole series of intermediaries separate the two.

I referred earlier to those remote tribes that have settled along the borders of the Nambikwara territory, on the fringes of the Amazonian forest. The Nambikwara know these tribes only by name, generally a nickname. Indeed, they avoid all contact with them. These tribes no doubt embody the quintessential "foreigner" – but a ghostly foreigner, a foreigner that does not really exist, that cannot be seen, or only rarely and fleetingly, and from whom one must then immediately flee. This foreigner is thus defined in a purely negative manner.

Within the Nambikwara's borders, the situation is more complex. I have already described how the "rainy season villages" break up into several small bands for the nomadic season. These bands are generally comprised of individuals who know each another, since they have lived together during the sedentary period, and they are often related, which does not necessarily mean that relations between them are always the most cordial.

There are, however, many villages whose relations with one another will vary along a spectrum, or on a continuous and nuanced scale, that constitutes the various relationships between neighboring and distant groups. First, there is the small band of twenty to thirty to which a given individual belongs and which forms, if I may put it this way, their "local homeland." Then, there are the parallel bands – the "sister" bands – comprised of individuals from the same village, who are relatives, allies, compatriots, but in a secondary and derivative sense. Finally, come the bands of the other villages, who are still Nambikwara, but who are perceived as more or less close and more or less friendly, depending on whether they belong to neighboring villages, with whom marriage unions may have taken place, or to distant villages, with whom contacts have been fewer and further between, if indeed there were any at all, and whose dialect is sometimes even unknown.

These bands, who roam the savanna during the entire nomadic period, maintain to varying degrees an ambivalent attitude toward one another in ways I have tried to specify. They fear and generally avoid one another, uncertain as they are of the sentiments and intentions of strangers. But, at the same time, they also have the sense that they are essential to one another. No matter how deprived the Nambikwara might be, they draw very fine distinctions between the various elements of their material culture, distinctions which often completely escape us. One northern band will thus be known for its walnut shell necklaces, which are considered more precious, and of greater quality, than similar ornaments from another region. Another band will possess certain seeds that can play an essential role in the winter economy, such as bean seeds, which are very rare and very much sought after. Yet another band will have skills in making pottery, whereas for others this technique will be entirely unknown.

It is thus only through contact with these potentially hostile and always dangerous bands, of which one must constantly be wary, that the essential articles for achieving economic balance can be procured. These articles can be divided into three categories: first and foremost, there are women, who represent a good that is all the more precious since in small Nambikwara bands the chief has polygamous privileges. Within a group of twenty or thirty, this privilege is enough to create a sustained imbalance between the sexes, with the young men of the band often lacking available spouses, unless they manage to obtain them, through means peaceful or warlike, from a neighboring tribe that is better endowed with women.

Then come bean seeds.

And, finally, pottery and even fragments of pottery. Indeed, the Nambikwara are largely ignorant of stonework, or at least of polished stone, and, insofar as they have ever had this knowledge, they would seem to have lost it in recent years. As a result, pottery fragments are the only heavy objects available with which they can easily fabricate their spindle weights. Every band is thus very keen to come by what I would hesitate to call ceramics, but rather ceramic fragments. Indeed, I was told by several Nambikwara that they had waged multiple wars over the previous few years whose sole objective was to come by bean seeds and pottery fragments.

I was lucky enough to take part in one of these encounters between neighboring bands. These run-ins are never impromptu, since, in the dry season, extraordinarily clear skies make it possible, every night, to spot the smoke billowing from the campfires of other bands. From day to day, these smoke signals can be seen to move closer or further away, in the former case producing extreme anxiety. Who are these Indians camping nearby? Who are these people who, at a distance of 10 or 15 kilometers, follow the same route as we do with their wives and children? Are they friends or enemies? Is there hope for friendly relations and the possibility of trade? Or, on the contrary, will they launch a sudden attack at dawn, as the Nambikwara are known to do? There are debates for days on end about what posture to adopt, and spies are dispatched to try to identify the strangers and their intentions.

If the signs are good, or if the meeting is necessary, the decision is made to confront the unknown. The women and children are sent to hide in the bush and the men set out alone to meet the other group. The latter has followed the same procedure. It is thus two groups of men who meet in the middle of the savanna and begin by calling out to each other in a manner and tone characteristic of this kind of meeting. It is a ritual form of communication, where voices are raised and the end of each word is drawn out in a nasal manner, either to enumerate grievances or, conversely, to express good intentions.

In the particular example I am referring to, after this exchange of declarations, the women and children were summoned; two encampments were formed, for the bands remained nonetheless separate, and dancing and singing commenced, with each group exclaiming at the end of their performances: "We cannot sing anymore, we cannot dance

... It is just awful! Please excuse us." And the other would protest in turn: "Not at all, it was lovely."

There must nonetheless have been a number of unspoken grievances between the two bands, for it was not long before discussions broke out between some of the men of the two groups which quickly took a violent turn. Other members of the groups intervened to mediate. And, suddenly, one felt things move in a different direction and in a rather peculiar manner. With gestures as rough and violent as in combat, they set out not to exchange blows but to inspect and try on one another's jewellery and ornaments – not clothing, since the Nambikwara are always completely naked, but pendant earrings, necklaces, bracelets – all the while commenting: "Let me see, this is pretty."

And so, most abruptly, we moved from near conflict to commercial exchange. This "reconciliation inspection," if we may call it that, performed the passage from hostility to collaboration, from fear to friendship, from possible war to potential deal.

On the following day, both groups rested, while a mysterious circulation of goods took place: fiber skeins, blocks of wax and resin, arrowheads were passed silently from one to another, with no signs of any transactions being concluded – no haggling, no discussions, and no expressions of thanks. Then, in the late afternoon, the two bands went their separate ways, each having traded away nearly all of their possessions ... I said "no haggling and no discussion" because these notions are foreign to the indigenous way of thinking. These were reciprocal gifts much more than commercial transactions. And yet, afterwards, the "gifts" are weighed and assessed, such that one of the two groups may belatedly realize that it was, or at least considers itself to have been, wronged in the process. New feelings of bitterness will then develop, which may turn increasingly aggressive and pave the way for new conflict. And this will either trigger a war – or lead to a new deal.

I alluded earlier to a certain continuity between the concepts of compatriot and foreigner. It would also seem that the notions of war and commerce, as well as those of antagonism and cooperation, also operate on a continuum. But we could go further still along these lines. Among the same indigenous population, I spent a few weeks with two bands that had gone beyond the stage of economic cooperation that I have just described. They had decided to merge by having all the children of one band be automatically engaged in marriage to all the children of the other band; this would, a few years down the line, effectively ensure the organic fusion of the two bands.

Yet these bands belonged to two remote regions and spoke different dialects. During the time I knew them, at which point their merger was probably only a few years old, they could only communicate with each other through one or two bilingual members who acted as interpreters. And yet there was already an emerging organization: one of the bands had given the new group its civil chief, the other its religious chief; and, as a result of the special characteristics of the Nambikwara kinship system, on which I will not elaborate here, the fact that the children were engaged to one another had transformed all the men of both bands into "brothers-in-law" and all the women of both bands into "sisters," at least theoretically. Thus, what we are dealing with here is a continuum, an institutional chain, that runs from war to trade, from trade to marriage, and from marriage to the merger of social groups.

This conceptual plasticity of concepts, which usually fall under the rubric of "foreign policy," is also to be found in another, geographically proximate example: that of the peoples of the Middle Xingu River, a right-bank tributary of the Amazon. The Xingu basin comprises several rivers, which run more or less parallel for part of their course. Clinging to the teeth of this giant comb, a dozen small tribes that are ethnically and linguistically distinct live in close contact with one another, although they represent linguistic groups that are the most remote in all of South America. These dozen tribes are distributed into approximately thirty-five villages, which, at the close of the past century, numbered in all twenty-five hundred to three thousand inhabitants.

How did these tribes come to be constituted in such close geographical proximity? Land ownership is defined along tribal lines: each tribe has its territory, with clearly defined borders; rivers are recognized as international waterways, but not the fishing weirs that often straddle them, which remain tribal property and are respected as such.

Furthermore, these tribes have developed industrial and commercial specializations, such as the manufacturing of hammocks or shell necklaces. Some have a monopoly on the manufacture of calabashes or walnut shell beads; others on the making of stone weapons and tools; and others still dedicate their industry to the making of indigenous salts from certain charred vegetables. Among all these groups, complex trade relations have developed, with one exchanging pottery for calabashes and another bows for salt and beads.

In addition, the tribes categorize one another as "good" and "bad" tribes, based on local tensions that may exist between them; visitors at different historical periods of time have all noted that some tribes were at war with one another and some avoided each other.

This latent hostility does not preclude the fact that in all villages there are some individuals who can speak all the various languages.

Indeed, each village is constantly hosting a number of visitors, and ceremonial life entails the presence of foreign groups, since one of the most important celebrations consists in wrestling matches with foreign villages, and certain rituals, such as initiation rituals, can only take place with the participation of foreign villages.

In addition, there are intermarriages between villages of different tribes. In some cases, these intermarriages give rise to new villages. Thus, an Aweti group and a Yawalapiti group have given rise through intermarriage to a new village, the Arawaiti, whose very name implies a dual origin. Here, again, there remains a wide range of relations between the groups, with no clear distinction between foreigners and nationals but, rather, a whole spectrum of variations that allows for the incorporation, or at least the partial incorporation, of foreign groups and, conversely – as in the case of the Nahukuá of Xingu, who are at war within their own linguistic group – for the introduction of distinctions within groups that might otherwise be seen as identical.

There is no doubt that the situation here is more complex, for we are dealing with much more developed peoples than those discussed earlier, but the overall picture is not without similarities to that of the simpler example I have sketched above. I will now try to highlight the general characteristics of this situation.

The foreign policy of a primitive people can be conceived in terms of two factors: the territorial and the human – i.e. their attitude in relation to land and their attitude in relation to the foreigner.

With respect to land, we can no longer hold on to the fiction, developed by an overly ideological sociology, of primitive peoples that cohere around a religious life and social organization that are entirely disconnected from their territory. Mr. Lucien Febvre was the first to object to this arbitrary account. The dispute that led him to challenge the old sociological school revolved around the famous Aranda population of Australia. More recent studies of the Aranda describe them as "landowners"; and this is even the title of a work published in Australia in 1936. Indeed, the notion of territory is always on indigenous peoples' minds. However, the notion may vary widely.

Let us now return to the Nambikwara example. When I described their territory earlier, I did so in almost entirely negative terms: poor soil, a desolate geography. It might therefore seem surprising that the Nambikwara would develop an attachment to this territory, as such, and attempt to defend its borders. Their conception of the territory is quite different from the one that has emerged from our feudal tradition. Their conception of land is not our conception of land. For us, the Nambikwara territory covers a specific land area; it is a space bounded by borders. For them, this reality appears as different as the X-ray image of a body would from the image of that same body seen by the naked eye. Territory is nothing in and of itself; it is reduced to a set of modalities, to a system of situations and values that would appear meaningless to a foreigner and might well even go unnoticed. These include the copses that, in some years, yield an abundance of wild seeds; regular hunting grounds; a grove of fruit trees. There is a whole indigenous map which, superimposed onto our civilized map, would reveal few if any points in common. In their situation, an indigenous group cannot grow attached to a specific territory, since its resources are far too variable and far too uncertain – every third year, or sometimes even two years out of three, there are fruits and seeds that do not produce any yield.

Conversely, it might prove useful to travel to very remote regions to take advantage of an exceptional harvest that local bands cannot consume themselves in its entirety. There is thus no notion of territory, of land in and of itself, but, rather, a very fluid and highly variable notion of the "value of the land" which, year after year, season after season, entails regular readjustments.

The same applies to certain Australian peoples who live predominantly on the foraging of a particular wild fruit – for instance, the tribes of central Australia who, for part of the year, are sustained by the indigenous bunya-bunya fruit and on the roots of wild lilies. When the harvest is bountiful and when, in addition, it ripens over such a short period of time that local bands cannot consume it all, these bands send around invitations to very remote tribes that are entirely foreign to them, sometimes as far as hundreds of kilometers away, and that are thereby authorized to enter the territory and take part in the harvest. This is a bit reminiscent of what happens with us in mushroom season, when the notion of land ownership is suspended and anyone can go anywhere, due to the very nature of the crop, which depends on the opportunity and the moment.

These harvests, which may attract up to two or three thousand people, are occasions for exchanges. The individual or collective property of chants and dances is confirmed by the testimonies of neighboring tribes; sometimes sites are rendered neutral to allow for encounters to which economic conditions would not otherwise lead.

A few observations can also be put forward with regard to the category of the foreigner. Primitive thought – and this may not in fact be as exceptional as it seems – has the common characteristic of always assigning a limit to the human. This limit may be very wide, or it may be very narrow – the limit of the human may end at the village or extend over vast territories, and even the better part of a continent, but there is always a point beyond which a man ceases to take part in the essential attributes of humanity.

This finds expression in two ways. On the one hand, extraordinary qualities are attributed to the foreigner, like those with which Cook was endowed by the indigenous peoples of Polynesia, who thought they recognized in him one of their gods; or the ones that the peoples of the Banks Islands had assigned to the early missionaries, whom they called "ghosts," their clothes "ghost skins," and the cats they brought with them "ghost rats." On the other, and quite to the contrary, foreign peoples are denied any human attribute whatsoever, as with the case of the Eskimos, who call themselves "excellent people" and foreigners, as a group, "lice eggs."

Yet this denial of human status only very rarely takes on an aggressive character. For if humanity is denied to certain groups, they are not comprised of men and, as a consequence, one does not behave in relation to them as one would with other human beings. In relation to these non-human groups, indigenous foreign policy – such as the silent trading that I described earlier – is reduced to a kind of "avoidance strategy." These groups are simply to be shunned, to be fled from; no contact is to be had with them.

Within the human group, however, we have seen nuances, degrees, diversity; and the hostility, which was absent in relations with the foreigner as such, we find organized in an incredibly artful way within the group itself, in its internal relations. Indeed, the indigenous group, as homogeneous as it may erroneously appear to us, is generally highly particularized and very divided. In the late nineteenth century, the Hopi of the southwestern United States numbered around three thousand, and they were divided into eleven villages that harbored feelings of jealousy and hostility toward one another. The Eskimos of the Cariboo, in the same period, numbered about five hundred, divided into ten bands. The Ona of the Tierra del Fuego comprised three to four thousand individuals, distributed into thirty-nine hordes, which were in constant conflict with one another. By 1650, the Choctaws numbered fifteen thousand souls, divided into some forty or fifty communities.[2]

As we can see, these apparently sizeable peoples are in fact subdivided into smaller units, between which antagonistic relations are not only very intense but also organized and stylized. In various regions of the world, the same artfulness that we devote to our foreign policy serves to organize the ways in which antagonisms – those arising within the social group – can be resolved, in a no doubt hostile yet not overly dangerous manner. These are the so-called blood customs of New Britain, in which each year the allied villages line up as if readying for battle; the refined distinctions made by the Yolngu of Australia, who have no fewer than six categories for analyzing the kinds of conflict between bands of the same tribe; and, finally, the very curious situations that can be found, or rather could be found, among the Creek confederacy in the southeast United States, where the different "towns" of the confederacy (since the elders called "towns" what were in fact hamlets) were divided into two categories, with an additional division that encompassed all the towns in a horizontal manner, so to speak.

These towns would be pitted against one another in ball games, which, in a telling way, the indigenous groups called "war's little brother." These matches had very specific rules, according to which training for them had to take place between certain camps, distinct from those that were to actually play the matches. Once a town had been defeated by another town a certain number of times, it had to join the same division and, as a result, lost the right to play against that team again. Quite complex mechanisms were thus put in place to settle disputes and antagonisms, after giving them an opportunity for expression and manifestation, even while paving the way for outcomes that ensured, in any event, the restoration of order.

The most profound way indigenous peoples conceive of these relations between groups, which may or may not be foreign to one another, is that which is so admirably expressed in the Fijian term *venigaravi*. The word can only be translated through periphrasis: it refers to the need for there to be two in order to establish social relations. The *venigaravi* are "those who face each other": sacrificial victim and high priest, pastor and parishioner, god and faithful, etc.

All the indigenous forms of organization I have sketched out or evoked here require that an effort be made for there always to be partners – partners between whom cooperation may be forged and antagonisms take shape. For, if one conclusion may be drawn from this presentation, it is that primitive facts help us to see that the aggressiveness of which we so often speak, and in which we are now trying to find the explanation for so many phenomena, is by no means an instinctual activity, unlike the psychological manifestations of certain instincts such as hunger, thirst or sexual drive.

There is, in fact, no innate aggression in these societies. The foreigner may be abolished; the foreigner may be destroyed; the foreigner may be eliminated. But, at the same time, there is no aggression directed toward him. Aggression emerges only as a function of another, antithetical, situation – i.e. cooperation; indeed, it is the counterpart of cooperation.

If we were to consider the lessons to be drawn from these observations, it would no doubt cause us to wonder whether the ideological and political evolution of our Western society has not led us to develop one of the terms of this opposition at the expense of the other. The entire force of modern Christian and democratic thought has been directed at the constant expansion of the limits of the human group, to the point where the notion of humanity has become coextensive with all human beings peopling the surface of the earth.

Yet, insofar as we have succeeded in this – and we have surely succeeded only imperfectly – we have lost something else. What we have lost is precisely the ability to think of this ever-expanding humanity as a set of concrete groups between which a constant balance must be found between competition and aggression, through pre-defined mechanisms for buffering the extreme forms that may arise in either direction. Or, rather, we have not been able to preserve this institutional framework outside the field of sports – i.e. games – whereas, in most primitive societies, it is called upon to solve the most important issues of social life.

We are thus invited to consider whether our current preoccupations – which would have us think about human problems in terms of open societies, of ever more open societies – do not in fact ignore a dimension of reality that is just as essential, and whether the ability of each group to think of itself as a group, in relation and in opposition to other groups, is not in fact what allows for a balance between, on the one hand, the utopian ideal of total peace and, on the other, the no less total war that results from the unilateral system in which our civilization is blindly engaged.

An anthropologist who passed away too soon and who, for many years, would visit at very regular intervals the same small group of indigenous people in central Brazil, not far from those I have told you about, reported that, every time he would leave, the Indians would break into tears. They were not so much sad that he was leaving as sorry for him to be leaving the only place in the world where life was worth living.

When one has been to these wretched villages, comprised of but a few straw huts in the middle of a bush desert, where a handful of people are slowly dying off in the impoverished surroundings to which they have been pushed by the progress of civilization, amidst the epidemics that civilization has offered them for their trouble, and when one realizes they can still conceive of this utter destitution as the only worthy and valuable existence there is, one cannot help but wonder if the perspective of the "closed society" is not in fact the way to achieve such spiritual heights and rich social experience, and if we would not be fools to let this source run dry and its lessons be lost.

Art

XI

Indian Cosmetics

The Kaduveo Indians, authors of the disturbing paintings reproduced in this issue, are slowly dying out in the south of Brazil, not far from the Paraguayan frontier. The southern part of the state of Mato Grosso which they inhabit has a strong appeal for the imagination: along the two banks of the Rio Paraguay lies the "Pantanal," the largest marshland in South America and one of the largest in the world, covering five hundred kilometers of ground, three-quarters of it flooded. From an airplane, the environs of the great rivers winding at random present a spectacle of huge bends and meanderings, provisionally abandoned by the waters. The riverbed itself is lined by a succession of pale arcs, as if Nature, herself an artist, had hesitated long before determining the present temporary outline of the river. But it is from the ground that the Pantanal takes on its dreamlike aspect: a landscape where flocks take refuge as on floating arks, on the summits of the low hills that have escaped the flood, while, in the lagoons, the thousands of birds form a rose and white canopy of feathers over endless spaces. Over this paradoxical territory, the Guaycuru Indians struggled until the nineteenth century against the Spanish conquerors. The complex structure of their warrior society, their divisions into castes differentiating between nobles, commoners and slaves, had something hieratic, which the elaborate style of their graphic art indirectly evokes. Of this once powerful nation, the Kaduveo tribe, formerly called the Eyiguayegui, is today one of the rare residues. Since the eighteenth century, travelers coming into contact with them have been dumbfounded by the prodigious tattoos and body paintings which are traditional to the tribe. The face, often the entire body, is covered with a network of asymmetrical arabesques, alternating with the patterns of a subtle geometry. The first descriptions are those of the Jesuit missionary Sánchez Labrador, who lived with the tribe from 1660 to 1670; the first drawings were published more than a century later, by the Italian painter and explorer Guido Boggiani. The largest collection – and no doubt the last, in view of the rhythm to which the tribe is heading toward extinction – is the one which we ourselves compiled in 1935.[1] Two documents are presented here, chosen from four hundred original native designs:[2] they are models of face paintings. In each, the motif, in the form of an arched pediment, represents, and is applied to, the upper lip; from that initial point of departure, the only correspondence with nature allowed, the design is developed freely over the face, often contradicting its symmetry, covering the chin, cheeks, nose, eyes and forehead. A distribution of motifs around a vertical median axis is nevertheless generally observed. Formerly, these designs were tattooed or painted. The latter technique only is used today. The artist – always a woman – works on the face or body of a companion with a thin bamboo spatula dipped in the blue-black juice of the "genipa" fruit. She improvises without model, sketch or established points of design. These highly developed compositions, at once unsymmetrical and balanced, are begun in one corner or another and carried out – without hesitation, going over or erasure – to their conclusion. They evidently spring from an unvarying fundamental theme, in which crosses, tendrils, fretwork and spirals play an important part. Nevertheless, each one constitutes an original work: the basic motifs are combined with an ingenuity, a richness of imagination, and even an audacity, which continually spring afresh. The genipa paint lasts only a few days; when it begins to wear off, it is removed, to be replaced by another decoration. Even half a century ago, the men were not above wearing these ornaments.

For the Americanist, the graphic art of the Kaduveo presents an enigma which is far from finding its solution and which, for the most part, everyone has carefully avoided posing. Body paintings are not rare in South America; but they are usually nothing more than linear drawings, or very simple geometric decorations, which are an inadequate base for so far advanced a refinement as appears here. Similarities have sometimes been drawn with the pre-Inca art of Ancon, particularly as concerns the composition of fretwork, and also with the pre-Colombian baroque of Marajó, and still more of Santarém, on the lower branch of the Amazon. But the likeness is only in the details, and the Kaduveo style, considered in its formal unity, presents a strong originality in relation to anything South or Central America has produced. Above all, it is not a "primitive" style, in the sense that theorists of art give to the term. On the contrary, this exquisite, meditated art, almost codified in its means of expression and its repertory of themes (of which the symbolism, though now lost, is nonetheless evident), evokes a very ancient culture, and one full of preciosities. On the purely graphic plane, it appears as the product of a long evolution. If one were pressed to look for aesthetic analogies, one would think of China, or India; there are insistent suggestions of stupas in these flames, tendrils and hooked beaks. But, for the ethnologist, these Asiatic recollections hold little promise.

The Kaduveo use their paintings only as ornaments. It is to be supposed, nevertheless, that at one time they had a more serious meaning. According to Sánchez Labrador, a decoration of the forehead coming down only to the eyebrows was the distinguishing mark of the ruling castes, whereas the vulgarity of painting the lower part of the face was left to slaves. Furthermore, in his day, only young women were painted. "It is rare," he writes, "for the old women to waste their time on these designs. They are content with those which time has wrought upon their faces." But the missionary, profoundly distressed by what this alteration of the face suggests of dissatisfaction with the work of the Creator, tends to elaborate explanations. In spending long hours over their minutely detailed arabesques, they may seek to defeat hunger; or rendered, as they are, virtually unrecognizable, they may possibly hope to escape their enemies more easily. But, in each case, defeat and escape is involved; and we have learned that such matters are rarely reduced to a game. Even the missionary, though ill-inclined to accept such a conclusion, is aware that these body paintings represent to the native a vital activity, and that they are in a sense their own object. He marks with concern men who spend whole days having themselves painted, forgetting the hunt, their fishing and their families. "Why are you so stupid?" they ask the missionaries. "Well, and why are we so stupid?" they would answer. "Because you don't paint yourselves like the Eyiguayegui." Indeed, there are other things to think of here besides simple utilitarian considerations.

Nothing is more dangerous for the ethnologist than to attempt to reconstruct a native mentality according to his own psychological experiences. Still, in the case of such a mentality as this, and where the customs have so obvious a sexual implication, it may be assumed that the reactions which it evokes are sufficiently profound to be universal, at least to a certain degree. Anyone who has come into contact with the Kaduveo can testify to the provocative efficacy of their face painting. The Kaduveo women have an erotic reputation which is solidly established on both banks of the Rio Paraguay; and many half-breeds, or Indians of other tribes, have come to settle on their territory and have married native women. The almost magical appeal of their facial and

Figure 1 Kaduveo child with painted face

bodily decorations is undoubtedly connected with this power. These delicate and subtle traceries, as sensitive as the lines of the face, but which sometimes accent them and sometimes falsify them, enhance them and at the same time contradict them, give to the feminine countenance something deliciously stimulating. They are the promise and outline of expert scoring. This graphic surgery grafts the loveliest constructions of art upon the base of the human body. And when Sánchez Labrador protests with anguish that it "opposes to the grace of Nature an artificial ugliness," he knows he is contradicting himself, since he affirms, almost in the same passage, that the most admirable tapestries cannot rival these native paintings. Actually, never has the erotic effect of cosmetics been so systematically – and no doubt so consciously – developed. Beside this achievement, the gross realism of our powder and rouge seems like a puerile effort.

The Eyiguayegui deserve to bear the name of "good savages" in the eighteenth-century sense. The lesson they teach is no less opposed to the eighteenth-century idea of the State of Nature. As far as "instinctual forces" are concerned, these paintings indicate an

Indian Cosmetics

Figure 2 Motif by a Kaduveo woman

independence, a mastery, no doubt much superior to the contrivances and remedies of modern man. This sovereign liberty to dispose of the body, reaffirmed by Indian art, certainly borders upon the sinful. From his point of view as a Jesuit missionary, Sánchez Labrador

156 *Art*

Figure 3 Motif by a Kaduveo woman

evinced a singular perspicacity by apprehending the demon in it. He himself underlines the Promethean aspect of this savage art when he describes the technical process employed by the natives in covering their bodies with dazzling designs of stars. "Thus, the Eyiguayegui looks upon himself as another Atlantus, who, not only in the shoulders and hands, but in the entire surface of his body, is the repository of a clumsily conceived universe." Perhaps this accounts for the exceptional character of Kaduveo art; through its intermediary, man refuses to be merely a reflection of the divine image.

Translated by Patricia Leblanc

XII
The Art of the Northwest Coast at the American Museum of Natural History

There is in New York a magic place where all the dreams of childhood have a rendezvous, where centuries-old tree trunks sing or speak, where indefinable objects lie in wait for the visitor with an anxious stare; where animals of superhuman gentleness press their uplifted little paws, clasped in prayer for the privilege of constructing for the chosen one the palace of the beaver, of guiding him into the realm of the seals, or of teaching him, with a mystical kiss, the language of the frog and kingfisher.[1] This place – to which disused but singularly effective museographic methods confer a supplementary prestige with the chiaroscuro of caves and crumbling heaps of lost treasures – can be visited daily from ten to five o'clock at the American Museum of Natural History. It is the vast gallery on the ground floor devoted to the Indians of the Northwest Coast which extends from Alaska to British Columbia.

Surely the time is not far off when the collections of the Northwest Coast will move from anthropological museums to take their place in art museums alongside those of Egypt, Persia and the Middle Ages. For this art is fully their equal, and, unlike them, it has displayed, during the century and a half of its known development, a prodigious diversity and apparently inexhaustible power of renewal. This was suddenly and so completely extinguished between 1910 and 1920 that today, aside from the ancient totem poles spared by museums, one can find along the entire coast nothing more than misshapen figurines roughly carved to be sold to tourists for a few cents.

Nevertheless, that century and a half witnessed the birth and flourishing of not one but ten different art forms: from the hand-woven blankets of the Chilkat – still unknown at the beginning of the nineteenth century and attaining at a single stroke the highest perfection of textile technique with the limited means of sharp yellow extracted from moss, black from cedar bark and coppery blue from mineral oxides – to the exquisite slate sculptures – as glossy as black obsidian and showing the flamboyant decadence (at the stage of the knick-knack) of an art suddenly in possession of steel implements which in turn destroy it – passing through the wild mode, which was to last only a few years, of the Tlingit dance headdresses blazoned with sculpted motifs of inlaid mother of pearl, covered with fur or the white down of wild birds and from which a hundred ermine pelts descend in cascades like curls. This incessant renewal, this sureness which, in no matter what direction, guarantees definitive and overwhelming success, this scorn for the path already followed, this ceaseless drive toward new feats which infallibly yields dazzling results – to come to know this our civilization had to await the exceptional destiny of a Picasso. It would not be inappropriate to emphasize that the daring ventures of this single man, which have left us breathless for thirty years, were known and practiced for over a hundred and fifty years by an entire indigenous culture. Indeed, we have no reason to doubt that this multiform art has developed at the same rhythm since its remotest origins, of which we are ignorant. Some stone objects excavated in Alaska show that this powerful art, easily recognized in even its archaic forms, has probably existed in its present location since very ancient times – this term being understood in the wholly relative sense it takes on whenever applied to American archaeology.

Be that as it may, at the end of the nineteenth century there still existed a continuous chain of villages along the coast and on the islands from the Gulf of Alaska to south of Vancouver. At its most flourishing period, the tribes of the Northwest Coast totaled one hundred to one hundred and fifty thousand souls, an insignificant number when one ponders the intensity of expression and decisive lessons of an art wholly developed in this far-flung province of the New World by a population whose density varied, according to the region, from 0.1 to 0.6 inhabitants per square kilometer.[2] To the north were the Tlingit, to whom we owe the purest sculpture and most precious ornaments; to the south, the Haida – rough and powerful sculptors; the more academic Tsimshian; the Kwakiutl who, in creating their dance masks, indulged in the most sumptuous fancies of form and color; the Bella Coola, in whose palette cobalt blue predominates; the Nootka of a more timorous realism; and, finally, to the extreme south, the Chinook and Salish, among whom the last rays of northern inspiration begin to vanish.[3]

Whence come these groups, often distinct from each other in language but whose art, in spite of local variations of style and inequalities of talent, attests to a common origin? My master, Marcel Mauss, delighted in suggesting that everything in the art and customs of the Northwest evoked for him a mysterious and very primitive China.[4] Indeed, it is impossible when confronting the decorative motifs of the Chilkat blankets and the Tlingit and Haida chests not to think of the ocellated bronzes of the first millennium of archaic China. The great American linguist Edward Sapir died convinced that the Na Dené, one of the most important linguistic families of the coast, was connected with Sino-Tibetan. Such commanding suggestions, however, meet with difficulty in finding a demonstration. Anthropologically the natives of Alaska and British Columbia are American Indians, doubtless members, as are all Indians of the two Americas, of a great Asiatic family, but separated for a sufficient number of millennia to justify the presence of specific characteristics totally absent in modern Mongolians: for instance, the predominance of the blood group O, which, overwhelmingly and unequaled in any other part of the world, is manifested from the Salish of the Northwest Coast to the natives of the Brazilian forest.[5]

Another hypothesis, often repeated since Cook reached the coast of Alaska by crossing the Pacific from the southern seas, is that of Polynesian affinities, more particularly with New Zealand. Like the Maori, the natives of the Northwest Coast built rectangular houses out of wooden planks; they also wove fringed blankets in a form common to the two regions, and in both groups wooden sculptures attained an exceptional level of development, characterized particularly by high posts ornamented with superimposed figures, similarly erected outside houses. Finally, as definite proof of kinship, there was the alleged discovery among the tribes of the Northwest of a highly specialized form of club, the New Zealand *patu mere*, so distinctive in form and decoration that its independent invention in two distinct parts of the earth seems totally inconceivable. Thus, the origin of the *patu mere* was soon to become the "mystery story" of American archaeology, and anthropologists applied themselves to each example with a subtlety worthy of Sherlock Holmes. To begin with, it was easily demonstrated that almost all specimens collected in America could have been brought there during the eighteenth and nineteenth centuries by travelers coming from the southern seas as Cook did. The specimens from the Northwest Coast seem the more doubtful since they were in the possession of the same tribes who, at the end of the eighteenth century, showed Cook silver spoons of Spanish style, introduced how, one wonders, into this hitherto unknown land. But one example, at least, resists all attempts at explanation: it was discovered by Tschudi in a pre-Incan tomb in Peru, with no doubt as to its Maori origin and no question of the impossibility of its surreptitious introduction by a traveler subsequent to the sixteenth century. From this one, why not admit the authenticity of all others, notably those of British Columbia? Alas, the authenticity of the Peruvian example is only too indisputable. The age of the tomb, however inviolate, in which it was found renders it contemporaneous with an epoch when the Maori had not yet reached New Zealand or had only just begun to settle there.[6] Even supposing they were already there, from New Zealand to American shores, the distance is five thousand miles! One is truly in the presence of the perfect crime – a crime against science alone; for even the most resolute adversaries of Dr. Paul Rivet's famous thesis of contacts between Polynesia and America in the pre-Columbian era[7] agree in recognizing the authenticity of the *patu mere* found in America, even while demonstrating, in the most convincing fashion that, from the point of view of history and geography, they should not have been able to be there.[8]

If we have laid out the debates of the specialists it is because they are but the expression, on a rational level, of the tragic mystery and austere anxiety which are the most striking characteristics of the art of the Northwest Coast. For spectators of the initiation rituals, the dance masks which suddenly open into two sections, allowing one to see a second face, and sometimes a third behind the second, attested to the omnipresence of the supernatural and the perpetual life of myth beneath the calm of everyday illusions. The primitive message was one of such violence that, even today, the prophylactic isolation of the display case does not manage to prevent its ardent communication. Wander for an hour or so across this room spiked with "*vivants piliers.*"[9] The expression of the poet, through a new and mysterious "*correspondance*," is the exact translation of the indigenous term designating these sculpted poles which supported the beams of houses – poles which were less things than living beings with "*regards familiers*," insofar as they too, in days of doubt and torment, issued "*de confuses paroles*," guiding the inhabitant of the house, advising and comforting him and indicating the path out of his difficulties. It would be more disturbing, even for us, to see them as dead tree trunks than not to hear their stifled murmur; just as, behind the glass of the display case, on the two sides of some dark visage, not to catch a glimpse of the "Cannibal Raven" flapping its beak-like wings and of the "Master of the Tides" presiding over the movement of the waters with a wink of his ingeniously articulated eye.

Indeed, most of these masks are contraptions that are simultaneously naïve and intense. A system of cords, pulleys and hinges permits the mouths to mock the terrors of the newly initiated, the eyes to mourn his death, and the jaws to devour him. This unique art unites in its figures the contemplative serenity of the statues of Chartres and the Egyptian tombs with the gnashing artifices of Halloween. These two traditions, of equal grandeur and parallel authenticity, the dismembered remnants of which amusement park stands and cathedrals today fight over, reign here in their primitive and undisturbed unity. This dithyrambic gift of synthesis, the almost monstrous faculty to perceive as similar what all other men have conceived as different, undoubtedly constitutes the exceptional feature of the art of British Columbia. Passing from display case to display case, from object to object, sometimes from one corner to another of the same object, one has the feeling of passing from Egypt to the twelfth century, from the wooden horses of merry-go-rounds to the Sassanids, from the Palace of Versailles (with its insolent emphasis on heraldry, crests and nobility and its almost depraved taste for metaphor and allegory) to the forests of the Congo. Look closely at the provision boxes, carved in bas-relief and set off with black and red. The ornamentation seems purely decorative. A strict application of canonical rules, however, permits the representation of a bear, a shark, a beaver without any of the limits which elsewhere constrain the artist: the animal is represented at once in full face, in profile, and from the back, and at the same time from above and from below, from without and from within. A butcher draftsman, by an extraordinary mixture of convention and realism, has skinned and boned, even removed the entrails, to construct a new being coincident in all points of its anatomy with the parallelepiped or rectangular surface and to create an object that is at once a box and an animal – many animals, and a man.[10] For the box speaks; it guards the treasures entrusted to it in the corner of a house which all proclaim is, itself, the inner part of some more enormous animal, which one enters by a door which is a gaping jawbone, and wherein rise up a hundred friendly and tragic aspects, a forest of human and nonhuman symbols. One observes the same transfiguration with the two admirable Tlingit wooden figures reproduced here. The two personages are literally clothed in animals; the abdomen of one grins like a jawbone while on the patella of the other appear two little moon faces. In a Kwakiutl legend recorded by Franz Boas, the natives tell of the mythological hero who appears first as a whale, who later approaches the shore as a man disembarking from the whale, which is no longer itself but his canoe. When he meets the local chief and his daughter, whom he wishes to marry, at a feast he presents them with the whale, which has now returned to its animal nature at the end of its third transmutation. Swanton[11] has recorded a Tlingit story of a woman who flees from bears and, arriving at a lake, sees a canoe floating on it. The canoe is wearing a dance hat and says to her, "run this way into the water." She runs into the water and reaches the canoe, which carries her into the sun. The canoe was a grizzly-bear canoe and could understand what was said, and after traveling for a long time it would stop suddenly. "This was because it was hungry and so they had to break out a box of fat in front of the bow to feed it." Would it not be astonishing if these objects which speak, dance and eat should not conserve, even in the prison of the museum, a little of their pulsating life?

These objects – beings transformed into things, human animals, living boxes – seem as remote as possible from our own conception of art since the time of the Greeks. Yet even here one would err to suppose that a single possibility of the aesthetic life had escaped the prophets and virtuosos of the Northwest Coast. Several of these masks and statues are thoughtful portraits which testify to a concern not only for achieving physical resemblance but also for intimating the subtlest essence of the soul. The sculptor of Alaska and British Columbia is not only the sorcerer who confers upon the supernatural a visible form but also the inspired creator, the interpreter who translates into eternal masterpieces the fugitive emotions of man.

No more profound or sincere homage has ever been rendered to the mission of the artist than that suggested by another Tlingit legend, which I will now recount following the version recorded by Swanton.[12] It is entitled "The Image that Came to Life" and tells the story of a young chief desperately in love with his wife, who dies of an illness in spite of the care of the finest shamans. The inconsolable prince goes from woodcarver to woodcarver begging them to carve a portrait of his wife, but not one could attain a perfect likeness. Finally, he met one who said to him: "I have seen your wife a great deal walking along with you. I never studied her face with the idea that you might want someone to sculpt it, but I will try if you will allow me." The woodcarver began work, finished the statue, and when the young chief entered the workshop he saw his dead wife sitting there, just as she had looked. Filled with a melancholy joy he asked the carver the price of this work. But the carver, sorry to see this chief mourning his wife, said: "It is because I felt your pain that I made it; so don't pay me too much for it." But the chief paid him very handsomely, in both slaves and goods. The chief had the feeling that his wife had come back to him and treated the image just like her, dressing it in his wife's clothes.

One day he had the impression that the statue began to move, and from that moment he examined it attentively every day, for he thought that at some point it would come to life. But, although the image grew daily more like a human being and was unquestionably alive, it could neither move nor speak. Sometime later the image emitted a sound from its chest, like that of cracking wood, and the man knew that it was ill. When he had it moved from its usual place, he found a small red-cedar tree growing there on the top of the floorboards. He left it until it grew to be very large, and it is because of this that cedars on the Queen Charlotte Islands are so magnificent. When people there come across a good tree, they say, "This looks like the baby of the chief's wife." The image, however, never becomes truly alive, and the nostalgic conclusion of the story remains marked with respect for the autonomy of the work of art, for its absolute independence vis-à-vis every sort of reality: "Day after day, the image of the young woman grew more like a human being, and, when they heard the story, people from near and far came to see her and the young cedar tree growing there, at which they were much astonished. The statue barely moved and never spoke, but whatever she wanted to say came to her husband in his dreams. It was through his dreams that he knew she was speaking to him."

When one compares the clumsy legend of Pygmalion with this sensitive and modest tale, filled with an exquisite reserve and such moving poetry, is it not the Greeks who seem the barbarians and the poor savages of Alaska who may pretend to the purer understanding of beauty?

South American Ethnography

XIII

The Social Use of Kinship Terms among Brazilian Indians

The kinship system of the Nambikwara Indians of the Western Mato Grosso is one of the simplest in Brazil. At the same time, it is typical of a sociological pattern, cross-cousin marriage, which according to our present information seems to have been very common throughout South America. The object of this article is to compare the familial organization of the Nambikwara with that of other tribes described in the older literature and to show that a certain kinship tie, the brother-in-law relationship, once possessed a meaning among many South American tribes far transcending a simple expression of relationship. This significance, still observable in Nambikwara culture, is both sexual and politico-social; and, owing to its complexity, the brother-in-law relationship may perhaps be regarded as an actual institution. Since the sixteenth century, travelers and sociologists have failed to devote sufficient attention to the phenomenon, probably because it could readily be interpreted as a development of the imported Iberian *compadre* relationship. In our opinion, on the contrary, the brother-in-law relationship, together with its remarkable implications, constitutes an indigenous aboriginal institution based on the pattern of native culture. Nevertheless, it presents a striking example of convergence, in which native and Latin-Mediterranean institutions show numerous apparent similarities, even while masking important structural differences.

The Nambikwara Indians are settled on the upper courses of the tributaries of the Tapajós River, between the eleventh and fifteenth parallels. Their territory consists of a semi-desert savanna, which contrasts with the narrow gallery forests along the main waterways. The fertile soil of these forests allows the natives to cultivate a few gardens in the rainy season, but during most of the year the Nambikwara subsist mainly by hunting and gathering wild food. Compared with the majority of Brazilian tribes, their cultural level is low. As they were discovered only in 1907, and as they had practically no contact with white civilization between the year of the Rondon–Roosevelt Expedition in 1914 and the time of our own fieldwork in 1938–9, their familial and social organization may be considered still intact.

The Nambikwara kinship system may be summarized as follows: all the father's brothers are classified together with the father and are called "father," and all the mother's sisters are classified with the mother and are called "mother." The father's sisters and the mother's brothers are classified together with the spouse's parents and the parents' parents in a single category which denotes simultaneously the cross-aunts and cross-uncles, the mother-in-law and father-in-law, and the grandparents. Passing to Ego's generation, the parallel cousins, both the children of the father's brothers and those of the mother's sisters are merged with siblings and are called "brother" and "sister." Turning to the children of the father's sisters and of the mother's brothers, a man calls all his female cross-cousins (to one of whom he is or will be married) "wife" and all his male cross-cousins "brother-in-law"; conversely, a woman calls all her male cross-cousins (among whom is her actual or potential husband) "husband" and all her female cross-cousins "sister-in-law." No terminological difference is made between actual and potential spouses. The members of the next younger generation are similarly divided into "sons" and "daughters" (Ego's own children and parallel nephews and nieces) and "sons-in-law" and "daughters-in-law" (Ego's cross-nephews and -nieces), since these are or may be the spouses of his children.

The system is somewhat complicated by secondary distinctions made between elder and younger siblings and by the fact that another kind of marriage – between a maternal uncle and his niece – is also practiced. This new pattern usually appears in the polygynous unions which, in the prevailingly monogamous Nambikwara society, are the privilege of the chief. This point needs some elaboration. Nambikwara polygyny results from the fact that, subsequent to a first marriage having all the characteristics of the common (i.e. the cross-cousin) form, a man may contract one or more unions of a somewhat different nature. Actually, the position of his new wives is not the same as that of his original one, and, although constituting real marriages, the later unions are psychologically and economically different from the first. The atmosphere in which they evolve is less conjugal and more like a kind of amorous friendship. The younger wives cooperate more extensively in the numerous tasks imposed on their husband because of his special social obligations. Furthermore, the activities of these women do not conform as closely as those of the first wife to the general pattern of the sexual division of labor. Finally, they are younger and are classified, in relation to the earlier wife, as "daughters" or "nieces." Such "oblique" unions (that is, between members of different generations) may also take place in monogamous marriages, but less frequently. Although their occurrence among the Nambikwara is an important point in our demonstration, the consequent modifications of the kinship system are not essential for the purposes of this article, and we may therefore omit any further mention of them. Our present observations will be limited to the special implications of the brother-in-law relationship, which is expressed through the reciprocal terms *asúkosu* (eastern dialect), *tarúte* (central and western dialect) or *iópa* (northern dialect).

It must be emphasized immediately that this useful translation of the native term is not in any way accurate. While the *asúkosu* is a man's male cross-cousin and also his potential brother-in-law, since the persons calling each other *asúkosu* (or *tarute* or *iópa*) call each other's sisters "wife," it is only in particular instances that one or more of the individuals involved is, in fact, the wife's brother or the sister's husband or both. The meaning of the term *asúkosu* is consequently much wider than "brother-in-law" as we understand it, including as it does approximately half the masculine members of a man's generation; the rest, of course, receive the name "brother" (consanguineous or classificatory). It should be noted that in the Nambikwara kinship system men alone have brothers-in-law and, conversely, women alone have sisters-in-law.

Only in the case of brothers-in-law are the Nambikwara conscious of a link between a special type of behavior and the position occupied by a kinsman in the relationship system. Generally speaking, there are no rules of avoidance or of privileged familiarity between particular kinds of relatives. The relations with the spouse's parents do not differ substantially from those with the parallel uncle and aunt and, although it is true that relations between consanguineous or classificatory siblings are rather reserved, the natives are unable to define this diffuse behavior. As a matter of fact, while siblings and parallel cousins do not avoid each other, they do not joke or even talk together unless there is a special reason for doing so. Sisters-in-law, on the contrary, comport themselves very freely. They laugh and joke together and render each other small services, such as rubbing each other's back with *urucu* paste. And these exceptional relations are even more marked with respect to brothers-in-law.

We have already mentioned the partial polygyny which exists in the group. The chief or shaman periodically withdraws several of the youngest and prettiest women from the regular cycle of marriages; consequently, young men often find it difficult to marry, at least during adolescence, since no potential spouse is available. The resulting problem is solved in Nambikwara society by homosexual relations, which receive the rather poetical name *tamindige ki'ándige* – "sham love." Relations of this kind are frequent among young men and are more publicly displayed than heterosexual ones. Unlike most adults, the partners do not seek the isolation of the bush but settle close to the campfire in front of their amused neighbors. Although the source of occasional jokes, such relations are considered childish and no one pays much attention to them. We did not discover whether the partners aim at achieving complete sexual gratification or whether they limit themselves to such sentimental effusions and erotic behavior as most frequently characterize the relations between spouses. In any event, the point is that homosexual relations occur only between male cross-cousins.

We never learned whether or not the same relations continue to exist between adult cross-cousins; it does not seem likely. Nevertheless, the freedom and demonstrativeness displayed by brothers-in-law toward one another are not characteristic of the relations between brothers or between the members of any other class of relatives. One often sees among the Nambikwara (who, in fact, like to indulge in expressions of affection) two or three men, married and sometimes the fathers of several children, walking together at dusk and tenderly embracing each other; always *tarúte ialásiete*, "[these are] brothers-in-law embracing [each other]." Certain games, too, such as the "scratch game" (in which the opponents try to scratch each other especially in the face), are commonly played by brothers-in-law.

But the close relationship between "cross-cousins actually or potentially allied through a sister's marriage" – the more accurate translation of the aboriginal term for brother-in-law – may extend far beyond the family tie. Actually, it is sometimes used to establish between individuals not belonging to the same kin group new links of a special nature, the function of which is to amalgamate into a single familial unit several formerly unrelated groups. This is brought out clearly in the following case.

During the past twenty years, several epidemics nearly destroyed the central, northern and western divisions of the Nambikwara. Several groups were decimated to such an extent that they could no longer successfully maintain a socially autonomous existence. In the hope of reconstituting functioning units, some of these, therefore, attempted to join forces. In the course of our fieldwork we met and worked with such a merged group made up of seventeen individuals using the northern dialect (Sabáne group) and thirty-four using the central dialect (Tarunde group). Each of the originally distinct groups, however, lived under the guidance of its own chief, although both leaders closely cooperated. It is probable that the demographic crisis did not by itself account for this situation, since the people of the second group formed merely a fraction of a more numerous unit from which it had split off for reasons unknown to us. However, from several events which occurred during our stay with them, we deduced that the break had been caused by political dissension, the details of which remained obscure to us. In any event, these groups now traveled and lived together, although two separate but contiguous camps were maintained in which the families formed distinct circles, each around its own fire. The most amazing feature of this curious organization was that the two groups did not speak the same language and were able to understand one another only through interpreters; fortunately, one or two individuals belonging to each group had sufficient knowledge of the other dialect to act as intermediaries. Even the two chiefs could not communicate directly. The problem of whether these dialects belong to the same linguistic stock need not be raised here; but the northern group undoubtedly must be classified with the Nambikwara cultural family because of the similarities of material culture and of the life pattern, and chiefly because of the psychological attitude of the people, who very evidently believed in their close affinity to the central group.

A more fundamental problem raised by the union of the two groups, namely the nature of the relations to be established between their respective members, was solved by the common statement that all the male members of the Sabáne group were to be acknowledged as the "brothers-in-law" (*tarúte̜*) of the male adults of the Tarunde group, and, conversely, the latter were to be acknowledged as "brothers-in-law" (*iópa̜*) by the former. Consequently, all the "wives" belonging to one group became the "sisters" of the "husbands" of the other and the "sisters-in-law" of the latter's wives; and all children of both sexes in one group became the potential spouses of the children in the other. As a result, these two groups will be welded into a single consanguineous unit within two generations.

The conscious and systematic nature of this solution cannot be doubted. When asked for their kinship relation to any male adult of the allied group, the male informants, irrespective of the group to which they themselves belonged, never gave a different answer but always emphasized that the question was meaningless since all the Sabáne men were their *tarúte̜,* or all Tarunde men their *iópa̜*. On the other hand, no one seemed to have a clear idea of the exact relationship between the women, the children, or the adults and the children of the two groups. Occasionally the correct theoretical relationship could be deduced; more frequently only the group name was given in reply to our queries: She calls the women from the other group "Sabáne" or "Tarunde." Thus, it may be assumed that the system was conceived and applied according to (and exclusively according to) the *tarúte* (or *iópa*) relationship. This inference is rather important because, of course, the same result could have been achieved by other means.

If the sole aim of the system had been to ensure intermarriage, it could have been brought about equally well in two other ways; perhaps we should say that two different interpretations might have been made of the same phenomenon. In the first place, the women might have been regarded as "sisters-in-law"; or, in the second place, all the men of one group and all the women of the other might have entered a brother–sister relationship. In both cases the result would have been the same as in the accepted interpretation, in which, indeed, these relationships are implied though not expressed. Nevertheless, the solution itself was actually based on the relationship between the male and his allied collaterals, the consequences of which must now be examined.

Two of the three possible interpretations implied the consideration of women; only one was purely masculine, and it is this last which was adopted by the natives. The reason for the choice is obvious, since the problem to be solved was a purely political one concerning the chieftainship, which is exercised by men, rather than the normal mechanism of filiation, the pattern of which seems to be matrilineal. In a simple system of cross-cousin marriage, such as that of the Nambikwara, the brother-in-law may be either the matrilateral or the patrilateral cross-cousin; nevertheless, the chosen interpretation stresses the male side in Nambikwara society, or, let us say, it shows a strong tendency in this direction. At the same time, we can see in such a solution a specifically social structure beginning to superimpose itself on the formerly simple familial units.

We do not intend in any way to base a theory of the origin of dual organizations on these restricted observations, the character of which is mainly anecdotal. However, this is a case where "the characteristic features of the sib organization are in some measure prefigured among sibless tribes";[1] as a matter of fact, in order to fulfill the main requirements of a system of exogamic moieties, it would be sufficient for the new unit, once fixed, to retain the recollection of its dual origin by preserving the habit of not mingling the camp-fires.

Moreover, the extension of the "brother-in-law" relationship provides an instance of the increasingly superior position of the men within the group, since it is through the men that group alliances are brought about, just as wars are waged by men.

The preceding observations have a further value, since with their help we may be able to interpret sociological information found in the older literature on South America, especially that dealing with the Tupi of the Brazilian coast.

There are striking similarities between several features of the Nambikwara kinship system and what may be inferred about the ancient familial organization of the coastal Tupi. When describing small details of Nambikwara daily life, one is often tempted to quote Jean de Léry or Yves d'Evreux, so accurately do their words apply to certain living features of Nambikwara society, notwithstanding the fact that they were written four centuries before this culture became known. As a matter of fact, several metaphysical themes are common to both cultures, and, indeed, certain names in the Nambikwara religious vocabulary have a conspicuously Tupi origin. The most important similarities, however, are those involving the kinship systems. In both cultures the same three principles of familial organization are stressed and are apparently similarly expressed: first, the dichotomy of the parents' brothers and sisters between parallel uncles and aunts, called "fathers" and "mothers," and cross-uncles and -aunts, called "fathers-in-law" and "mothers-in-law"; second, the marriage of cross-cousins with the correlative assimilation of parallel cousins to "brothers" and "sisters"; and, finally, the avuncular marriage, which, among the ancient Tupi, seems to have taken the form of a preferential union between the mother's brother and the sister's daughter.

An excellent text by Anchieta gives evidence of the occurrence of the first principle, as well as showing signs of the existence of the other two:

> In questions of relationship they never use the word *ete* (true) since they call their father's brothers "father," their brothers' sons "son," and their father's brothers' sons "brother"; when they wish to designate their actual father or son, they say *xeruba xemonhangara*, "my father who engendered me," or, for a son, *xeraira xeremimonhanga*, "my son whom I engendered." I never heard an Indian call his wife *xeremireco ete*, but simply *xeremireco* or *xeracig*, "mother of my children," and I never heard a woman refer to her husband as *xemenete*, "real husband," but simply *xemena* or *xemembira ruba*, "father of my children." They use

these terms indifferently for their husband or lover. If the husband calls one of his wives *xeremireco ete*, he means the most esteemed or best loved wife, and she is often the last one he took.[2]

This text also shows that the Tupi encountered a difficulty in their kinship system, namely, how to distinguish classificatory parents or children from the consanguineous ones. This stresses the structural similarity between their kinship system and that of the Nambikwara, since the latter met with the same problem. Apparently the Tupi, like the Nambikwara, felt no need for special terms, but, when it was necessary, made comments based on physiological considerations. When the Nambikwara are asked to point out the real status of their consanguineous children, they add to the name for "son" or "daughter" another word, the meaning of which is "child" or "little one." The physiological implication of this new term is perfectly clear, since it is ordinarily used to designate newly born animals, while the former terms are applied only to relationships within the human family. Complementary indications regarding the assimilation of the father's brother to a classificatory father may be found in Soares de Souza.[3]

The old authors give numerous examples of cross-cousin marriage and of marriages between uncles and nieces. Here again, Anchieta will be our main source:

> Though many Indians have several nieces, and very attractive indeed, nevertheless they do not use them as wives. However, brothers have such authority over sisters that they consider their nieces as belonging to them and that they are entitled to marry them and to use them ad libitum if they wish. In the same way they give their sisters to some and refuse them to others. Taragoaj, an important chief of the village of Jaribiatiba in the plain of San Vicente, had two wives, one of whom was his niece, his sister's daughter.[4]

Both types of marriage are treated as symmetrical institutions in the same document "because the fathers give them the daughters and the brothers the sisters."[5] Furthermore, cross-cousin marriage is referred to by Staden – "They make presents also of their daughters and sisters"[6] – and by Soares de Souza,[7] Claude d'Abbeville[8] and others. With a sound sociological feel, Anchieta establishes a link between the custom of a man marrying his sister's daughter and the recognition of the male as the only one responsible for conception – a theory also shared by the Nambikwara. On this matter, Anchieta writes:

They call the brothers' daughters "daughter" and treat them as such. Therefore they would not have sexual intercourse with them, since they believe that the true kinship link has its origin in the father, whom they consider the only agent, while the mother, according to them, is merely a container in which the children are formed ... For that reason, too, they use the sisters' daughters "ad copulam" without sin ... For the same reason, the father will give his daughters in marriage to their uncles, their mother's brothers, a thing which, until now, was never done with the nephew who is the brother's son ...[9]

Cross-cousin marriage seems to have a very wide distribution throughout South America.[10] But, among the Tupi, avuncular marriage in particular aroused the interest of early travelers. For instance, Léry notices: "As to the uncle, he marries his niece";[11] and Thevet: "As soon as they are born, the maternal uncle lifts them from the ground and keeps them for his future wives."[12] De Magalhães Gandavo expresses himself as follows: "It is their custom to marry the women who are their nieces, the daughters of their brothers or sisters; these are considered their legitimate and true wives. Fathers of the women cannot refuse them, nor can any persons other than their uncles marry them."[13] But this statement seems to be doubly inaccurate. For other references to the same phenomenon one may turn to Nóbrega,[14] Vasconcellos[15] and Soares de Souza.[16]

Regarding polygyny and the sharp differentiation made among the Nambikwara between the first wife who devotes herself to feminine activities and the younger wives who are their husband's companions and share his tasks, it may be recalled that de Magalhães Gandavo[17] refers to a special category of women, single indeed, who shared in masculine activities.[18]

The preceding similarities may perhaps allow us to establish a valid comparison between our observations concerning the extension of the "brother-in-law" relationship among the Nambikwara and what seems to have been a very similar institution among the ancient Tupi. We first quote Yves d'Evreux:

> They scattered part of the French through the villages so that they might live according to the custom of the land, which consists in having *chetouasap*, that is to say, hosts or god-sibs [*compères*], giving them merchandise instead of money. Such hospitality or god-sib relationship is very close among them, for they regard you as their child as long as you stay with them. They hunt and fish for

you and, what is more, they used to give their daughters to their god-sibs [compéres].[19]

The same author refers later to the "French who were established in the villages in a god-sib relationship [compérage]."[20] Evidence of the aboriginal institution may also be found in Jean de Léry:

> It is worth remarking that the words *atour-assap* and *coton-assap* differ, because the first signifies a perfect alliance between them and between them and us, so much so that the belongings of the one are common to the other. And also that they cannot have the daughter or sister of the first named.[21]

From this one may infer, conversely, that marriage is authorized with the sister and the daughter of the *coton-assap*. Therefore, the *coton-assap* is granted a double privilege: first, marriage with his partner's sister, which makes him a "brother-in-law"; and, second, marriage with his partner's daughter, which is equivalent to his assimilation to the rank of "maternal uncle"; then, because he is considered a theoretical brother of his partner's wife, he also becomes a theoretical brother-in-law. Actually, therefore, both privileges have the same result.

One more similarity between the Tupi and Nambikwara brother-in-law relationship remains to be pointed out. All the texts quoted agree that there existed among the Tupi a kind of authority held by young men over their sisters. Cross-cousin marriages seem to have resulted chiefly from a reciprocal exchange of their respective sisters by the male cross-cousins. (The same holds for the giving of a daughter by a father.) The potential or actual brothers-in-law then enter into a relationship of a special nature based upon reciprocal sexual services. We know that the same thing may be said of the Nambikwara brothers-in-law, with the difference that, among the Tupi, the sisters or daughters of the brothers-in-law provided the object of these services, whereas among the Nambikwara the services are directly exchanged in the form of homosexual relations.

We may now summarize our observations. The ancient Tupi acknowledged two forms of marriage – namely, cross-cousin marriage and avuncular marriage. The first was usually practiced in the form of an exchange of sisters by two male cousins; the second appears to have been a right to the sister's daughter exercised by the mother's brother or granted to him by his sister's husband. In both cases the marriage is the result of an agreement between cross-cousins, actually or potentially brothers-in-law, which is the definition we retained as a convenient translation of the Nambikwara terms *tarúte̜* and *iópa̜*. Now, this special "brother-in-law" relationship could be established, under the name of *chetouasap* (Evreux) or *coton-assap* (Léry), between individuals not united previously by any kinship tie, or else only more remotely related, or even between strangers (as was the case of the French and the Indians). The reason for such a step was to ensure intermarriage and by this means to amalgamate familial or social groups, previously heterogeneous, into a new homogeneous unit. One recognizes here the same process described in the analysis of the relations between the newly joined groups, Sabáne and Tarunde.[22]

The objection may be raised that the old authors have interpreted inaccurate observations in the light of European data. Since we shall suggest the use of the word *compérage* – borrowed from the French – to identify the institution, which we consider to be an authentic aboriginal one, it will be useful to discuss briefly this aspect of the problem.

Without any doubt there is a striking analogy between the facts related above and the Latin-European institution of compérage. Originally the *compère* and the *commère* were connected with each other, and both with the child's parents, through the mystical link of *parrainage*. However, the relation was very soon secularized in all small rural communities, or, rather, wherever the familial structures were of greater importance than the social ones; it was then used to establish an artificial link of kinship, or, more precisely, as is the case among the Nambikwara, to express in kinship terms a purely external relationship of spatial promiscuity.[23] The stranger or newcomer was adopted by means of the reciprocal appellation of *compère* or *commère* which he received from – and returned to – his male adult contemporaries. On the other hand, since the stranger usually assimilated himself to the group by marrying within his new community, the terms *compère* and "brother-in-law" soon became synonymous, so that men allied by marriage usually called each other only by the first term. In all small communities of Mediterranean Europe and of Latin America, the *compère* or *compadre* is an actual or a potential brother-in-law. No doubt in certain regions of Central and South America the analogy between the European and aboriginal institution has helped the latter to become fixed and modernized. Thus, in Mexico, the primitive institution of the *moste* – that is, of the heads of families bound to exchange gifts at certain periods – now expresses itself by means of the "compadre" relationship, the Spanish term providing an easy translation of the earlier Otomi.[24] The formal analogy between the institutions, however, cannot hide the fact that they are really opposite in character. In Latin-Mediterranean society, the formerly mystical and, actually, social link of *compérage* may be changed, through marriage, into a real kinship tie. Among the ancient Tupi, as among the Nambikwara, the actual kinship provides the type of link used to establish wider relations.

This being admitted, there are two strong reasons why our authorities cannot have constructed a pseudo-institution based on a European pattern from inconsistent observations. In the first place, men as well acquainted with religious problems as were Yves d'Evreux, Cardim and Léry could not have assimilated a relationship whose first consequence and probable aim was to permit new forms of marriage to the relationship between godfathers and parents, the main purpose of which, especially since the thirteenth century, had been to impose new and very rigid restrictions upon marriage. At the time they were writing, the matter was of immediate interest and was being discussed by the Council of Trent, where the earlier rules were somewhat mitigated. But there is a much stronger argument: from the moment of the arrival of the European missionaries, both institutions, the European and the aboriginal, actually coexisted among the Indians, at least among those who were baptized, and neither they nor their European priests ever interpreted the Christian "god-father" relationship in terms of the native "brother-in-law" institution. On the contrary, and much more logically, since the new relationship placed restrictions on marriage, they considered it as a modality of the relation of paternity; thus, they assimilated the "god-father" to a classificatory "father."

> They [the newly baptized children] regarded their god-fathers as their true fathers and called them *Cherou*, that is to say, "my father," and the French called them *Cheaire*, that is to say, "my son," and the little girls *Cheagire*, "my daughter."[25]

Therefore, it cannot be doubted that the *compérage* is quite distinct from its European parallel.

A sufficient number of convergent indications have been recorded so that we may consider the outstanding character of the "brother-in-law" relationship a specific feature of South American sociology, constituting the core of an original institution of *compérage* which appears clearly among the Nambikwara and which, as suggested by the documents presented in this article, may formerly have had a much wider distribution on the continent.

XIV

On Dual Organization in South America

In a recent issue of *American Anthropologist*, Professor Robert H. Lowie refers, with exceedingly kind comments, to a letter which I wrote him in 1938 from Campos Novos (Mato Grosso) during my fieldwork among the Nambikwara. At the time I was writing I certainly never thought that it would ever deserve Professor Lowie's attention; nor do I believe today that the suggestions hastily presented in it justify the opening of a discussion. However, in view of Professor Lowie's enlightening article,[1] I should like to take this opportunity to make some observations on the methodological approach to one of the main problems of South American sociology.

My letter was written in response to a previous suggestion by Professor Lowie that "the appearance of matrilineal moieties on the Bororo–Canella level indicates the local origin of such institutions among hunters-gatherers or at best incipient farmers."[2] I suggested an alternative hypothesis, namely that the dual organization was retained by those tribes (and many others in South America) as a vestige of a cultural level undoubtedly higher than that which they now display, but which existed in a relatively recent past. Professor Lowie observes that this suggestion recalls the Graebner–Schmidt interpretation of parallel organizations in Australia – a rather embarrassing association which I shall try to show that I do not deserve[3] – and, while admitting that the possibility should be kept in mind, he objects that, until a particular model is produced, "either alternative seems equally admissible."

Two parts, I believe, should be distinguished in Professor Lowie's argument. First there is the theoretical question of knowing if, as Professor Lowie suggests, the ruder levels possess a creative capacity making it possible for them to develop spontaneously complex types of social organizations. Second, we have to say whether this was actually the case in South America. While I fully and entirely agree with

Professor Lowie on the first point, I believe that, as to the second, the facts point in quite another direction.

Sociologists and anthropologists may thank Professor Lowie for having challenged, at last, what he calls "the dogma of human uninventiveness." There is little doubt he is right when he states that he is "more than ever impressed with the amazing fertility of ideas that confront us on the ruder levels."[4] In material things, as well as in social custom and religious belief, people of low culture are capable of creative and amazing achievements, and there is certainly nothing in the dual organization which places it beyond their reach. Not only do I agree with Professor Lowie on this point, but I have perhaps been able to put forward a concrete example of it which presented itself during my stay among the Nambikwara of the Western Mato Grosso. Among this group, which belongs to one of the lowest cultural levels existing in South America, I met with two bands speaking different dialects, the members of which were able to communicate with each other only through interpreters. The two bands, however, had decided to merge, and, in order to achieve this result, they were making special use of their kinship system, which is based on the terminology typical of cross-cousin marriage. The two bands made the common statement that all the male members of one group would consider as sisters the women of the other group, and conversely. Consequently, all the children of both sexes in one group became the potential spouses of the children of the other, and both groups were to be welded into a single consanguineous unit within two generations. Then it would be sufficient for the components of the new unit to retain the recollection of their dual origin – for instance by preserving their respective sets of personal names to be confronted with a typical system of exogamic moieties.[5] This observation does not stand alone. We have numerous instances, from the Xingu area and from the West Indies, of new social units resulting from the merging of two groups or more.

Facts of this kind clearly establish, on an experimental basis, the validity of Professor Lowie's assumption that human cultures, even the more primitive, are able to evolve, from elementary stages, new forms of organization. The remaining problem is to ascertain if dual organization in South America was actually developed directly on the ruder levels; and here I cannot agree with Professor Lowie.

I should be the first to point out – against myself – that the occurrence among the Nambikwara of a social process – the result of which is to produce a system equivalent, from a functional point of view, to a dual structure – is not at all the same thing as the occurrence among the Gê of a developed, fully expressed, conscious institution like the matrilineal moieties. Indeed, nothing could be more dangerous than to acknowledge in the first case something like a "stage" in the process which leads to the true dual organization. The example of the Nambikwara gives proof of a theoretical possibility as well as of a practical ability; it does not allow us to attempt an historical reconstruction. On the other hand, and from the point of view of the Americanist, the answer to the problem raised by Professor Lowie does not lie in abstract considerations; it depends on whether we may consider the Gê, or the Bororo, or the Nambikwara, as true hunter-gatherers or true incipient farmers, or whether their cultural position is not, in fact, different. I shall now try to elaborate this point.

In my 1938 letter I suggested that the low economic level of the tribes of Central and Western Brazil should be interpreted more as the result of a pre-Columbian process of acculturation than as an original condition. To this suggestion, Professor Lowie objects that it will remain a mere possibility "until a particular model is produced of which the Bororo–Canella organization is the demonstrably attenuated replica."[6]

One is tempted to give an answer that is perhaps too easy: the dual organization existed in Peru and Bolivia, with the probably pre-Incan division between "upper" and "lower"; and it is Professor Lowie himself who, commenting upon the social organization of the Bororo, remarks that it recalls Bandelier's description of Tiahuanaco.[7] Looking further north, the dual principle, or at least its basic pattern, existed among the Aztecs, with the ritual fights between the Order of the Eagle and the Order of the Jaguar – two animals, it should be remembered, which are also the fundamental characters of Tupi mythology, and of the mythology of other South American tribes, as everyone knows who is familiar with the theme of the "Jaguar of the Sky" and the ritual raising of the harpy eagle on the plazas of villages. This is especially significant as there are also striking similarities between Aztec and Tupi ritual. Indeed, one would be tempted to suggest that the particular model, of which the lower cultures of the tropical lowlands are the attenuated replica, should be sought among the elaborate systems of Peru and Mexico.

The facts are not so simple, however. In modern times, only Colonel Fawcett came to believe that some mysterious Eldorado was still standing in the deserted savanna of Central Brazil. What I am suggesting is far more modest: when we look at the higher and at the lower cultures of Central and South America, we find an enormous number of themes and patterns which are common to both. It could easily be shown, for instance, that the apparently mysterious spectacles-like ornaments on several Maya figures from Piedras Negras, Copán and Uxmal are still actually worn in Central Brazil. The dual organization is but one of them. The terribly confused and homogeneous character of the distribution of those common traits, scattered throughout the continent, present among the lower as well as among the higher levels, makes extremely unlikely the possibility of accounting for the occurrence of each by as many historical processes of diffusion. Such an explanation, needless to say, would remain purely hypothetical. On the contrary, it seems that this overall situation can be looked at as a huge phenomenon of syncretism, itself the result of innumerable migrations and mixtures, all of which should have taken place far before the start of what we call the pre-Columbian history of South America – i.e. the beginning of the high cultures of Mexico and Peru. When these started, a common cultural basis was already built up which was more or less homogeneous throughout Central and South America.

Now could the low cultures of the savanna constitute such a basis for the further development of the higher cultures? Certainly not. One cannot imagine, for instance, a sudden transition from, let us say the Gê level, to the early Maya or even the early Mexico. The only conclusion is that this common basis was somewhat higher than what we find presently in central South America, though obviously much more primitive than what we can now reconstitute of the beginnings of the high civilizations.

We have numerous pieces of evidence that such a level was once widespread. First, archaeology suggests that, in a relatively recent past, centers of cultures clearly higher than those now confronting the fieldworker were scattered throughout tropical South America: for instance, the West Indies, Marajó, Cunani, the lower valley of the Amazon and of the Tocantins, the plain of the Mojos, Santiago del Estero, and the huge petroglyphs of the Orinoco valley and elsewhere, the carving of which undoubtedly required the cooperation of large groups of workers. History confirms to some extent the same picture: the cultures which Orellana encountered on the whole course of the Amazon seem to have been quite developed. Shall we assume that, at the time when all these cultures were flourishing, the ruder levels were not participating to some extent in this cultural climax of tropical South America?

Furthermore, it is perhaps an example of too much refinement to label the matrilineal dual organization found in South America as "the Bororo–Canella organization" and, likewise, to try to explain it as a phenomenon peculiar to the tribes of the savanna. For the dual organization also exists – or existed – among very different tribes: limiting myself to the lowlands, I shall mention only the Tereno, Parintintin and Munduruku, all well known to Professor Lowie. This does not include the Tereno of the southern tip of Mato Grosso and the Palikur, who are especially significant since, as members of the Arawak stock, they belong to the higher cultural level of the tropical area. It should also be added that unmistakable traces of the dual organization exist among the Tupi-Kawahib of the Upper Machado, and that we are consequently able to define an almost continuous area of dual organization which extends from the right bank of the Tocantins to the Madeira, south of the Amazon. I question the possibility of interpreting the dual organization in exclusive relation with the ruder levels, when we know positively that they shared it with their northwestern neighbors of the forest area, whose cultural level, featuring extensive farming and head-hunting, was undoubtedly much higher.[8]

The social organization of the savanna people cannot be isolated from that of the Tupian tribes of northern Mato Grosso. Conversely, one may ask if there is a sound basis for the grouping of the Bororo together with tribes that seem to be on a ruder level. The main argument for this assimilation is a text of von den Steinen from which one is tempted to infer that, prior to contact with the Brazilian army, the Bororo were an exclusively hunting tribe and ignorant of agriculture: "the women, who were used to digging up the roots in the bush, started cutting down the young trees, carefully turning over the soil in order to discover roots. This hunting tribe lacked a true agriculture, and above all the patience to wait for the tubers to grow."[9] But these were the soldiers' gardens, not the natives', and von den Steinen himself notices that "the Bororo did not care much for the gifts of civilization."[10] When one reinserts the text on agriculture into the lively picture drawn by the German ethnologist of the dreadful process of acculturation which was taking place as a result of the "pacification" of the Indians, one hesitates to give more importance to it than that of an anecdotal remark. What inference can be drawn from it? That at the time the Bororo had no gardens of their own? This would hardly be surprising, as they were being pursued and exterminated for several years by the Brazilians. Or that they were more interested in looting the soldiers' gardens than in tilling the soil? But fortunately we have more precise information; I shall not mention here Colbacchini, whose statements on this point can be interpreted both ways.[11] But in 1901, among the Bororo of the Rio Ponte de Pedra (a then little-known tributary of the São Laurenço), Cook noticed fields of "a small yellow corn."[12] In 1905, Frič[13] visited the villages on the Rio Vermelho, which were then untouched by civilization. He stated: "The Bororo plant very little in the Colonia Theresa Christina and for this reason, perhaps, Professor von den Steinen, who only saw them plough under compulsion, believed that they had never been an agricultural nation. Mr. Frič, visiting those still living in a wild state, discovered many plantations carefully kept." Of special significance is the harvest ritual described by the same author. He witnessed a "ceremony of blessing, to taste the corn before which would mean certain death." It consisted

> in first washing the half-ripe husk and placing it before the *aroetorrari* (the medicine man), who by uninterruptedly dancing and singing for several hours, and by incessant smoking, works himself into a state resembling hypnotic ecstasy, in which condition, trembling in every muscle, he bites into the husk, uttering shrieks from time to time. A similar ceremony is repeated whenever a large animal such as a tapir, wild pig, etc., or some large fish such as *Jahu, Dorado* (salmon), etc., is shot. It is the firm belief of the Bororo that should anyone touch unconsecrated meat or maize before the ceremony has been completed, he and his entire tribe would perish.

It is very difficult to imagine that the Bororo, whose culture collapsed almost completely (except for one or two villages of the Rio Vermelho) between 1880 and 1910, would have taken the care and found the opportunity to elaborate a harvest ritual for a newly acquired agriculture, unless they possessed it previously.

Thus, the real issue is to know if anywhere in South America we can speak of pure hunters and gatherers and of incipient farmers. It is true that, in present times, many tribes appear to belong to these types; and it cannot be denied that some of them (as the Guayaki of Paraguay and the gathering tribes of the Orinoco) seem very primitive. However, the number of tribes lacking agriculture entirely is extremely small, and each one is isolated among groups belonging to a higher cultural level. I submit that their particular history would better account for their presence than the hypothesis of a former archaic cultural level of which they should be considered as survivals. As regards the other ones, they are undoubtedly crude farmers, relying partially or principally on hunting, fishing or gathering, but this leaves open the question of whether they are incipient farmers, or whether they were able only partially to retain farming, on account of new living conditions.

In several recent articles, Father J. M. Cooper has proposed distinguishing the tribes of tropical South America into two main groups, which he calls the Silval and the Marginal. He divides in turn the

Marginal (in the tropical area) into two sub-groups: the Savannal and the Intrasilval.[14] Only the main division has to be considered here. This division may be useful for practical purposes, but it would be very dangerous to try to use it to support an attempt at historical reconstruction. There is absolutely no proof that the tropical savanna was a dwelling place in archaic times; but there are, on the contrary, many indications that the "Savannals" are doing their best to retain in their present habitat something like a "silval" pattern of life. In presenting the following observations I shall leave entirely aside the tribes of the Chaco, which furnish Father Cooper with the main basis for his argument, and which I consider quite distinct from the groups inhabiting the vast area of the tropical lowlands.

There is no geographical distinction clearer to the mind of the South American native than that between the savanna and the forest. The first one is improper for cultivation, as well as for gathering and collecting wild food: both its vegetation and its animal life are sparse. On the contrary, the forest offers an abundance of wild plants and game and its soil is moist and fertile. The opposition between the agricultural life of the forest and the hunters and gatherers of the savanna may be a cultural opposition, but it has no ecological significance. The most suitable place for gardening, for hunting, for fishing and for collecting wild food is the forest and the barren banks of some rivers in the forest area. Then it is impossible to distinguish between a pre-horticultural level retained by the tribes of the savanna and a cultural one based on gardening in the forest, for the people of the forest are not only the best gardeners (though not the only ones), they are at the same time the best collectors and gatherers (though not the only ones), because there are many more things to gather in the forest than elsewhere. In both areas we find both collecting and cultivation, while the only difference is that the two patterns are simultaneously more developed in one area than in the other. This point was completely misunderstood by Nordenskiöld, who is responsible for many confusions between geographical and cultural determination. For instance, it is not, as he states, the lack of paripinnate palm trees which should be held responsible for the eventual lack of basketry in some part of the Chaco[15] but only perhaps the ignorance among the Indians of the Chaco of the technique of basket-making from fan-shaped leaves: the baskets of the Guiana Indians are made indifferently from both types. Geographical determinism is practically non-existent in the forest area: it is the plants which are substituted; the cultural pattern is maintained. The determinism of the savanna, on the other hand, is purely negative. It does not offer new opportunities but only limits those of the forest. There is no savannal culture. The savannal culture is but an attenuated replica of the "silval." Pre-horticultural people as well as gardeners would have chosen the forest as a dwelling place, or stayed in the forest, if only they had an opportunity to do so. If the savannals are not in the forest it is not on account of a savannal culture of their own; it can only be because they were driven out of it. In this way were the Gê driven toward the interior by the great migrations of the Tupi.

One may readily admit that in some cases the new environment was not entirely negative. The Bororo may have become predominantly hunters on account of the special richness of game on the borders of the marshlands which occupy the middle course of the Paraguay River; similarly, fishing may have taken a larger part in the economies of the Xingu tribes than it eventually did in their undoubtedly more northern place of origin. Nevertheless, and whenever it is possible, the savannal tribes cling to the forest, and to forest-like conditions. All the gardening is made in the gallery forest which, even in the savanna, accompanies the main waterways. It would be impossible to do it elsewhere. The stupidity of the mythical deer which tries to cultivate manioc in the savanna filled the Bakairi with mirth, according to von den Steinen.[16] Long trips are undertaken to the nearest forests in order to get items indispensable to cultural life – for instance, the big bamboos used as containers and for making musical instruments. But it is the character of the techniques related to wild food which is the more striking. While among the forest tribes (in the Guiana for instance) they constitute a careful, almost scientific exploitation of the natural resources (let one recall the elaborate process of extracting starch from the trunk of palm trees, the fermentation of wild seeds buried in the ground, and the still more complicated techniques which, at the level of wild plants, must have led to the discovery of the utilization of poisonous varieties), among the savannal tribes they consist mostly of a crude form of gathering and consuming which seems to have originated in a sudden need to make up for the lack of basic staples. Then even collecting and gathering appear in the savanna to have a secondary and acculturated character.

All this is apparently very far from dual organization. But I have tried to show, first, that dual organization is not, in tropical South America, the special property of the ruder levels, but that they share it with more developed tribes; and, second, that those ruder levels do not appear to constitute a specific pattern of culture or a survival of an archaic condition, but are more probably an attenuated replica, on account of newly unfavorable geographic surroundings, of the higher life of the forest area. I had previously suggested that what I called the

Central and South American syncretism demands the hypothesis of some kind of a cultural homogeneity which should have existed on a middle cultural level in ancient times. It is probably on this middle level that dual organization took shape. The syncretism was undoubtedly the result of innumerable cultural borrowing processes, the traces of which are forever lost. Thus, we are compelled to take it as a starting point in South American history. From this starting point two kinds of historical events must have taken place: on the one hand, the birth and development of the high cultures of the highlands; on the other, under the influence of wars, migrations and clashes, the breaking down of the original level and the adaptation of the weaker tribes, which were driven into the savanna, to their new and poor environment. As to the original, syncretic level, perhaps its features are better preserved among the intensive farmers of the Orinoco–Amazon area. This conception shall not be regarded, I hope, as a replica of the Graebner–Schmidt interpretation of the parallel Australian problems. But it appears to me as providing a less unsatisfactory approach to the basic problem of South American sociology, namely the occurrence of dual organization at both extreme levels – the higher and the lower of the South American scale of cultures.

XV

The Tupi-Kawahib

Tribal Divisions and History

The Tupi-Kawahib are not mentioned in the literature before 1913–14, when they were discovered by General Cândido Mariano da Silva Rondon, who headed the Brazilian Military Commission. Little information about them is contained in the reports of the Commission (*Missão Rondon*, 1916; Rondon, 1916).

The Tupi-Kawahib declined rapidly in population within a few years. The three hundred individuals who comprised the Takwatip clan in 1915 were reduced in ten years to only fifty-nine persons – twenty-five men, twenty-two women and twelve children. In 1938, there were only five men, a woman and a small girl. Thirty years ago, the entire Tupi group probably included from two thousand to three thousand persons; now only a hundred or a hundred and fifty of them are alive. Epidemics of influenza, during 1918–20, are largely responsible for the decline in population. Several cases of paralysis of the legs, observed in 1938 (Lévi-Strauss, n.d.), suggest that poliomyelitis may have reached this remote region.

According to the linguistic and historical evidence presented by Nimuendajú (1924, 1925), the Tupi-Kawahib and Parintintin are the remnants of an ancient Tupi tribe, the Cabahiba. Since the eighteenth century, it has often been stated that the Cabahiba had once lived in the upper Tapajós basin. The language of the Tupi-Kawahib closely resembles that of the Parintintin, and both are related to the language of the Apiacá of the Tapajós River. After the destruction of the Cabahiba by the Mundurucú, the Tupi-Kawahib settled on the Rio Branco, a left tributary of the Roosevelt River (lat. 10°–12° S, long. 61°–62° W). From the Rio Branco they were driven to their present territory on both sides of the Machado (or upper Ji-Paraná) River, from the Riosinho River in the southeast to the Muquí and the Leitao River in the north and the northwest. These three waterways are small tributaries of the Machado River. The native groups mentioned by both Rondon and Nimuendajú (1924, 1925) are clans with special geographical localization. According to Nimuendajú's informant, the Wiraféd and Paranawát (Paranauad) were settled on a tributary of the right bank of the Riosinho River. The Takwatib Eriwahun (Nimuendajú), or Takwatip (Lévi-Strauss), who had once lived on the Tamuripa River, a right tributary of the Machado River, halfway between the Riosinho and the Muquí rivers, were brought by General Rondon to the Rio Machado, where they lived until 1925, when the last six members of the group joined the Telegraphic Post of Pimenta Bueno. The Ipotewát, mentioned by Rondon, are no longer an autonomous unit. According to information recorded in 1938, they were then living on the upper Cacoal between the Riosinho and Tamuripa rivers. Living downstream were the Tucumanfét. The Paranawát, mentioned by Rondon and Nimuendajú, lived on the Rio Muquí in 1938. They numbered about a hundred individuals and had refused to have any contact with white people. When the remnants of the previously unknown Mialat were discovered in 1938 on the upper Leitao River, there were only sixteen members of the group (Lévi-Strauss, n.d.). The now extinct Jabotifet were formerly settled between the upper Cacoal and Riosinho rivers.

Culture

Subsistence

Farming – The Tupi-Kawahib cultivate gardens in large clearings near their villages and hunt game in the dense forest. They raise both bitter and sweet manioc; five kinds of maize – a white one with large kernels, a dark red variety, a kind with white, black and red kernels, one with orange and black kernels, and a red "chine"; small broad beans; peanuts; hot peppers; bananas; papayas; cotton; and calabashes. Digging sticks and stone axes were formerly used for preparing and tilling the fields.

Wild foods – The Tupi-Kawahib gather several wild foods. To facilitate the collection of Brazil nuts, which are abundant in the region, they clear the forest around each tree. They collect two kinds of cacao beans, which are eaten raw, and several kinds of berries. To harvest the small pyramidal seeds of an unidentified tall forest grass (*awatsipororoke*), the natives tie several of the stems together before the ears are ripe, so that the seeds will fall together in small heaps.

The tapir, peccary, forest deer, great anteater, and numerous kinds of monkeys (figure 4) and birds are hunted. Wild bees are killed in the hive by closing the entrance with a pad of leaves of an unidentified poisonous tree, and the honey is collected in coarse containers of bark or leaves. Fish are shot with arrows or drugged with a saponine-rich vine that is used in dams constructed of branches and mud in shallow places in rivers. When the Tupi-Kawahib were first observed by Whites, they kept chickens in conical sheds made of sticks set in the ground in a circle and tied together at the top. There was no dog in the Mialat village discovered in 1938.

Figure 4 Life in a Tupi-Kawahib village: a monkey being skinned

Food preparation – Game is singed and smoked in the skin, either intact or in pieces. Babracots are about 5 feet (1.5 m) high and are constructed on four posts. Game is smoked for twenty-four hours; during the night, an attendant takes care of the fire. The babracot for drying beans is made of several branches placed on transverse sticks, which are supported on the prongs of a three-forked branch.

Maize chicha (*ka-ui*) (figure 5) is made by drying the kernels and grinding them in a mortar with a few Brazil nuts or peanuts for seasoning. The coarse flour is mixed with water in large bowls, and small children spit saliva in the gruel. After the chicha ferments a few hours, it is put on the fire and kept just below the boiling point for two or three hours. Fresh gruel is constantly added to compensate for the

Figure 5 Life in a Tupi-Kawahib village: production of corn beer

evaporation. The beverage is drunk as soon as it is cold or during the next two or three days.

Manioc tubers are grated and roasted in large plates. Popcorn is made of maize and of the wild seed *awatsipororoke*. Pama berry seeds are eaten roasted. In contrast to the neighboring Nambikwara, the Tupi-Kawahib are fond of highly seasoned foods. They cook hot peppers and broad beans in a stew. A kind of salt is prepared by burning acuri palm leaves, sifting the ashes, and washing them with water. Both the water, which is dark brown and bitter, and the ashes, which form a gray astringent powder, are used as condiments.

Houses

When Rondon discovered the Tupi-Kawahib, their square huts had no walls; the gable roof of palms was supported on posts set in the ground. Hammocks were swung from the posts. In 1915 the Takwatip village comprised about twenty houses, each from 12 to 18 feet (3.5 to 5.5 m) long, arranged in a circle about 60 feet (18 m) in diameter. Two large houses in the center of the circle, each from 36 to 42 feet (11 to 12.5 m) long, were occupied by the chief, Abaitara, and his wives, children and court. Cages for harpy eagles and huts for fowls were in the open space of the circular plaza. There were no fortifications surrounding the village. Quite different was the Mialat village discovered in 1938. Of the four square houses, each about 30 feet (9 m) long, situated in a row, two were used for living quarters and two for food storage. The roof frame was supported by posts, irregularly spaced and set back under the projecting roof, so that the house resembled a square mushroom. The storage quarters had no walls. Each of the other two houses was surrounded by a continuous palisade about 6 feet (2 m) high, which gave the appearance of a wall but actually did not support the roof, as there was an opening a few inches wide between the lower edge of the roof frame and the top of the palisade. The palisade, which had loopholes for shooting arrows, was made of longitudinal sections of palm trunks, fastened edge to edge, the convex surface turned outward. The exterior was decorated in *urucu* paste with jaguars, dogs, harpy eagles, snakes, frogs, children and the moon.

Platforms were built along the paths leading to the villages as lookouts from which the moves of hostile groups could be observed (Rondon, 1916).

Tree trunks were used to bridge small waterways.

Dress and ornaments

According to Rondon (1916), men wore a garment of woven cotton resembling drawers. In 1938, Tupi-Kawahib men were naked except for a small conical penis sheath made of the two halves of a leaf plaited and sewed. Women wore a short, cylindrical skirt of woven cotton string, which reached half-way to the knees (see figure 7). Modern Tupi-Kawahib women tattoo their faces with a sharpened deer bone and genipa, applying a geometrical design on the chin and two large symmetrical curved stripes on the cheeks, running from the chin to the ears. Men used to paint themselves with genipa or *urucu* dye when monkey hunting (Rondon, 1916). Both sexes wear bracelets, earrings, necklaces and rings made of mollusk shells, nutshells, wild seeds, game teeth, and deer bones cut in rectangular plates (figures 6 and 7). For

Figure 6 Life in a Tupi-Kawahib village: a Tupi-Kawahib mother and her baby

Figure 7 Life in a Tupi-Kawahib village: a child carrier

ceremonies, men wear a cap without a top made of a large band of woven cotton, over which feathers are stuck. The chief wears a heavy tuft of feathers hanging down his back. Both sexes pluck their pubic hair and eyebrows, using the thumb nail and a half shell. "Eyebrows wearer" is the derogatory equivalent of "civilized." Woven cotton bands are worn around the ankles, the arm and the wrists.

Transportation

The Tupi-Kawahib made canoes of the bark of large trees (Rondon, 1916). A baby straddles its mother's hip, supported by a cotton sling (see figures 6 and 7).

Manufactures

Spinning – Spinning is done by women. A Tupi-Kawahib spindle consists of a small stick, with a round wild seed for the whorl. It is very light and is used more for winding thread in balls than for spinning.

Textile arts – Cotton armlets and anklets are woven by women on primitive vertical looms. Women's skirts are woven and small hammocks are netted with cotton string, and carrying sacks are woven with tucum string.

Basketry – The Tupi-Kawahib weave flat sieves and baskets of bamboo strips and palm leaves and fire fans of palm leaves, often decorating the fans with feathers. An ingenious rucksack for carrying large objects or animals is made by knotting two palm leaves together.

Pottery – The earthenware seen in 1938 consisted of hemispherical bowls, large ones for preparing chicha and small ones for individual meals, and large, circular plates for roasting flour. None were decorated. Informants, however, speak of a purple dye obtained from a wild leaf which was used in former times for painting geometric designs.

Weapons – Tupi-Kawahib bows are about 5 feet 8 inches (1.7 m) long and are made of a black palm wood. The section is circular and the ends are carved to form a knob and shoulders for fastening the string. The grip is wrapped with cotton. Arrows are of three types: those tipped with a large bamboo splinter, for hunting mammals; those with a blunt point, for bird hunting; and arrows which have short feathers and four to seven bamboo points arranged as a crown around a small ball of string, for fishing. Feathering is flush and tied (Arara type), flush and sewed (Xingu type), or arched (eastern Brazil type). Arrow poison is unknown. When shot, the arrow is grasped between the first and middle fingers, which also draw the string, or else it is held between the thumb and finger, and the string is drawn with the other three fingers.

To defend the paths leading to their villages, the Tupi-Kawahib set pointed rods or stakes obliquely into the ground, either singly or fencelike. The stakes are from 1 foot (30 cm) (Lévi-Strauss, n.d.) to 4 feet (1.2 m) (Rondon, 1916) in height, so as to impale the foot or the body, and are hidden under foliage taken from the surrounding forest.

Other implements – Boxes for holding feathers are made of hollowed sections of acuri palm trunks; a longitudinal segment serves as a cover.

A manioc grater consists of a wooden board with embedded palm thorns. Spoons and containers are made of calabashes. Ordinary combs and smalltooth combs are of the composite type. Drills and knives are made of iron pieces fastened onto sticks with wax and wrapper cotton.

Social and political organization

The Tupi-Kawahib are divided into several patrilineal sibs, each localized in one or more villages occupying a defined territory. There is a strong tendency toward village exogamy, which is regarded less as a binding rule than as a means of ensuring good relations between neighboring sibs. Endogamic marriages are possible, although infrequent. Residence seems to be patrilocal, although contrary practices have been recorded. Consequently, the majority of individuals in any village belong to one eponymic sib but are nevertheless associated with a few people belonging to different allied sibs. Besides the four group names mentioned by Rondon (1916) and Nimuendajú (1924), no fewer than fifteen new sib names were recorded in 1938 (Lévi-Strauss, n.d.). As this list is certainly incomplete, the ancient sib organization must have been complex. In addition to sib divisions, each village was divided into two age classes, "the youths" and "the elders." The function of these age classes seems to have been mostly ceremonial.

Chieftaincy is hereditary, passing from the father to son. In former times, the chief was attended by a hierarchy of officials. He possessed judicial power and imposed the death sentence, the convicted person being bound and thrown into the river from a canoe. When the Rondon Commission first met the Takwatip chief Abaitara, he was apparently extending his domination over a large number of sibs and trying, by means of successful wars, to establish his hegemony over others.

Warfare

Rondon mentions the decapitation of enemies killed in warfare but does not state that head trophies were prepared.

Life cycle

Childbirth – A couvade is observed, during which both parents eat only gruel and small animals. Nuts of all kinds are forbidden them.

Marriage – The Tupi-Kawahib practice marriage between cross-cousins and between a maternal uncle and his niece. In the latter case, an adult man may be betrothed to a baby girl, who remains under his care and to whom he gives presents until they marry. Although marriage is generally monogamous, a chief may have several wives, usually sisters or a woman and her daughter. To compensate for the shortage of women thus created, the chief lends his wives to bachelors and to visitors, and fraternal polyandry, associated with the levirate, is practiced within the group. In a polygynous family, one wife has authority over the others, regardless of the differences of age or of previous family relationship.

The existence of homosexuality is not openly acknowledged, but a word meaning "passive pederast" is commonly used as an insult.

Death – The deceased at the time of Rondon's visit was buried inside his hut under his hammock, which, with his weapons, ornaments and utensils, was left undisturbed. Mourners, i.e., relatives, cut their hair (Rondon, 1916).

Aesthetic and recreational activities

Art – Painting on house walls has already been mentioned.

Narcotics – Strangely enough, the Tupi-Kawahib do not cultivate or use tobacco (for chicha, see p. 191).

Games – Children play with crude toys made of plaited or twisted straw. In a disk game, "the youths" are matched against "the elders"; each age group alternately shoots its arrows at a rolling wooden disk thrown across the plaza by a pitcher. In another archery contest, they shoot arrows at a dummy representing a man or an animal. There is a belief that to shoot at a wooden dummy may bring death; to avoid the risk, the dummy is made of straw.

Dance and music – Festivals were given by the chief, who assumed the title "Owner of the Feast." Festivals were preceded by hunting expeditions to obtain small animals, such as rats and marmosets, which were smoked and strung together to be worn as necklaces. During the feast, men playfully carried a flute player on their shoulders.

In 1938, the Mialat chief entertained his people several times with a musical show in which songs alternated with dialogue. He himself played the numerous roles of the comedy, humorously enacting the adventures of several animals and inanimate objects which were mystified by the japim bird. Each character was easily recognized by a musical leitmotif and a special register of the voice.

Musical instruments – The main musical instruments were pottery trumpets (Rondon, 1916), panpipes with thirteen pipes, short flageolets with four holes, whistles and gourd rattles. A clarinet without stops was made of a piece of bamboo about 4 feet (1.2 m) long; a small piece of bamboo in which a vibrating strip was cut formed the reed.

Magic and religion

We have no indication of the magical and religious beliefs of the Tupi-Kawahib. The chief is certainly endowed with shamanistic powers: he treats patients and improvises songs and dances in order to tell and enact his dreams, which are considered to have a premonitory significance. At the end of his musical show, he may become delirious and try to kill anyone in sight.

Although nearly all the sibs have animal or vegetable names, totemism does not seem to exist, for the eponymic plants or animals are freely eaten.

Even today, the Tupi-Kawahib capture great harpy eagles, rear them carefully in large square cages, and feed them game, such as birds and monkeys. It is likely that this custom has a magical or religious background, though nothing positive is known in this respect.

Bibliography

Claude Lévi-Strauss, "Notes on the Tupi Indians of the Upper Gy-Paraná," undated manuscript.
Missão Rondon: apontamentos sobre os trabalhos realizados pela Commissão de linhas telegráphicas ..., Rio de Janeiro, 1916.
Curt Nimuendajú, "Os Indios Parintintin do Rio Madeira," *Journal de la Société des américanistes*, new series, 16 (1924), pp. 201–78.
—— "As Tribus do Alto Madeira," *Journal de la Société des américanistes*, new series, 17 (1925), pp. 137–72.
Cândido Mariano da Silva Rondon, *Lectures Delivered by Colonel Cândido Mariano da Silva Rondon*, Rio de Janeiro, 1916.

XVI

The Nambikwara

TRIBAL DIVISIONS AND HISTORY

The Nambikwara (Nambikuara, Mambyuara, Mahibarez) have been identified only recently. Nambikwara, meaning "long eared," was originally a Tupi nickname used since the eighteenth century for the little-known tribes of the western and northern parts of the Serra dos Parecis. These tribes had large ear and lip plugs, like those of the Suya and Botocudo, and were called Beiços de Pau, "Wooden Mouths," by the rubber collectors and gold miners. About 1830, they began to make hostile sorties from the region of the upper Sangue River. When, in 1907, General Cândido Mariano da Silva Rondon discovered significant tribes in the Serra do Norte, he identified them with the Nambikwara of the old literature. Thus, Nambikwara designates a tribe other than the "Long Ears," or "Wooden Mouths," to whom it was originally applied.

Extending northwest from the Papagaio River more or less to the confluence of the Comemoração and the Barão de Melgaço rivers, branches of the Machado (Ji-Paraná) River, the region of the Nambikwara (see map, p. 227) is bounded on the south by the right tributaries of the Guaporé River and, further west, by the whole of the Comemoração de Floriano River. The northern boundary is unknown but probably runs more or less along the 11th parallel between the Roosevelt and Papagaio rivers (Lat. 10°–15° S, long. 57°–61° W).

The first classification of the Nambikwara was made by Roquette-Pinto (1938, pp. 216–17), who listed four main groups. Lévi-Strauss (n.d.), using linguistic data, distinguishes three main groups. Two of these, which are subdivided into two groups each, clearly belong to the same linguistic family, but the linguistic affiliation of the third group, which is undivided, is doubtful. These groups are Eastern Nambikwara (Roquette-Pinto's Kôkôzu, Cocozu) between the Papagaio and Juína rivers; Northeastern Nambikwara (Roquette-Pinto's Anunze) in the basins of the Camararé and Doze de Outubro rivers; Central and Southern Nambikwara (Roquette-Pinto's Uaintaçu, which includes his Kabishi, Tagnani, Tauitê, Tarutê and Tashuitê) between the Guaporé River basin in the south and the Tenente Marques, Iké and Roosevelt rivers in the north and northwest; Western Nambikwara (new), closely related to the central and southern groups and living on the headwaters and in the upper basin of the Roosevelt River; and Northern Nambikwara (new), speaking its own language and living north of the central group.

The Indians mention other tribes north of the Nambikwara; one called Saluma, Saruma or Solondé is almost certainly the Mundurucú; another may be the Tapanyuma.

In 1907, Rondon estimated the total Nambikwara population to be twenty thousand. In 1912 Roquette-Pinto met between one thousand and fifteen hundred. It is doubtful whether the total population, which has been decimated by several recent epidemics, now greatly exceeds fifteen hundred.

The Nambikwara language was previously thought to be isolated, but its distinctive trait – the use of classificatory suffixes dividing the universe into about ten categories – is strongly reminiscent of Chibcha.

Nambikwara culture, although less primitive than that of the Sirionó to the southwest, is strikingly simple in comparison with that of the neighboring Paressí to the southeast and of the Tupi-Kawahib to the northwest. Their lack of the hammock, their custom of sleeping on the ground, their crude ceramics (the Eastern Nambikwara entirely lack pottery), the nakedness of both sexes, their nomadism, their use of temporary shelters during most of the year, the general poverty of their material culture, and the simplicity of their social organization distinguish them from the higher cultures of the Guaporé River area, to which they nevertheless probably belong.

CULTURE

Subsistence

The Nambikwara habitat is a savanna-like plateau about 500 to 1,500 feet (150 to 500 m) above sea level with an arenaceous soil which comes from disintegrated sandstone bedrock. Except for narrow gallery forests along riverbanks, the region is infertile, having only shrubs and small trees with thorns or thick bark.

In this unproductive environment the Nambikwara have a dual subsistence pattern. They are both semi-nomadic bush dwellers and incipient farmers. During the dry season, women, accompanied by their children, forage with digging sticks for wild fruits, seeds and roots and catch grubs, rats, bats, spiders, snakes, lizards and other small creatures, while men hunt what large game they can find with bows and arrows and collect wild honey.

When rains come, the Nambikwara settle in temporary villages, and the men open circular gardens in the gallery forest by burning and felling the trees with stone (now steel) axes. They till the soil with pointed sticks and raise both bitter and sweet manioc, several kinds of maize which are different from those of their more civilized neighbors (Roquette-Pinto, 1938, p. 297n.), beans, gourds, cotton, *urucu*, and a variety of small tobacco with tiny leaves. Despite the difficulty of fishing in the deep, clear tributaries of the Juruena River, they have moderate success using fish arrows, basket traps, and a drug made of a vine.

Food preparation – Game is usually only half-cooked in hot ashes, but it is sometimes smoked on rectangular or pyramidal babracots. Manioc is grated on thorns of the catizal palm (*Iriartea* sp.) imbedded in palm wood plants. To remove the poisonous juice of bitter manioc, the pulp is either squeezed in a strip of bark twisted spirally or buried for several days to allow the juice to drain off. Balls of the pulp are then sun-dried and packed in leaves in baskets or buried at marked places. In times of scarcity, perhaps months later, the half-rotten balls are made into flat cakes, hastily cooked in hot ashes, and eaten.

The Nambikwara cannot bear to eat salt, which they do not know how to prepare, or pepper, which they do not cultivate. Even hot food is cooled with water before it is eaten. Wild honey, too, is diluted with water. The only condiment is a variety of cumaru bean which has a strong, bitter almond taste. It is boiled in pots; afterward the liquid is drunk and the beans are mixed with food, especially with grasshoppers crushed in mortars. Armadillo meat is often ground with maize flour.

Domestic animals and pets – The Nambikwara have many pets, especially monkeys, coatis, parrots and other birds. Domesticated animals were unknown until the Rondon Commission introduced chickens and dogs. Although at first extremely afraid of dogs, the Indians quickly adopted them and treated them with the same deep affection they show all their tame animals. Even now they are terrified by oxen seen at telegraph stations, and call them by the name given to the deadly spirits of the water and the bush. They do, however, hunt and eat horses and mules as if they were wild game.

Houses

The surprising variety of house types suggests recent borrowing from neighboring tribes. The Nambikwara, like the Sirionó, may formerly have lacked houses entirely. During most of the year, even at the present time, they build only scanty temporary shelters for a single night. These consist of branches of palms stuck into holes dug in the sand to form a half or quarter circle on the side from which the sun, the wind or rain are expected (figure 8). Each individual family builds its own shelter and lights its own fire in the opening. During the rainy season, villages consisting of one or more beehive huts are built on slight hillocks above the course of a secondary stream. Some of the Eastern Nambikwara build only shelters, although larger and stronger than the ones described. The beehive hut is very light, each about 10 to 20 feet (3 to 6 m) in diameter. The frame consists of several long, supple poles, bent so that both ends can be stuck into the ground and tied together at the top, where they cross. Circular branches running horizontally are tied to the poles at different levels. The Central and Western Nambikwara have a more elaborate hut whose perimeter is about 50 feet (15 m). It has a central post from the base of which several forked poles run obliquely to support the bent poles of the external frame. All types of huts are thatched with horizontal layers of palm leaves, those of Central and Western Nambikwara are exactly like the houses of their southern neighbors, the Kepikiriwat.

A gabled house without walls was also observed by Roquette-Pinto, who recorded other kinds of temporary huts. Some were built by sticking two branches into the ground, bending them over and attaching them to a horizontal pole tied to two perpendicular posts and covering them with bunches of grass.

The Nambikwara, although all their neighbors use hammocks, sleep on bare ground or on flat pieces of bark from the paxiuba palm. Because of this custom, the Paressí nicknamed them Uaikoakôre, "Those Who Sleep on the Ground."

Figure 8 Nambikwara family shelter

Clothing and adornment

Both sexes are naked, except that men sometimes tie a small tuft of buriti straw to their belt to cover the sex organs. Both men and women wear a thin, cotton-thread belt strung with white or black beads cut from river mollusk shells or from tucuma palm nuts. Such beads, with larger triangular pieces of mollusk shells, are also used for necklaces, earrings, bracelets and other ornaments (figure 9). Men wear grass or reed pins through their upper and lower lips; and, through their nasal septum, a larger pin made of a jacu (*Penelope*) feather mounted on a stalk covered with plaited cotton thread and porcupine quills and trimmed with a red toucan feather ring. Both sexes wear armlets and anklets of woven cotton, buriti straw, feathers, parts of dried

Figure 9 Nambikwara woman piercing a mother-of-pearl earring

birds, fur, or mollusk or crawfish shells. Women wear one or more bracelets cut from the tail of the great armadillo and double bandoleers of plaited cotton dyed with *urucu* and decorated with porcupine quills. Hair ornaments are confined to men: circlets of plaited straw, of straw and toucan feathers, or of fur with feather pendants. War dress consists of a jaguar-skin bonnet (figure 10) with a long, plaited buriti-straw tail painted with red stripes and dots hanging down from the nape of the neck. A similar but shorter headdress may be worn in daily life.

Hair is groomed with a composite comb. It is cut with a shell, either all around the head at the level of the ear lobe, or only across the forehead, the back and sides being allowed to fall loose. Body painting consists mainly of *urucu* smeared uniformly, but some groups roughly

Figure 10 Nambikwara man wearing a jaguar skin headdress

trace black dots and stripes with genipa juice on the chest and legs. Face and body hair is generally pulled out, especially by women; men often have a sparse moustache and beard.

Transportation

Canoes are unknown. Small waterways are crossed on a fallen tree, large ones by swimming, sometimes with the help of large floating bundles of buriti palm stems. Babies straddle their mother's hip supported by a large sling of bark or woven cotton.

Manufactures

Spinning – Women spin cotton with a crude drop spindle made of grass stalk. The whorl is a wild fruit, a potsherd, or a conical piece of sun-dried clay. Cotton thread is rolled in a ball and, like everything else in a Nambikwara household, wrapped in leaves. Women and men twist tucum and buriti fibers on their thighs to make string.

Weaving – Weaving is limited to cotton bands and belts, which men make on small, rough looms of the "Arawak" type (figure 11).

Basketry – Men make long, open-mouthed, cylindrical baskets using bamboo strips and a hexagonal, open weave. Fire fans are plaited of palm leaves. The Northern Nambikwara used palm leaves to weave low square baskets for storing the manioc and maize flour.

Pottery – Pottery is unknown among the Eastern Nambikwara. In other groups, women make coarse pots of varying sizes. They mix the clay with ashes, fire the pot in the open, and wash it while it is still hot in an infusion of resinous bark.

Implements – Stone ax heads were formerly fixed with wax and strings in the loop of a bent handle. Knives and drills are made of a crude flint chip or piece of iron fastened with wax and thread at the end of a piece of wood or between two pieces of wood, which form the handle. Women hollow small cylindrical mortars in tree trunks by means of fire. Fire is made with a fire drill, crude rubber serving as tinder. The Indians burn almecega (*Tetragastris balsamifera*) resin for light. Knives are thin, sharp-edged pieces of wood.

Figure 11 Nambikwara man weaving a bracelet

Weapons – The Nambikwara bow is about 5 to 7 feet (2 m) long, the section being flat, semicircular or concave according to the group. The grip is wrapped with cotton. The arrow is released between the thumb and the first finger, the three other fingers being placed on the string (secondary release). Four types of arrows are used: (1) featherless fishing arrows with three to five prongs; (2) bird arrows with a blunt point; (3) big-game arrows with a lanceolate bamboo point; and (4) poisoned arrows, used chiefly for hunting monkeys, with several barbs which are attached to the point with cotton wrapping and which break easily in the wound, being, therefore, usually protected by a bamboo sheath. The last three have a bamboo shaft and "Arara" feathering. Sewed feathering is known by the central and northern groups but seldom used. For warfare, big-game arrows with serrated bamboo points are used.

Nambikwara arrow poison is a curare prepared by grating the root of a *Strychnos* shrub and by infusing (Eastern Nambikwara) or boiling (Central and Northern Nambikwara) it until the water evaporates and leaves a thick brownish substance, which is smeared on a wax-coated arrow point. It can be preserved in tiny pots for several months. Among South American arrow poisons, it is remarkable because it is made of only one vegetable substance and is prepared openly – in some groups by the chief or shaman, in other groups by anyone – without magical practices or taboos. Its great toxic properties were studied by Vellard (1939).

Other poisons of unknown composition are used for amorous or political revenge. They are in the form of powders and are kept in tubes made of feather quills, bamboo or other woods, each ornamented with paintings and cotton or bark wrappings.

Clubs are carved in the shape of a flattened or cylindrical pointed spade; the handle is often adorned with black and white plaiting of philodendron bark and bamboo strips. Their purpose is mostly ceremonial.

Social and political organization

Kinship terms identify parallel cousins with siblings and cross-cousins with potential or actual spouses. Cross-uncles and cross-aunts are called by the same terms as parents-in-law and grandparents; parallel uncles and parallel aunts are equated with parents. Similarly, parallel nephews and parallel nieces are classed with children and cross-nephews and cross-nieces with children-in-law. Marriage is between cross-cousins or between the maternal uncle and his niece. Monogamy is the rule, but polygyny is the privilege of the chief and other important men. Polygyny is usually with several sisters (sororal) or with a woman and her daughters by a former union. The first wife runs the household, subsequent wives being assistants to the husband. The deficiency of available women which results from polygyny is compensated by homosexuality between adolescent male cross-cousins (Lévi-Strauss, 1943a).

The village is ruled by a chief, but each of the nomadic bands into which it splits during the dry season is led by a secondary chief. Chieftainship is not hereditary; the chief, when old or sick, designates his successor from the ablest men of the group. The chief's authority is slight; it depends wholly on the good will of the family heads.

Relations between neighboring bands are inspired both by fear and by the desire to exchange goods. Warfare, therefore, is closely connected with barter. Groups not acquainted with one another use ritual speech when they meet.

Before starting a war expedition, a divinatory rite is performed with special songs and dances. An arrow is hidden by the shaman, the outcome of the expedition being presaged by its appearance the following day.

Life cycle

Childbirth – After the delivery of a child, the placenta is buried in the bush and both parents are subjected to rigid prohibitions concerning food, the use of ornaments, and social contacts.

Puberty – The initiation rite for young men consists of piercing their lips and nose and giving them their adult personal name. At her first menstruation, a girl is isolated for several months in a special shelter outside the village, where she is given ritual food by her mother. At the end of the rite, she takes a long bath in the river; this also constitutes the first step of the marriage ceremony.

Both cross-cousin and avuncular marriages (see pp. 175–6) are often planned by parents for their infant children. Marriage is celebrated by festivals, banquets and dances. The union is pronounced by the chief. Fish and fishing are important both before and during the ceremony.

Separation is frequent, the chief cause being that the man seeks a younger and prettier woman. There is no social sanction for adultery, except that the seducer is advised by his companion to go away for a while so as to avoid the husband's revenge. A murderer also flees vengeance.

Death – Some groups of Nambikwara bury their dead in a circular pit, the corpse being placed in a crouching position. Others leave the corpse to decompose in an elongated ditch and later wash the bones in the river, put them in a basket, and bury them in the village, which is then abandoned. Weapons, implements, adornments and other property of the deceased are destroyed, but his garden – if he owned one – is abandoned only for a few months. Later anybody may cultivate it.

Aesthetic and recreational activities

Art – Most Nambikwara groups are completely ignorant of drawing, although some groups decorate calabashes with dots and straight and sinuous lines. These are conventionalized reproductions of realistic designs found among other groups.

Music and dance – Music is clearly tonal, with melodic structures easy to identify. The end of a melody is usually marked with several shrill sounds, which are repeated after each coda. Music is both instrumental and choral and usually accompanies dances.

Dances are performed under the leadership of the chief. Men and women stamp rhythmically on the ground while turning in a circle. Usually, dancers close one nostril with the left hand to make their singing nasal. Only men perform war dances, forming one or more rows and stepping forward and backward in front of the leader. In the second phase of the dance, they attack a post, a symbolical enemy, with bows and arrows and clubs. Most of the dances and songs are connected with hunting or seasonal ceremonies, but they may be used at any time for mere entertainment.

Musical instruments – Flageolets have four holes and an air duct; three are usually played together, accompanied by a rhythm trumpet made of a piece of bamboo with a hollow calabash fixed to its bottom. Nose flutes are made of two pieces of calabash glued together with wax and pierced with three holes. One hole is blown with one nostril while the other nostril is closed with the thumb; the other two holes vary the notes. Nose flutes are also played in unison. Double and treble whistles have the air duct cut in the middle of the pipe, so that they can be blown at either end. Panpipes are of two kinds: the common type has five pipes; the other type consists of two or three reeds cut obliquely at the mouth end. In the latter type, all pipes produce approximately the same note.

Drinks and narcotics – Drinks are made with crushed manioc or maize mixed with water, or of palm fruits, especially *Mauritia* sp., *Acrocomia* sp., and *Oenocarpus distichus*. A slightly alcoholic beverage is prepared of wild pineapples mixed with water.

The Nambikwara are ardent smokers. They cultivate a tobacco with tiny leaves, which they dry between two pieces of wood, crush with their hands and store in small calabashes. Cigarettes are rolled in special leaves and tied with grass.

Magic and religion

The Nambikwara believe in the existence of a diffuse power or substance which may occur in objects and in living beings. It is manifest mostly in poisons, some of which are real (see Weapons, pp. 207–8), some purely magical. To the latter belongs the resin of the barrigudo tree (a Bombacaceae), which is kept in tubes like the true poisons. When thrown by a special technique at an enemy, it is believed to make him swell like the trunk of the tree and die.

There are also dangerous spirits of the bush and of water, which may appear in the shape of an animal, especially the jaguar, or in a particular form of their own. Death is identified with these spirits. Men's souls are believed to be reincarnated as jaguars, whereas women's and children's souls are taken away by wind and thunder, never to return.

The highest being is the Thunder, with which any man, though usually a shaman, may have personal contact through revelations and visions. Women, however, except when very old, and children are deprived of these privileges. Women are also forbidden, under pain of death, to see the sacred flageolets (see Musical instruments, p. 210) played at the ceremonies marking the beginning and the end of the dry season.

Shamanism and medicine

The shaman is sometimes distinct from – but more frequently identified with – the political chief. He is distinguished by having the privilege of polygyny, playing the leading role in ceremonial life, and possessing special supernatural powers. He treats patients by sucking out the disease or by fighting it with small ritual arrows called "thunder arrows." In addition to magical cures, the Nambikwara treat sickness with numerous medicinal plants, which are used externally or internally according to the disease. For eye infection, which is very frequent, they apply the infusion of a special bark with the help of a container made of leaves.

Folklore, lore and learning

The only legend recorded by Lévi-Strauss (n.d.) is a flood tale relating the destruction of human life and its re-creation through several incestuous marriages between the offspring of an old woman, who was the only being who escaped the disaster.

The only basic numbers used for counting are one and two, but the natives can reckon higher figures by combining these.

Colors are classified differently according to the dialects. The Eastern, Central, Southern, and Western Nambikwara agree in putting yellow and green in the same category, whereas the northern group identify red and yellow and class green, blue and black together.

Some Nambikwara groups call stars by the same name that designates the spirits. The year is divided into two seasons and an indeterminate number of lunar months. The day includes six main stages, each based on the position of the sun. Space is divided into two sections that are perpendicular to each other, one corresponding to the apparent movement of the sun and the other to the direction of the main waterways.

BIBLIOGRAPHY

Commission Rondon, *Publicações*, Rio de Janeiro, 1911.

Claude Lévi-Strauss, "The Social Use of Kinship Terms among Brazilian Indians," *American Anthropologist*, 45/3 (1943a).

—— "War and Trade among the Indians of South America," *Renaissance*, I/1–2 (1943b), pp. 122–39.

—— "Tribes of the Machado–Guaporé Hinterland," undated manuscript.

Cândido Mariano da Silva Rondon, *Lectures Delivered by Colonel Cândido Mariano da Silva Rondon*, Rio de Janeiro, 1916.

Theodore Roosevelt, *Works*, vol. 6, London, 1924.

Edgar Roquette-Pinto, *Rondonia*, Rio de Janeiro, 1912a (repr. Archivos do Museu Nacional, vol. 12, 1917; São Paulo, 1935; Biblioteca Pedagógica Brasileira, 39 [1938]).

—— "Os Indios Nambikuara do Brasil Central," paper delivered at the International Congress of Americanists, London, 1912b.

—— *Die Indianer Nhambiquara aus Zentral-Brazilien, Brasilianische Rundschau*, Rio de Janeiro, 1912c.

—— "Os Indios da Serra do Norte," paper delivered at the Pan-American Congress of Washington, 1917.

Max Schmidt, "Ergebnisse meiner zweijährigen Forschungsreise in Matto Grosso, September 1926 to August 1928," *Zeitschrift für Ethnologie*, 60 (1929), pp. 85–124.

Rodolfo R. Schuller, "Die Bedeutung der Bezeichnung Njambiquara für südamerikanische Indianer," *Petermanns Geographische Mitteilungen*, 58/2 (1912), p. 207.

—— "The Linguistic and Ethnographical Position of the Nambicuara Indians," *American Anthropologist*, 23 (1921), pp. 471–7.

Antonio Pyreneus de Souza, "Notas sobre os costumes dos indios Nhambiquaras," *Revista do Museu Paulista*, 12/II (1920), pp. 389–410.

Jehan Vellard, "A preparação do curare pelos Nambikwaras," *Revista do Arquivo Municipal*, 59 (1939), pp. 5–16.

XVII

Tribes of the Right Bank of the Guaporé River

INTRODUCTION

The native culture of the region irrigated by the northern tributaries of the Guaporé River is one of the least known in Brazil. Since the eighteenth century, explorers, travelers and missionaries have used the Guaporé River as a thoroughfare, and in more recent times hundreds of rubber tappers have worked along its banks and along the lower course of its tributaries. It is likely, therefore, that a thorough study of the tribes of the Guaporé River will show them to have suffered severely from the effects of that continuous traffic, perhaps almost to the point of extinction.

Unlike most South American rivers, the Guaporé River is not the axis of a homogeneous culture area; it is a frontier rather than a link. The Mojo–Chiquito culture area extends from the left bank toward the Andes; the heterogeneous tribes on the right bank have a definitely Amazonian culture (see map, p. 227). Geographic factors may partly account for this lack of symmetry. The flat landscape of the Llanos merges into the marshy lands of the left bank; whereas the right bank, alternately marshy and steep, marks the farthest extension of the highlands of western Brazil. The highlands and the right bank of the Guaporé River define the limits of the culture area to which probably belong the tribes of the southern part of the upper Madeira River basin, such as the Kepikiriwat, discovered in 1914 by the Rondon expedition (*Missão Rondon*, 1916).

TRIBAL DIVISIONS

Two areas must be distinguished. One is the right bank of the lower Guaporé River between the Rio Branco and the Mamore River, which is occupied by the Chapacuran tribes. The basins of the Rio Branco and of the Mequenes and Corumbiara rivers comprise the second area, where some of the languages seem to be Tupian. The Arua (not to be confused with the Arua at the mouth of the Amazon) and Macurap live along the Rio Branco (lat. 13° S, long. 62° W); the Wayoro on the Colorado River (lat. 12° 30′ S, long. 62° W); the Amniapä, Guaratägaja (Snethlage, 1937a), and Cabishinana (Lévi-Strauss, n.d.) on the Mequenes River (lat. 13° S, long. 62° W); and the Tuparí (lat. 12° S, long. 62° W) and Kepikiriwat (lat. 11° S, long. 63° W) on the headwaters of the southern tributaries of the Machado (Ji-Paraná) River. Linguistically distinct from both Chapacuran and Tupian are

1 the Yabuti (Japuti) and Aricapu, on the headwaters of the Rio Branco (lat. 12° 30′ S, long. 62° W), whose language shows affinities with the Gê dialects (Snethlage, 1937) but who are strongly influenced culturally by their neighbors;
2 the Huari (Massaca) on the Corumbiara River (lat. 14° S, long. 61° W) (Nordenskiöld, 1924a), who are linguistically linked to the Puruborá (Burubora) of the headwaters of the São Miguel River on the boundary between the two areas, but who, culturally, display strong similarities to their northern and northwestern neighbors the Kepikiriwat (Levi-Strauss, n.d.), Amniapä, Guaratägaja and Tuparí (Snethlage, 1937); and
3 the Palmella, on the right bank of the Guaporé River between the mouths of the Rio Branco and the Mequenes River (lat. 13° S, long. 63° W), who, until the late nineteenth century, were the southernmost representatives of the Cariban linguistic family in South America (Severiano da Fonseca, 1895). The unknown Indians who live on the right bank of the upper Guaporé River in the region of Villa Bella probably belong to the southern Nambikwara (Cabishí).

CULTURE

Subsistence and food preparation

The tribes of the upper Guaporé River, especially those upstream, rely for food mainly upon maize and peanuts. Manioc is of secondary importance to the natives living between the Guaporé and Machado rivers. Hualusa, peppers, papaws, gourds, *urucu*, cotton and tobacco are widely cultivated. Black beans are grown by the Guaratägaja and Wayoro. Gardens are tilled with digging sticks and weeded with chonta knives. An exceptional feature of the area is the raising of grubs in the dregs of maize beer, which is kept in long bamboo containers (Snethlage, 1937). On the Guaporé River, as on the Pimenta Bueno River, grubs are allowed to breed freely in the trunks of wild palm trees, which are left standing for that purpose when forests are cleared for gardens (Levi-Strauss, n.d.). Clearing and tilling gardens are cooperative enterprises; helpers are entertained with beer, snuff and dances. Crops are sometimes stored on large covered platforms. Certain tribes keep peanuts in large bamboo tubes.

Fish are shot with multipointed arrows or are drugged. The natives blow whistles to attract birds and then shoot them from small watchposts. Throughout the area, they either trap game in pitfalls or shoot them with plain arrows. The Amniapä, Kepikiriwat and Pawumwa also use poisoned arrows, and the Pawumwa, blowguns.

Flat cakes of maize and manioc are grilled on clay plates. Instead of grating manioc tubers, the Guaratägaja mash them with a small stone pounder. Wayoro mortars are pieces of bark. The Amniapä consider boiled mushrooms a special delicacy, a culinary dish noticed elsewhere only among the Nambikwara. Game is roasted in the skin on pyramidal babracots.

Domesticated animals

The Guaporé River tribes keep dogs, hens and ducks.

Houses

The beehive hut, built around a high central post, seems to be common to the area. Each house is divided by mats into several family compartments. Tupari houses shelter up to thirty-five families; those of the Wayoro may contain more than a hundred occupants. Houses along the Pimenta Bueno River are smaller. In some villages, Snethlage (1937) saw a painted woven screen set up in the middle of the hut as a kind of altar. These tribes sleep in hammocks, those of the Wayoro and Makurap being unusually large. Amniapä and Kepikiriwat men use small, concave wooden benches.

Dress and adornment

Among the Huari, Kepikiriwat and probably all the southeastern tribes, both men and women cut their hair high above the forehead and depilate the temples and eyebrows (figure 12). They wear wooden or resin labrets in the upper and lower lips and pins of various types in the nasal septum. Women go completely naked except for these and other ornaments – shell beads, cotton necklaces, belts, bracelets, and tight cotton armlets and anklets. Kepikiriwat, Huari and Guaratágaja men use a small conical penis sheath of leaves. Men of other tribes, except the Tuparí, wear a short skirt of buriti fiber (figure 13). Ear ornaments of tucuma-nut rings strung together like a chain are used by the Huari and Kepikiriwat. Skin caps (Wayoro), feathered circlets (Huari) and strips of fiber (Amniapä) are worn on festive occasions. Shell disk necklaces (figure 14) are used by all tribes except the Tuparí.

Figure 12 Indians of the Pimenta Bueno River

Figure 13 Indians of the Pimenta Bueno River

Body painting with genipa juice is especially well developed among the Amniapä, who, by means of maize cobs, apply elaborate patterns, such as crosses, dots, circles and hatchings.

Transportation

Carrying nets of tucum fiber are used instead of baskets. All the tribes, except, perhaps, the Huari, have canoes.

Manufactures

Spinning and weaving – Both rolled ("Bororo") and drop ("Andean") spindles are known. Fringed bands are woven on looms similar

Figure 14 Indians of the Pimenta Bueno River

to those of the Itene (Moré). Hammocks, which seem to reach a record length among some of the upper Guaporé River tribes, are made by extending a single warp between two perpendicular posts and twisting it with a double weft. Arm bands are knitted around a circular piece of wood with a bone or wooden needle (Macurap and Aricapu).

Pottery – Pottery is generally crude, and the clay used for its manufacture is not tempered. Calabash containers are especially common.

Figure 15 Huari ax (copied from Nordenskiöld, 1924b, fig. 26)

Weapons – To make an ax, the Wayoro insert a stone blade into a wooden handle, lash the head, and smear it with wax; the Huari use a vine or split branch bent double over the butt and tightened with bast and wax (figure 15).

Arrow feathering is of the "Xingu" (flush) sewn type (Tuparí, Arua) or of the "Arara" (arched) type (Huari, Kepikiriwat). Arrow points are made of plain or indented bamboo splinters, bone points, or the spikes of sting rays. The Tuparí paint arrow feathers. A tribe of the Pimenta Bueno region, known only through some implements found in the possession of the Kepikiriwat, paint red, black and white earth between the feathering of the arrow shaft. The Amniapä use three-pointed arrows for birds; the Kepikiriwat use similar arrows with less feathering for fishing. Arrows poisoned with curare and the point protected with a bamboo sheath are attributed to the Kepikiriwat, Amniapä and Pawumwa.

The Pawumwa use blowguns.

Clubs are used only as dance paraphernalia, except among the Huari, who fight with large, double-edged clubs, 4 to 5 feet (1.2 to 1.5 m) long, decorated with a basketry casing around the handle.

Social organizations

Sibs which are named after animals but which have no corresponding food prohibitions are found among the Macurap and Yabuti (patrilineal and exogamous) and the Arua (matrilineal). It is doubtful whether such clans exist among the Kepikiriwat, who have moieties that function at ceremonial ball games and probably on other occasions. Prisoners taken from another tribe are incorporated into the captor's clan, where they pay a small tribute but enjoy great freedom. Nothing is known about chieftainships, except that Guaratägaja chiefs distribute game among the men of the community. Intertribal commerce seems to be well developed.

A ceremony used by the Amniapä to receive a neighboring tribe includes a mock battle, the offer of benches, and a crouched salutation accompanied by ceremonial wailing.

Life cycle

The couvade, accompanied by abstention from fish, is attributed to the Macurap. They also require that a girl's parents consent to her marriage. Postmarital residence during the first weeks is matrilocal; later it is patrilocal. A widow remarries only with the permission of the clan's head.

The Tuparí bury their dead outside the village in a prone position; the Amniapä bury their dead inside their huts in a crouched position. Burial among the Macurap is similar to that among the Amniapä, but a pottery vessel is placed on top of the grave. The Wayoro practice urn burial, at least for children, and paint their corpses red. The Guaratägaja burn the house of the deceased; the Cabishiana burn the possessions of the deceased.

Cannibalism

According to Snethlage (1937), the Amniapä and Guaratägaja admit cannibalism and eat not only the barbecued bodies of their enemies but even their own tribesmen and women who are put to death for a crime.

Aesthetic and recreational activities

Art – Among many tribes, especially among the Kepikiriwat, each family possesses many calabashes which are used as beer cups during feasts. Women decorate the calabashes with incised or pyrograved geometric designs.

Games – Games in which a ball is propelled with the head are played between moieties (Kepikiriwat) and between villages or tribes (Amniapä). The Amniapä keep score with maize grains; the Kepikiriwat play to win arrows.

Dances and masks – Dancing and singing are generally practiced by both men and women, sometimes, as for instance among the Arua, in the form of patterned amorous challenges. The Macurap and the Amniapä dance in front of an altar or round an especially erected ceremonial tree. The Amniapä use calabash masks with features attached or painted on. Masks are kept in the dome of the hut, but they do not seem to be the object of worship or prohibition. Masked dancers costume themselves with a drapery of fibers and hold a stick topped with the wax image of a bird.

Musical instruments – Sacred gourd rattles are used only by Arua, Yabuti and Aricapu shamans and are unknown among the Tuparí and Guaratägaja, who use jingling belts garnished with fruit shells. The Yabuti, Amniapä and Guaratägaja use rhythm trumpets with a gourd or bamboo resonator (figure 16, left). The Amniapä and Guaratägaja call the trumpets, and also their masks, "gods." Clarinets are played in pairs by a single musician (Macurap, Arua). True panpipes are made of four closed and four open tubes placed in two rows (Arua) (figure 16, bottom right). A unique type of pseudo-panpipe consisting of a series of two to eight whistles (the latter in two rows), each with a sound orifice and a wax deflector, is used ceremonially among the other tribes (figure 17); two notes may be played at the same time on these instruments. End flutes (figure 18) of the Mataco type with four stops and whistles are used by the Tuparí, Guaratägaja and Amniapä. Snethlage (1939) mentions instrument playing of "disciplined orchestras."

Narcotics and beverages – A narcotic snuff of crushed angico, tobacco leaves and the ashes of a certain bark is blown by the shaman during feasts. For healing purposes he blows it into the nose of the patient, through one or two tubes that terminate in a hollow nut, often shaped like a bird's head. Snuff is carefully prepared with small mortars, pestles and mixing brushes and is kept in bamboo tubes.

Beer is made from manioc, maize and sweet potatoes. The Guaratägaja use a special leaf to cause fermentation.

Religion, folklore and mythology

Indians of the Guaporé River region seem to believe in the existence of an invisible fluid which may be good or evil. By appropriate gesticulations, the shaman captures, manipulates and incorporates it into food, into the sick, or into the bodies of enemies. On the Rio Branco, the

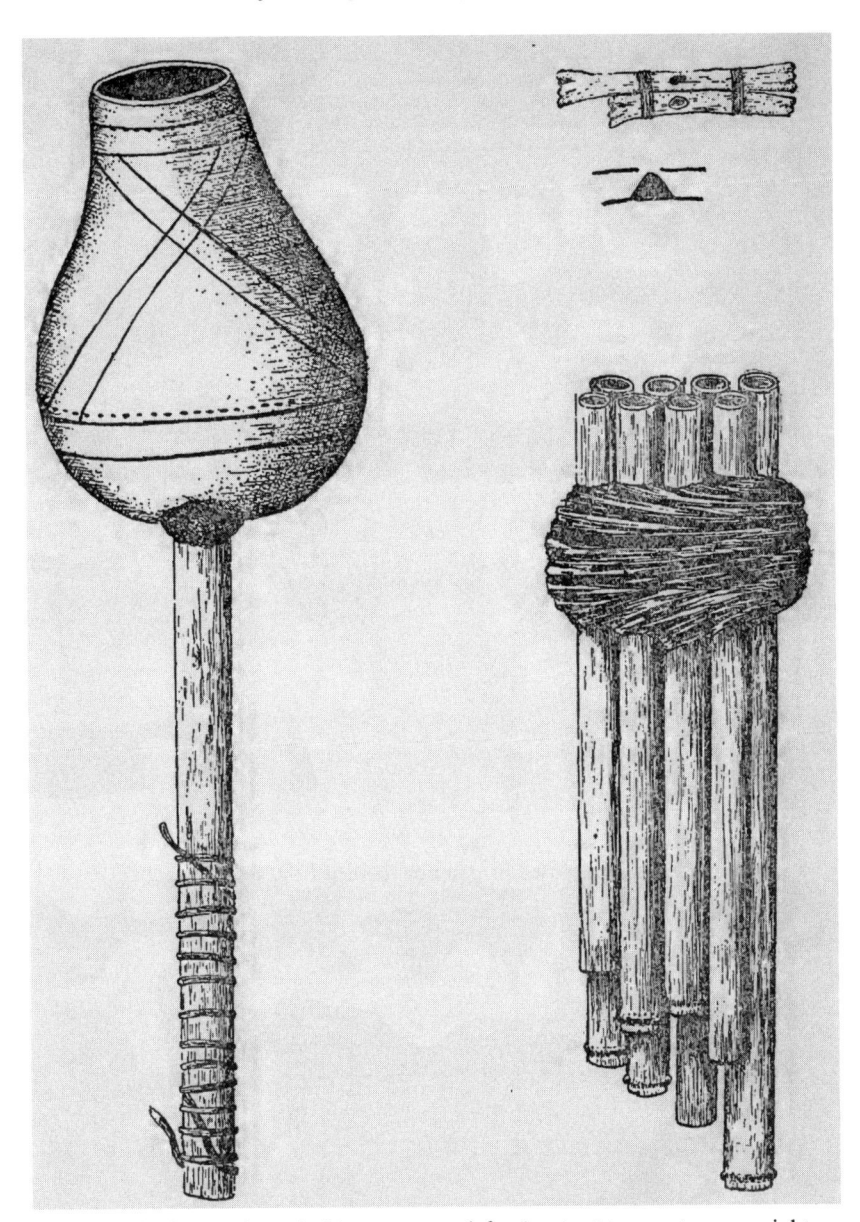

Figure 16 Guaporé musical instruments: left, *Amniapä* trumpet; upper right, *Guaratägaja* bird whistle; bottom right, *Arua* double pan flute (copied from Snethlage, 1939)

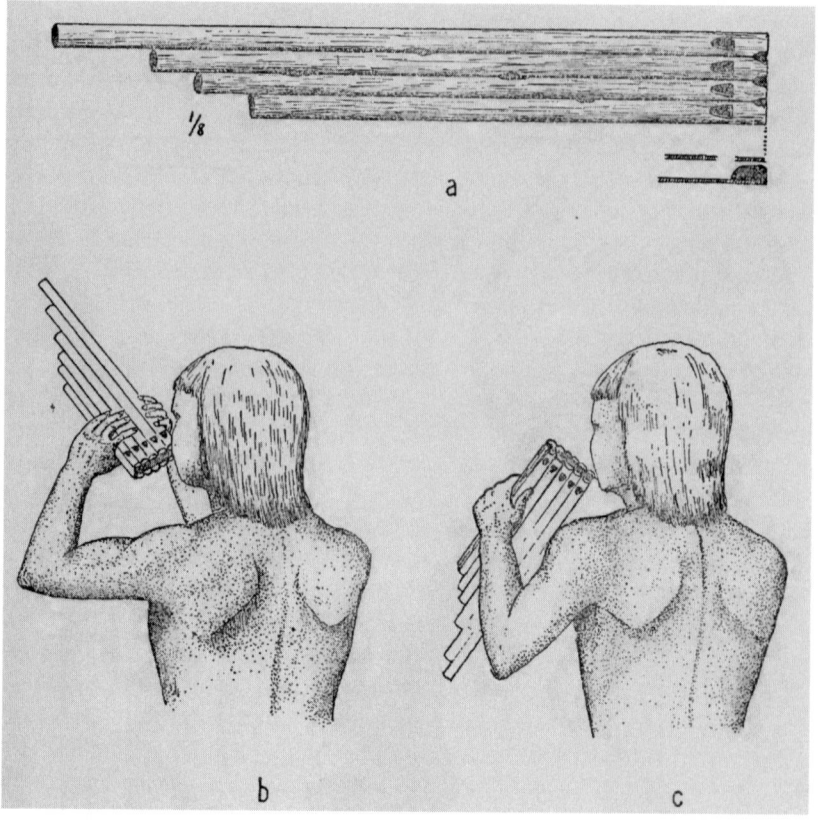

Figure 17 Macurap pseudo-panpipe (copied from Snethlage, 1939)

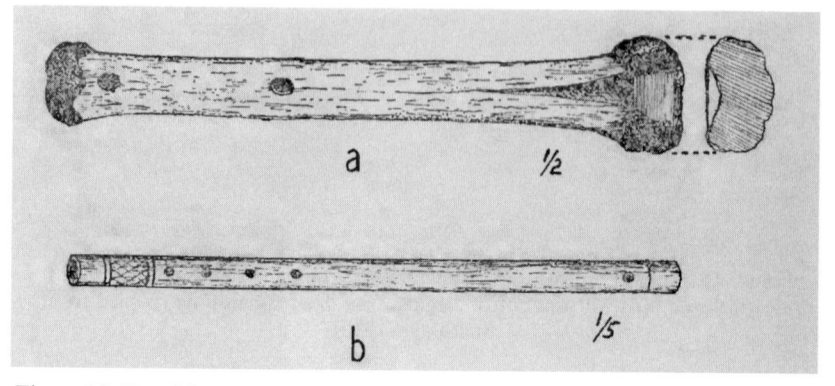

Figure 18 Huari flutes made of bone (copied from Nordenskiöld, 1924b, fig. 43)

shaman's outfit includes a snuffing tube, a magic board with a handle and a feathered stick. The board is used as a tablet upon which to mix the snuff; the feathered stick seems to acquire a mystic weight when filled with the magic fluid, which makes it difficult to carry toward the altar. The shaman kneels in front of a plaited screen which forms the altar and is the center of most ceremonies; he speaks to the screen and leaves food and beer nearby. The Wayoro ceremonies are forbidden to women and children.

Shamanistic cures follow the widespread pattern of sucking, blowing and spitting on the patient.

Ghosts play a considerable role in the beliefs of the Guaporé River Indians. According to the Arua, ghosts are the souls of the dead returning from the Kingdom of Minoiri to harm their enemies and to protect their friends, chiefly shamans. Snethlage (1937, p. 141) stated that he distinctly heard the noise which the ghosts are supposed to produce.

The Amniapä and Guaratägaja attribute the creation of the world to Arikuagnon, who married Pananmäkoza and was the father of the culture hero Arikapua. Another culture hero was Konanopo, the teacher of agriculture. The mythical being Bärabassa is held responsible for the great flood from which only one couple survived to repopulate the world. Other mythical beings are Ssuawakwak, Lord of the Winds that cause thunder, and Kipapua, Master of the Spirits who play supernatural musical instruments. Sun and Moon were the first men; together they tilled a garden; Sun burnt his brother and as a punishment was sent to the sky by his father, Sahi. Two mythical brothers were regarded by the Arua as creators of the world and bringers of darkness and of fire. Disguised as birds, they stole fire from the old man who was its keeper. When the brothers were old, a flood threatened to destroy mankind, but their sister saved two pairs of children from the best families by putting the children afloat in wooden troughs.

In three tales from the Arua, recorded by Snethlage (1937), a mother-in-law falls in love with her daughter's husband, a married couple live alternately as toads and as human beings, and a deer brings agriculture (also from the Bacaïri of the upper Xingu River).

BIBLIOGRAPHY

Roger Courteville, *Le Matto-Grosso*, Paris, 1938.
P. H. Fawcett, "Bolivian Exploration, 1913–1914," *Geographical Journal*, 45 (1915), pp. 219–28.

Gonçalves da Fonseca, "Navegação feita da cidade do Gram-Pará até a boca do Rio de Madeira ...," *Collecção de noticias para a historia e geografia das nações ultramarinas, que vivem nos dominios portuguezes, ou lhe são vizinhas*, Lisbon, vol. 4, n° 1, 1826.

J. D. Haseman, "Some Notes on the Pawumwa Indians of South America," *American Anthropologist*, new series, 14 (1912), pp. 333–49.

Claude Lévi-Strauss, "Tribes of the Machado-Guaporé Hinterland," manuscript, undated.

Missão Rondon: apontamentos sobre os trabalhos realizados pela Comissão de Linhas Telegráficas, Rio de Janeiro, 1916.

Erland Nordenskiöld, *Forschungen und Abenteuer in Südamerika*, Stuttgart, 1924a.

—— *The Ethnography of South-America seen from Mojos in Bolivia*, Göteborg, 1924b.

Cândido Mariano da Silva Rondon, *Lectures Delivered by Colonel Cândido Mariano da Silva Rondon*, Rio de Janeiro, 1916.

João Severiano da Fonseca, *Viagem ao redor do Brasil, 1875–1878*, 2 vols, Rio de Janeiro, 1880–1.

Emil Heinrich Snethlage, *Atiko y: Meine Erlebnisse bei den Indianern des Guaporé*, Berlin, 1937.

—— *Musikinstrumente der Indianer des Guaporé-Gebietes*, Berlin, 1939.

Map.

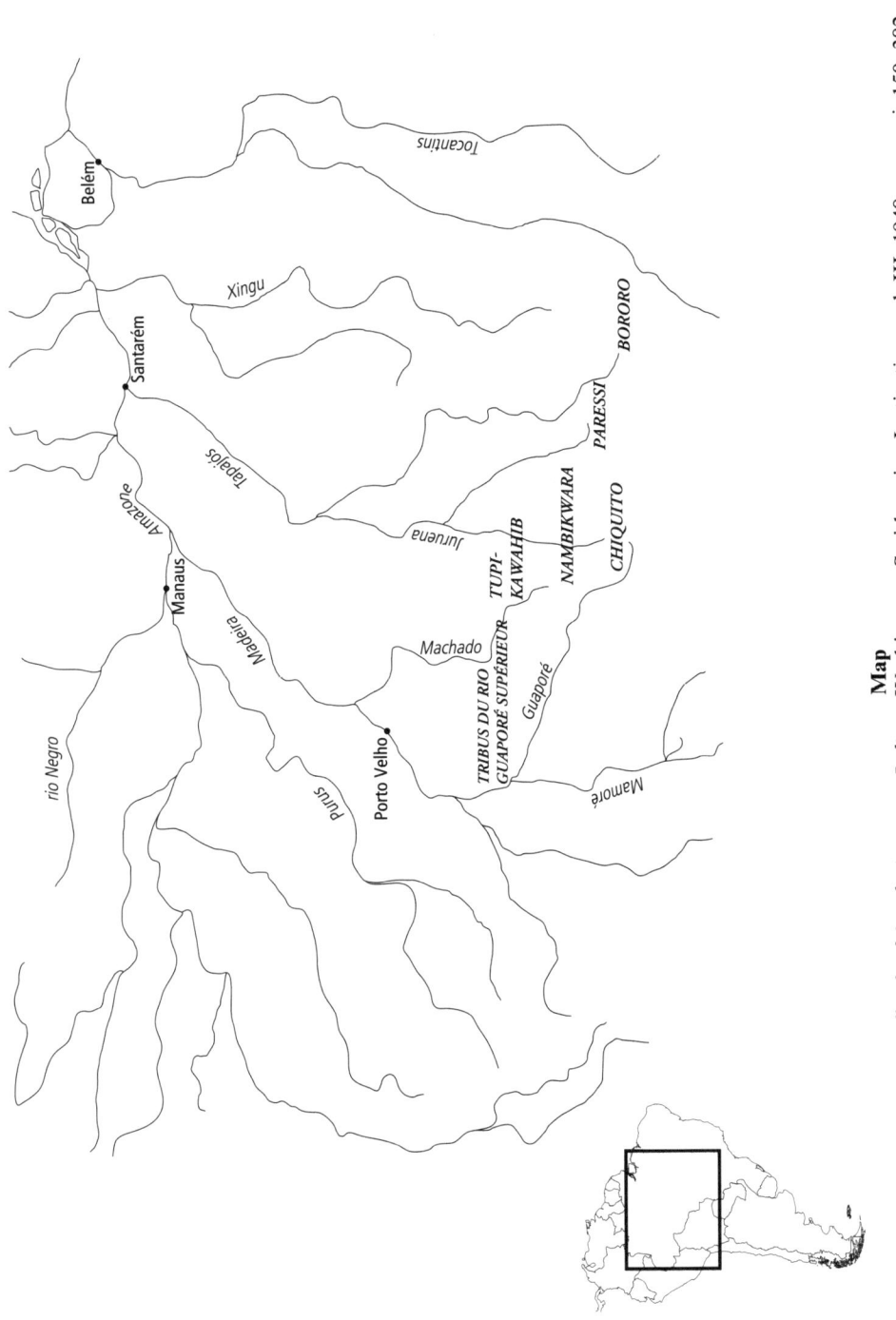

From Julian Steward (ed.), *Handbook of South American Indians*, Washington, Smithsonian Institution, vol. III, 1948, pp. xxvi, 150, 382.

Sources

Chapter I

"French Sociology," in Georges Gurvitch and Wilbert E. Moore (eds), *Twentieth Century Sociology*, New York, Philosophical Library, 1945, pp. 503–37.

Chapter II

"Souvenir of Malinowski," *VVV*, I/1 (1942), p. 45.

Chapter III

"L'œuvre d'Edward Westermarck," *Revue de l'histoire des religions*, 129 (1945), pp. 84–100.

Chapter IV

"The Name of the Nambikuara," *American Anthropologist*, 48/1 (1946), pp. 139–40.

Chapter V

Comptes rendus, *L'Année sociologique*, 3rd series, I (1940–8), pp. 329–36, 353–4.
Two of these reviews originally appeared in English, in slightly different versions: "The Cheyenne Way," *Journal of Legal and*

Political Sociology, 1 (1942), pp. 155–7; and "Sun Chief," *Social Research*, 10/4 (1943), pp. 515–17.

Chapter VI

"La technique du bonheur," *Esprit*, no. 127 (1946), pp. 643–52; first appeared in *L'Âge d'or*, no. 1 (1945), pp. 75–83.

Chapter VII

"Guerre et commerce chez les Indiens de l'Amérique du Sud," *Renaissance*, I/1–2 (1943), pp. 122–39.
Also appeared in Portuguese, in *Revista do arquivo municipal de São Paulo*, 87 (1942), pp. 131–46.

Chapter VIII

"The Social and Psychological Aspects of Chieftainship in a Primitive Tribe: The Nambikuara of Northwestern Mato Grosso," *Transactions of the New York Academy of Sciences*, 7/1 (1944), pp. 16–32.
A French version was published under the title "La Théorie du pouvoir dans une société primitive," in Boris Mirkine-Guetzévitch (ed.), *Les Doctrines politiques modernes*, New York, Brentano's, 1947, pp. 41–63.

Chapter IX

"Reciprocity and Hierarchy," *American Anthropologist*, 46/2 (1944), pp. 266–8.

Chapter X

"La Politique étrangère d'une société primitive," *Politique étrangère*, 14/2 (1949), pp. 139–52.

Chapter XI

"Indian Cosmetics," *VVV*, I/1 (1942), pp. 33–5.

Chapter XII

"The Art of the Northwest Coast at the American Museum of Natural History," *Gazette des beaux-arts*, no. 24 (1943), pp. 175–82.

The original French version was published, without illustrations or notes, in Michel Izard (ed.), *Claude Lévi-Strauss*, Cahiers de l'Herne, no. 82 (2004), pp. 145–8.

Chapter XIII

"The Social Use of Kinship Terms among Brazilian Indians," *American Anthropologist*, 45/3 (1943), pp. 398–409.

Chapter XIV

"On Dual Organization in South America," *America Indígena*, 4/1 (1944), pp. 37–47.

Chapter XV

"The Tupi-Cawahib," in Julian Steward (ed.), *Handbook of South American Indians*, Washington, Smithsonian Institution, vol. III, 1948, pp. 299–305.

Chapter XVI

"The Nambicuara," in Julian Steward (ed.), *Handbook of South American Indians*, Washington, Smithsonian Institution, vol. III, 1948, pp. 361–9.

Chapter XVII

"The Tribes of the Right Bank of the Guaporé River," in Julian Steward (ed.), *Handbook of South American Indians*, Washington, Smithsonian Institution, vol. III, 1948, pp. 371–9.

Notes

Introduction

1 Didier Eribon, *Conversations with Claude Lévi-Strauss*, Chicago, University of Chicago Press, 1991, p. 68.
2 Claude Lévi-Strauss, *Structural Anthropology*, New York, Basic Books, 1963, p. 328.
3 Eribon, *Conversations with Claude Lévi-Strauss*, p. 91.
4 Claude Lévi-Strauss, *The Savage Mind*, London, Weidenfeld & Nicolson, 1966, p. 247.
5 See Gildas Salmon, "Symbole et signe dans l'anthropologie structurale," *Europe*, nos. 1005–6 (2013), pp. 110–21.
6 The title *Structural Anthropology Zero* emerged in 2011 in the course of a discussion with Laurent Jeanpierre and Frédéric Keck, as we envisaged the publication of a critical edition of these little-known articles. With this original project having fallen through, I am grateful to them for letting me use the title on which we had settled together.
7 *Introduction to the Work of Marcel Mauss*, London, Routledge, 1987.
8 Those who have offered commentary on this article, which represents a pivotal moment in twentieth-century French philosophy, include Maurice Merleau-Ponty, Claude Lefort, Gilles Deleuze, Jacques Derrida, Jacques Lacan, Roland Barthes, Pierre Bourdieu, Jean Bazin and Jacques Rancière.
9 See especially Pierre Clastres, *Society against the State: Essays in Political Anthropology*, New York, Zone Books, 1987.
10 Carlos Fausto and Marcela Coelho de Souza, "Reconquistando o campo perdido: o qui Lévi-Strauss deve aos ameríndios," *Revista de Antropologia*, São Paulo, XLVII/1 (2004), pp. 98–9. See Vincent Debaene, "Claude Lévi-Strauss aujourd'hui," *Europe*, nos. 1005–6 (2013), pp. 11–36.
11 The page number in parentheses refers to the present edition.
12 Eribon, *Conversations with Claude Lévi-Strauss*, p. 56. See also Roman Jakobson and Claude Lévi-Strauss, *Correspondance, 1942–1982*, Paris, Seuil, 2018, pp. 174–85.
13 This silence was by no means specific to Lévi-Strauss and indeed characterized all the contributions to the special edition of *Esprit* (though this was not the case for contemporary publications in *Temps Modernes* about the United States). Letters to his parents show that Lévi-Strauss had read Claude McKay, for

example, and happily spent time in Harlem, particularly at the Savoy Ballroom, but, as in his writings of the 1930s on São Paulo, which occasionally mention black and mixed-race populations, he seems to conceive of racial discrimination as a historical remnant rather than as a pressing social and political issue.

14 The references for the original publications are available at the end of this volume.
15 See the polemical review of *The Cambridge History of the Native Peoples of the Americas*, Vol. 3: *South America*, published in *L'Homme* (nos. 158–9, pp. 439–42). Lévi-Strauss was to make a total of five contributions to the *Handbook of South American Indians*: the three articles that are included here rely in large part on material collected first-hand; they do not draw on the long article summarizing the available information on the tribes of the upper Xingu or on the ethnobotanical study (which was published in the sixth volume in 1950) on the native uses of wild plants in tropical America.
16 Eribon, *Conversations with Claude Lévi-Strauss*, p. 44.
17 On this long article of 1945 and the originality of what Lévi-Strauss calls "the French point of view" (p. 50), see Vincent Debaene, *Far Afield: French Anthropology between Science & Literature*, Chicago, University of Chicago Press, 2014, pp. 51–66.
18 The argument that follows is directly inspired by the work of Laurent Jeanpierre on the intellectual sociology of exile, in particular "Les structures d'une pensée d'exilé: la formation du structuralisme de Claude Lévi-Strauss," *French Politics, Culture and Society*, 28/1 (2010), pp. 58–76.
19 See Laurent Jeanpierre, "La politique culturelle française aux Etats-Unis de 1940 à 1947," in Alain Dubosclard et al., *Entre rayonnement et réciprocité: contributions à l'histoire de la diplomatie culturelle*, Paris, Publications de la Sorbonne, 2002, pp. 85–116.
20 See Jeanpierre, "Les structures d'une pensée d'exilé," pp. 63–5.
21 An interesting chronicle of his progress can be found in the abundant correspondence he had with his parents, then in hiding in the remote Cévennes region of France. See Claude Lévi-Strauss, *"Chers tous deux": lettres à ses parents (1931–1942)*, Paris, Seuil, 2015.
22 See Laurent Jeanpierre, "Une opposition structurante pour l'anthropologie structurale: Lévi-Strauss contre Gurvitch, la guerre de deux exilés français aux Etats-Unis," *Revue d'histoire des sciences humaines*, no. 11 (2004), pp. 13–44.
23 See Gildas Salmon, "Symbole et signe dans l'anthropologie structurale," and *Les Structures de l'esprit: Lévi-Strauss et les mythes*, Paris, PUF, 2013.
24 Eribon, *Conversations with Claude Lévi-Strauss*, p. 14. See Lévi-Strauss, in *"Chers tous deux,"* letters of March 1933, pp. 272–6. See also Emmanuelle Loyer, *Lévi-Strauss: A Biography*, Cambridge, Polity, 2018, pp. 78–82.
25 "Model" is to be understood here not as a reality to be imitated but as a system revealing properties that cannot be readily observed otherwise. Models are generally formal, but the Nambikwara offered a rare empirical case of a social reality reduced to its essential properties.
26 See Emmanuelle Loyer, *Paris à New York: intellectuels et artistes français en exil 1940–1947*, Paris, Grasset, 2005.
27 On this point, see the very influential 1949 conference of the British sociologist T. H. Marshall, entitled "Citizenship and Social Class" (republished in *Citizenship and Social Class, and Other Essays*, Cambridge, CUP, 1950).
28 The report by the British economist William Beveridge in 1942 laid the

theoretical bases for the welfare state. The relevant passage can be found in *Tristes Tropiques*, without, however, the discussion of forms of reciprocity that preceded it.
29 See the note on *Tristes Tropiques* in Claude Lévi-Strauss, *Œuvres*, Paris, Gallimard, 2008, pp. 1676–8.
30 Eribon, *Conversations with Claude Lévi-Strauss*, p. 50.
31 Daniel Fabre, "D'Isaac Strauss à Claude Lévi-Strauss: le judaïsme comme culture," in Philippe Descola (ed.), *Claude Lévi-Strauss, un parcours dans le siècle*, Paris, Odile Jacob, 2012, p. 281.
32 Quoted in Loyer, *Lévi-Strauss*, p. 293.
33 See Wiktor Stoczkowski, *Anthropologies rédemptrices: le monde selon Lévi-Strauss*, Paris, Hermann, 2008, pp. 139–84.
34 Lévi-Strauss, *"Chers tous deux,"* p. 559.
35 Lévi-Strauss, *Tristes Tropiques*, New York, Atheneum, 1984, p. 24.
36 Ibid. Regarding this formulation, see above, pp. 27–9.
37 Eribon, *Conversations with Claude Lévi-Strauss*, p. 50.
38 Lévi-Strauss, *Tristes Tropiques*, p. 406.
39 Document written for the Peace Aims Group Council of Foreign Relations, cited in Loyer, *Lévi-Strauss*, p. 233.
40 *Conversations with Claude Lévi-Strauss*, p. 256.
41 Claude Lévi-Strauss, "Diogène couché," *Les Temps Modernes*, no. 110 (1955), p. 1194.
42 Eribon, *Conversations with Claude Lévi-Strauss*, p. 256.
43 See the note to *Tristes Tropiques* in *Oeuvres*, pp. 1711–12.
44 See Stoczkowski, *Anthropologies rédemptrices*, pp. 26–33.
45 Ibid., pp. 224–42.
46 Claude Lévi-Strauss, "The Three Humanisms," in *Structural Anthropology*, vol. 2, Chicago, University of Chicago Press, 1976, pp. 271–4.
47 Lévi-Strauss, "Reflections on Liberty," *The View from Afar*, Chicago, University of Chicago Press, 1985, p. 282.
48 Lévi-Strauss, *Tristes Tropiques*, p. 57.
49 Claude Lévi-Strauss, in an interview with Victor Malka in 1983 (*L'Arche*, no. 317 (1983), p. 57). On this question, see the essential study by Fabre, "D'Isaac Strauss à Claude Lévi-Strauss."
50 Lévi-Strauss, *Tristes Tropiques*, pp. 24–7.
51 Ibid., p. 30.
52 Ibid., p. 24.
53 Lévi-Strauss, *Tristes Tropiques*, p. 128. See Vincent Debaene, "Portrait de l'ethnologue en Lazare," in Michel Izard (ed.), *Claude Lévi-Strauss*, Cahiers de l'Herne, no. 82 (2004), pp. 102–4.
54 Lévi-Strauss, *Tristes Tropiques*, p. 129.
55 Ibid.
56 "In Pointe-Rouge (one of the camps on the island), to a young and most distinguished scholar, who was to pursue his research in New York … No, you are not French, you are a Jew, and the Jews who call themselves French are worse than the foreign Jews." André Breton, "Troubled Waters," *Martinique: Snake Charmer*, Austin, University of Texas Press, 2008, p. 68.
57 Lévi-Strauss, *Tristes Tropiques*, p. 29.
58 See Stoczkowski, *Anthropologies rédemptrices*, pp. 213–42.
59 Lévi-Strauss, *Tristes Tropiques*, pp. 149–50.

60 Ibid., p. 23.
61 Lévi-Strauss, "Diogène couché," p. 1217.
62 Maurice Blanchot, "Literature and the Right to Death" [1947], in *The Work of Fire*, Stanford, CA, Stanford University Press, 1995, pp. 300–44; Jean Cayrol, *Lazare parmi nous*, Paris, Seuil, 1950.
63 Lévi-Strauss, *Tristes Tropiques*, pp. 24 and 41, respectively. See Vincent Debaene, "Cadrage cannibale: les photographies de *Tristes tropiques*," *Gradhiva*, no. 27 (2018), pp. 90–117.
64 See "En marge de *Tristes tropiques*," in *Œuvres*, pp. 1628–50.
65 Jeanpierre, "Les structures d'une pensée d'exilé."
66 Lévi-Strauss drew a parallel between the extermination camps, the destruction of archaic societies, and that of plant and animal species in a little-known and uncommonly vitriolic text: the speech he made when he was awarded the Erasmus Prize in 1973 ("Discours de Claude Lévi-Strauss," *Praemium Erasmianum*, Amsterdam, Stichting Praemium Erasmianum, 1973, pp. 24–8). On these questions, see Salvatore D'Onofrio, *Lévi-Strauss face à la catastrophe*, Sesto San Giovanni, Mimésis, 2018.
67 "Discours de Claude Lévi-Strauss," pp. 27–8.
68 See Maurice Blanchot, "Man at Point Zero," in *Friendship*, Stanford, CA, Stanford University Press, 1997, pp. 73–82.

Chapter I French Sociology

1 The "double oppression" from which Mauss was suffering is no doubt an allusion to his forced retirement from the Collège de France and the requisition of his apartment, in 1942, which drove him to live in a small "cold, dark and dirty" ground floor apartment (in his own words, from a letter to Ignace Meyerson).
2 *American Anthropologist*, new series, 37 (1935), p. 394.
3 Fred Eggan (ed.), *Social Anthropology of North American Tribes*, Chicago, University of Chicago Press, 1937.
4 Emile Durkheim, *The Rules of Sociological Method*, 2nd edn, New York, Free Press, 1982.
5 Robert Redfield, *The Folk Culture of Yucatan*, Chicago, University of Chicago Press, 1941, Preface, p. x, and p. 343.
6 Robert H. Lowie, *The History of Ethnological Theory*, New York, Farrar & Rinehart, 1937.
7 Talcott Parsons, *The Structure of Social Action*, New York, McGraw-Hill, 1937.
8 John Sholtz, "Durkheim's Theory of Culture," *Reflex*, 1935; Harry Alpert, "Emile Durkheim and the Theory of Social Integration," *Journal of Social Philosophy*, 6 (1941), pp. 172–84.
9 Harry Alpert, *Emile Durkheim and his Sociology*, New York, Columbia University Press, 1939.
10 Alfred L. Kroeber, "History and Science in Anthropology," *American Anthropologist*, 37 (1935), p. 559, n. 14.
11 On this point, see René Hubert, *Les sciences sociales dans l'Encyclopédie* (1923) and René Maunier, *Introduction à la sociologie* (1929).
12 On this point, see Marcel Mauss, "Divisions et proportions des divisions de la sociologie," *Année sociologique* (1924–5), pp. 98–176.
13 Eng. trans. as *A Geographical Introduction to History*, New York, Alfred A.

Knopf, 1925. See also the article "History," by Henri Berr and Lucien Febvre, in *Encyclopedia of the Social Sciences*, 7, pp. 357–68.
14 Albert Demangeon, *La Plaine picarde*, Paris, 1905; and (in collaboration with Lucien Febvre) *Le Rhin*, Paris, 1935.
15 Marc Bloch, "Le Salaire et les fluctuations économiques à longue période," *Revue historique*, January–February 1934, and *Les Rois thaumaturges*, Strasbourg, 1924; *Les Caractères originaux de l'histoire rurale française*, Oslo, 1931; *La Société féodale*, Paris, 1939. The review edited by Bloch from 1929, *Annales d'histoire économique et sociale*, is sociological as well as historical.
16 English translations: *The Rise of the Celts*, New York, Alfred A. Knopf, 1934; and *The Greatness and Decline of the Celts*, London, Routledge, 1934.
17 Marcel Granet, *Fêtes et chansons anciennes de la Chine* (Paris, 1919); *La Polygynie sororale* (Paris, 1920); *La Religion des chinois* (Paris, 1922); *Danses et légendes de la Chine ancienne* (2 vols, Paris, 1926); *La Civilisation chinoise* (Paris, 1929); *La Pensée chinoise* (Paris, 1934). Most of them have been translated.
18 Marcel Granet, *Catégories matrimoniales et relations de proximité dans la Chine ancienne* (Paris, 1939).
19 See all the work of the "Centre International de Synthese," directed by Henri Berr with the cooperation of many sociologists, as well as *Les Sciences sociales en France*, by Raymond Aron, Albert Demangeon, Jean Meuvret and others (Paris: Centre d'études de politique étrangère, 1937). Also, the earlier article by Emile Durkheim and Paul Fauconnet: "Sociologie et sciences sociales," *Revue Philosophique*, May 1903.
20 See also Paul Fauconnet, "The Durkheim School in France," *Sociological Review*, 19 (1927), pp. 15–20.
21 Durkheim, *The Rules of Sociological Method*, Preface.
22 Emile Durkheim, "Jugements de valeur et jugements de réalité', *Revue de métaphysique et de morale* (1911); Célestin Bouglé, *Leçons de sociologie sur l'évolution des valeurs* (1922).
23 Gabriel Tarde, *Les Lois de l'imitation*; *Essais et mélanges sociologiques*; *La Logique sociale*, (1895); *Études de psychologie sociale*; *Les Lois sociales* (1898); *L'Opinion et la foule* (1901).
24 Maurice Halbwachs, *Les Cadres sociaux de la mémoire* (Paris, 1925); Charles Blondel, *La Conscience morbide* (Paris, 1914); 'Les Volitions", in *Nouveau traité de psychologie*, ed. Georges Dumas.
25 In French colonial possessions, specialized institutes carry on sociological as well as linguistic, archaeological and ethnological research. The most important are the Ecole Française d'Extrême Orient, the Institut de L'Afrique Noire, the Institut des Hautes Études Marocaines and the Institut des Hautes Études Sahariennes. In connection with socio-anthropological research in the French colonial possessions, the following works may be cited: Alfred Grandidier, *Histoire de Madagascar (1876–1917)*; Maurice Delafosse, *Haut-Sénégal Niger* (3 vols, 1912); *The Negroes of Africa*, trans. F. Fligelman (Washington: Associated Publishers, 1931); Henri Labouret, *Les Tribus du Rameau Lobi* (1931); *Les Manding* (1934); *Les Pêcheurs de Guet N'dar* (1935); Robert Montagne, *Les Berbères et le Makhzen* (1930); *Villages et kasbas berbères* (1930).
26 Arnold van Gennep, *Le Folklore* (1920); *Le Folklore de la Bourgogne* (1934); *Le Folklore du Dauphiné* (2 vols, 1932–3); *Le Folklore de la Flandre et du Hainaut* (2 vols, 1935–6); *Manuel de folklore français contemporain*, vols 3 and 4 (the first two to be published), 1937–8.

27 See Georges Gurvitch, "The Sociological Legacy of Lucien Lévy-Bruhl," *Journal of Social Philosophy*, 5 (1939), pp. 61–70.
28 See also Roger Lacombe, *La Méthode sociologique de Durkheim* (1926).
29 Célestin Bouglé, "La Méthodologie de François Simiand et la sociologie," *Annales sociologiques*, series A, no. 2 (1936).
30 Bloch, "Le Salaire et les fluctuations économiques à longue période."
31 Durkheim, *The Elementary Forms of Religious Life*, New York, Free Press, 1995, p. 418.
32 Ibid.
33 Ibid., p. 1.
34 Ibid., p. 85.
35 Ibid., p. 228.
36 Ibid., p. 421.
37 Ibid., p. 2.
38 *The Rules of Sociological Method*, p. 120.
39 Ibid., p. 130.
40 Ibid., p. 135.
41 *Année sociologique*, vol. 1. Eng. trans. as *Incest: The Nature and Origin of the Taboo*, New York, Lyle Stuart, 1963.
42 *The Rules of Sociological Method*, p. 121; and, further, the basic distinction (borrowed by Alfred Radcliffe-Brown) between cause and function, together with the first sociological definition of the idea of function: "We must determine whether there is a correspondence between the fact being considered and the general needs of the social organism" (ibid., p. 123). Thus, Durkheim hoped to eliminate the search for intention in the interpretation of social processes.
43 *The Elementary Forms of Religious Life*, p. 232.
44 Ibid., p. 233.
45 Ibid., pp. 233–4.
46 *The Rules of Sociological Method*, p. 109.
47 Ibid.
48 Ibid., p. 111.
49 Ibid., p. 112.
50 Ibid., p. 121.
51 Ibid.
52 Ibid., p. 122.
53 Ibid., p. 123.
54 Ibid.
55 Ibid.
56 Ibid.
57 Ibid., p. 117, n. 10.
58 Ibid., pp. 97–8.
59 Kroeber, "History and Science in Anthropology."
60 Ibid., p. 560.
61 A. P. Elkin, review of W. Lloyd Warner, *A Black Civilization*, in *Oceania*, I (1937–8), p. 119.
62 Robert Hertz, *Mélanges de sociologie religieuse et de folklore* (ed. Marcel Mauss), Paris, 1928.
63 Africanists such as Marcel Griaule, Bernard Maupoil, Michel Leiris, Denise Paulme, Roger Bastide; and Americanists such as Jacques and Georgette

Soustelle, Claude Lévi-Strauss, Henri Lehmann, Alfred Métraux and George Devereux – the latter two Americans but trained in Paris – and many others, have resolutely associated themselves, almost all of them, with the Musée de l'Homme and the Institut d'Ethnologie of Paris University, both directed by Professor Paul Rivet. For that reason, their work is mainly anthropological in character and cannot be considered here. But none of them would disclaim his indebtedness to the Année sociologique school, and especially to its master, Marcel Mauss.

64 Kroeber, "History and Science in Anthropology."
65 Ibid., p. 560.
66 Ibid.
67 Durkheim, *The Rules of Sociological Method*, p. 77.
68 Ibid., p. 75.
69 Ibid., pp. 75ff.
70 Marcel Mauss and Paul Fauconnet, article "Sociologie" in *La Grande Encyclopédie* (Paris, 1901).
71 Ibid.
72 Ibid.
73 *The Rules of Sociological Method*, p. 111.
74 For instance, Mauss discusses the validity of the opposition drawn by Durkheim in *The Division of Labor in Society* between "organic" and "mechanical" solidarity. (Mauss, "Fragment d'un plan de sociologie générale," *Annales sociologiques*, series A, no. 1, 1934).
75 To make matters clear, I shall quote Mauss further: "It can now be seen more clearly of what in our opinion the unity of the sacrificial system consists. It does not come, as Smith believed, from the fact that all the possible kinds of sacrifice have emerged from one primitive, simple form. Such a sacrifice does not exist. ... All the sacrificial rituals we know of display a great complexity." But, "if sacrifice is so complex, whence comes its unity? It is because, fundamentally, beneath the diverse forms it takes, it always consists in one same procedure, which may be used for the most widely differing purposes. This procedure consists in establishing a means of communication between the sacred and the profane worlds through the mediation of a victim, that is, of a thing that in the course of the ceremony is destroyed" (Henri Hubert and Marcel Mauss, *Sacrifice: Its Nature and Function*, Chicago, University of Chicago Press, 1964, pp. 95–7). This treatment may hardly be called "categorizing unscientific experience."
76 See his enlightening reviews of contemporary publications in the *Année sociologique*. Most of them could have been written today.
77 *The Rules of Sociological Method*, pp. 161–2.
78 Emile Durkheim, "Représentations individuelles et représentations collectives," *Revue de métaphysique et de morale*, (1898).
79 Mauss and Fauconnet, "Sociologie."
80 Mauss, "Rapports réels et pratiques de la psychologie et de la sociologie," *Journal de psychologie* (1924), p. 904.
81 Ibid., p. 903.
82 *The Elementary Forms of Religious Life*, pp. 422–3.
83 Ibid., p. 429.
84 *The Rules of Sociological Method*, Preface, p. 32.
85 *The Elementary Forms of Religious Life*, p. 445.

86 Mauss, "Rapports réels et pratiques de la psychologie et de la sociologie", pp. 910–11.
87 A different approach to Gurvitch's thought may be found in the excellent essay by Roger Bastide: "A sociologia de Georges Gurvitch," *Revista do Arquivo Municipal de São Paulo*, vol. 68 (1940).
88 *The Rules of Sociological Method*, pp. 151–5.
89 Henri Hubert and Marcel Mauss, *A General Theory of Magic*, London, Routledge, 2001, p. 131.
90 Bronisław Malinowski, "Culture," in *Encyclopedia of the Social Sciences*, Vol. 4, p. 236.
91 Lucien Lévy-Bruhl, *La Mythologie primitive*, Paris, 1935, p. 317.
92 Mauss, "Fragment d'un plan de sociologie générale descriptive."
93 Ibid., p. 56.
94 Ibid., p. 34.

Chapter III The Work of Edward Westermarck

1 Edward Westermarck, *The History of Human Marriage*, London, Macmillan, 1891.
2 Westermarck, *The Origin and Development of the Moral Ideas*, London, Macmillan, 1906, 1908.
3 Westermarck, *L'Origine et le développement des idées morales*, trans. Robert Godet, 2 vols, Paris, Payot, 1928.
4 Westermarck, "The Magic Origin of Moorish Designs," *Journal of the Royal Anthropological Institute of Great Britain*, XXXIV (1904).
5 Westermarck, "Midsummer Customs in Morocco," *Folklore: The Journal of the Folklore Society*, 16 (1905), pp. 27–47.
6 Westermarck, *Marriage Ceremonies in Morocco*, London, Macmillan, 1914.
7 Westermarck, *Ritual and Belief in Morocco*, London, Macmillan, 1926.
8 Pp. 109–30 of *Festkrift Tillägnad Edvard Westermarck*, Helsinki, 1912; republished in Rivers, *Psychology and Ethnology*, 1926.
9 Westermarck, "Methods in Social Anthropology," Huxley Memorial Lecture, *Journal of the Royal Anthropological Institute of Great Britain and Ireland*, 66 (1936), p. 223.
10 Ibid.
11 Ibid., p. 224.
12 Westermarck was recently keen to demonstrate that progress in zoological observation had confirmed his theory. See "On Primitive Marriage: A Rejoinder to Mr. V. F. Calverton," *American Journal of Sociology*, XLI/5 (1936), pp. 565–84.
13 Westermarck, "The Magic Origin of Moorish Designs."
14 Westermarck, "Methods in Social Anthropology," p. 232.
15 Ibid., p. 236.
16 W. H. R. Rivers, *Psychology and Ethnology*, London, Kegan Paul, 1926, p. 10.
17 Emile Durkheim, "Sur l'évolution générale des idées morales," *Année sociologique* (1905–6), p. 385.
18 See Westermarck, *The History of Human Marriage* and *The Origin and Development of the Moral Ideas*, chap. XL; and James G. Frazer, *Totemism and Exogamy*, vol. IV, London, Macmillan, 1910.

Notes to pp. 71–118

19 Westermarck, *The History of Human Marriage*, p. 319.
20 Ibid.
21 Westermarck, "Methods in Social Anthropology," p. 241.
22 Ibid.
23 Alfred Radcliffe-Brown, Presidential Address to the Anthropology Section of the British Association, 1931; see Westermarck, "Methods in Social Anthropology," pp. 248, 237.
24 Westermarck, "On Primitive Marriage: A Rejoinder to Mr. V. F. Calverton," p. 584.

Chapter IV The Name of the Nambikwara

1 Emilio Willems and Egon Schaden, "Stature of South American Indians," *American Anthropologist*, 47/3 (1945), pp. 469–70.
2 Morris Steggerda, "Stature of South American Indians," *American Journal of Physical Anthropology*, I/1 (1943).

Chapter VI Techniques for Happiness

1 This study was written in 1944.
2 Margaret Mead, *And Keep Your Powder Dry*, New York, William Morrow, 1943.
3 Namely, the young admirers of Frank Sinatra, whose excesses were widely talked about in 1942–3; young hoodlums that move in packs; and young women who, during the war, manifested their patriotism by offering their company and sexual favours to soldiers [*publisher's note*].

Chapter VII War and Trade among the Indians of South America

1 Curt Nimuendajú, *The Apinayé*, Washington, Catholic University of America, Anthropological Series, no. 8, 1939, and the other works of this admirable anthropologist on the Šerenté and the Ramkokamekra.
2 These observations are the subject of a separate study, "The Social Use of Kinship Terms among Brazilian Indians," to be published shortly (here, chapter XIII).
3 Claude Lévi-Strauss, "Contribution à l'étude de l'organisation sociale des Indiens bororo," *Journal de la Société des américanistes de Paris*, 2 (1936).

Chapter VIII The Theory of Power in a Primitive Society

1 In Emile Durkheim, *The Rules of Sociological Method* (New York, Free Press, 1982, p. 123): the function is the "correspondence between the fact being considered and the general needs of the social organism."
2 In his "Études de la nature" (1784), Bernardin de Saint Pierre suggested that nature devised melon ribs to make the fruit easier to divide on the family table, and that it made fleas black so that they could more easily be caught on white skin.

240 Notes to pp. 121–45

3 Claude Lévi-Strauss, "The Social Use of Kinship Terms among Brazilian Indians," *American Anthropologist*, 45/3 (1943). See chapter XIII of this volume.
4 Michel de Montaigne, "Of Cannibals," *Essays*, Book I (end of the chapter).
5 Closest English equivalent: "to have a rough time of it, to go through the mill."
6 Robert H. Lowie, *The Origin of the State*, New York, 1927, pp. 76–107; K. N. Llewellyn and E. A. Hoebel, *The Cheyenne Way*, University of Oklahoma Press, 1941, Part II, chap. 5.
7 Bronisław Malinowski, *Crime and Custom in Savage Society*, 3rd edn, New York, Harcourt, Brace, 1940, p. 46.
8 See the late F. E. Williams's remarkable analysis in *Papuans of the Trans-Fly*, Oxford, Clarendon Press, 1936, pp. 167–9.
9 Robert H. Lowie, *Primitive Society*, New York, Boni & Liveright, 1920, at the beginning of chapter XIII.
10 Quoted in Governor-General Félix Eboué's Memorandum on "Native Policy," issued on November 8, 1941 (*French Colonial Policy in Africa*, special issue no. 2, New York, 1944).
11 Ibid.

Chapter IX Reciprocity and Hierarchy

1 V. Frič and P. Radin, "Contributions to the Study of the Bororo Indians," *Journal of the Royal Anthropological Institute of Great Britain and Ireland*, 36 (1906); Antonio Colbacchini and César Albisetti, *Os Boróros Orientais*, São Paulo, 1942.
2 Colbacchini and Albisetti, *Os Boróros Orientais*, p. 126.
3 Ibid., p. 43.
4 Ibid., p. 111.
5 Ibid., p. 97.
6 Ibid., pp. 196–7.
7 J. K. Bose, "Social Organization of the Aimol Kukis, and Dual Organization in Assam," *Journal of the Department of Letters* [University of Calcutta], 25 (1934).
8 Colbacchini and Albisetti, *Os Boróros Orientais*, p. 30.
9 Claude Lévi-Strauss, "Contribution d l'étude de l'organisation sociale des indiens Bororo," *Journal de la Société des Américanistes de Paris*, 2 (1936).
10 Colbacchini and Albisetti, *Os Boróros Orientais*, pp. 30, 136.
11 Lévi-Strauss, "Contribution d l'étude de l'organisation sociale des indiens Bororo."
12 Colbacchini and Albisetti, *Os Boróros Orientais*, pp. 31, 35, 95.
13 Robert H. Lowie, "A Note on the Social Life of the Northern Kayapó," *American Anthropologist*, 45 (1943).

Chapter X The Foreign Policy of a Primitive Society

1 Mrs. Margaret Meade, who related this account to me.
2 Robert H. Lowie, "Some Aspects of Political Organization among the American Aborigines," Huxley Memorial Lecture, *Journal of the Royal Anthropological Institute of Great Britain and Ireland*, 78 (1948).

Chapter XI Indian Cosmetics

1 Lévi-Strauss would revise this assessment in *Tristes Tropiques*: "For a long time I remained convinced that I had made my collection at the last possible moment. I was, therefore, greatly surprised two years ago to receive an illustrated account of a collection made fifteen years later by a Brazilian colleague. Not only did his documents seem as expertly executed as mine, but very often the designs were identical" (pp. 185–7) [Editor's note].
2 In the original publication of this article in the journal *VVV*, the Kaduveo drawings were reproduced "in negative" – i.e. the lines appeared white on a black background. We have here reestablished the contrast of the original drawings with black lines on a white background.

Chapter XII The Art of the Northwest Coast at the American Museum of Natural History

1 On the occasion of the first publication of the French version of this article in 2004, Lévi-Strauss explained: "[This old article] dates from a time when diffusionist speculation – which Radcliffe-Brown called conjunctural history – was still in vogue. We have since become more prudent, for, even if the problems persist, we are more aware of the fact that our solutions to them will very likely remain hypothetical. To today's readers, sketches of prehistoric contact between different cultures might seem outmoded. If they would be so kind as to remember, in all fairness to these pages, that they were written more than sixty years ago." *Claude Lévi-Strauss*, Cahiers de l'Herne, 2004, p. 145.
2 I am referring here to the figures provided by A. L. Kroeber in *Cultural and Natural Areas of Native North America*, Berkeley, University of California Press, 1939.
3 The more important works on the northwest coast are Franz Boas, *The Social Organization and Secret Societies of the Kwakiutl Indians*, Report of the U.S. National Museum for 1895; *Tsimshian Mythology*, 31st Annual Report of the Bureau of American Ethnology, 1916; J. R. Swanton, *Contributions to the Ethnology of the Haida*, Memoirs of the American Museum of Natural History, VIII, 1915; *Social Condition, Beliefs and Linguistic Relationship of the Tlingit Indians*, 26th Annual Report of the Bureau of American Ethnology, 1908; and the contributions by the same authors to the works and publications of the Jesup North Pacific Expedition.
4 In his Huxley Memorial Lecture entitled "Une catégorie de l'esprit humain: la notion de personne, celle de 'moi'," *Journal of the Royal Anthropological Institute of Great Britain and Ireland*, 68 (1938).
5 The predominance of the blood group O among the Salish was established by Gates and Darby, "Blood Groups and Physiognomy of British Columbia Coastal Indians," *Journal of the Royal Anthropological Institute of Great Britain and Ireland*, 64 (1934). Among the Brazilian Indians, Ribeiro and Berardinelli found the percentage, skeptically received at first, of 100 percent group O for a band of Tupi Indians. This result, however, was entirely confirmed by Dr. J. A. Vellard and myself during our expedition of 1938 among the Nambikwara Indians. North American anthropologists have found among different stocks of North and Central American Indians percentages averaging from 60 to

almost 90 percent. One can hardly doubt that pure American Indians, from either North or South, belonged entirely to the O group. There is not a single instance of a similar, or even comparable, predominance of one blood group anywhere else in the world.
6 On the excavations of Von Tschudi, see M. E. Rivero and J. D. Von Tschudi, *Antiguedades Peruanas*, Vienna, 1851. Concluding a thorough analysis of the Tschudi case, Dr. Dixon, a resolute adversary of the Polynesian theory, confesses: "*On the basis of the data available* we appear to have reached an *impasse*" (emphasis in the original). Roland B. Dixon, "Contacts with America across the Southern Pacific," in *The American Aborigines*, ed. Diamond Jenness, Toronto, University of Toronto Press, 1933, p. 342.
7 Dr. Paul Rivet's theory is well known. It appears in its latest form in his book *Les Origines de l'homme américain*, just published by Les Editions de l'Arbre, Montreal, 1943.
8 After having convincingly established the almost practical impossibility of pre-Columbian contacts between Polynesia and America, Dr. Dixon concludes: "When all the many instances are sifted and critically weighed, there remains a very small residue of perhaps two or three facts which renders the acceptance of trans-Pacific contact not only just, but apparently inescapable" ("Contacts with America across the Southern Pacific," p. 353). The question is, when one reaches such a conclusion, if all the other evidence which was previously dismissed as dubious or equivocal should not be reconsidered in a more favourable light. Probabilities are worthless when they receive no confirmation; but, as soon as the fact to which they testify is established on independent grounds, they gain singularly in strength and reinforce each other. This does not prevent me from agreeing with Dr. Dixon as to the tremendous difficulties with which we are confronted – "on the basis of the data available," to borrow a useful argument from him – when trying to understand how and when the contact may have taken place and to evaluate its bearing upon the development of American cultures.
9 Quotations from Baudelaire, even short, cannot be translated without profanation. These come from the sonnet *Correspondances*, the fourth poem of *Spleen et Idéal* in *Les Fleurs du Mal*, with its mysterious Alaskan-like atmosphere.
10 The great Franz Boas, who died a few months ago, has applied the inexhaustible resources of his analytical genius to the interpretation of the labyrinth of themes, rules and conventions of the art of the Northwest Coast. See Boas, "The Decorative Art of the Indians of the North Pacific coast," *Bulletin of the American Museum of Natural History*, 9 (1897), and the book by the same author entitled *Primitive Art*, Oslo, 1927.
11 John R. Swanton, "Tlingit Myths and Texts," *Bulletin of the Bureau of American Ethnology*, 39/1 (1909), pp. 1–451: "The Origin of Copper," pp. 254–5.
12 Ibid., pp. 181–2.

Chapter XIII The Social Use of Kinship Terms among Brazilian Indians

1 Robert H. Lowie, "Family and Sib," *American Anthropologist*, 21 (1919), p. 28.
2 José de Anchieta, "Informaçao dos casamentos dos Indios do Brasil," *Revista Trimensal del Instituto Historico e Geographico Brasileiro*, 8 (1846), p. 259.

3 Gabriel Soares de Souza, "Tratado descriptivo do Brazil em 1587," *Revista do Instituto Historico e Geographico Brasileiro*, 14 (1851), pp. 316–17.
4 Anchieta, "Informaçao dos casamentos dos Indios do Brasil," p. 259.
5 Ibid., p. 261.
6 Hans Staden, *The True History of his Captivity*, ed. Malcolm Letts, London, Routledge, 1928, Vol. 11, chap. 18, p. 146.
7 "Tratado descriptivo do Brasil em 1587."
8 Claude d'Abbeville, *Histoire de la mission des pères capucins en l'isle de Maragnan et terres circonvoisins*, Paris, 1614.
9 Anchieta, "Informaçao dos casamentos dos Indios do Brasil," pp. 259–60. The same interpretation is made by Manoel de Nóbrega, *Cartas do Brasil 1549–1560*, Rio de Janeiro, 1931.
10 For instance, Breton gives clear evidence of its occurrence among the Antillean Caribs: "First cousins whom we call father's brother's sons call each other 'brothers' and the father's brothers are also called 'fathers.' The children of brothers do not marry, but they may contract marriages with the children of their father's sisters." *Dictionnaire caraïbe-françois*, Auxerre, 1665, p. 11.
11 Jean de Léry, *Voyage faict en la terre du Brésil*, ed. Paul Gaffarel, Paris, 1880, II, chap. 17, p. 85.
12 André Thevet, *La Cosmographie universelle*, Paris, 1575, p. 932.
13 Pero de Magalhães Gandavo, *The Histories of Brazil*, New York, Cortes Society, 1922, Vol. II, chap. 10, p. 89.
14 Nóbrega, *Cartas do Brasil*, p. 148.
15 Simão de Vasconcellos, *Chronica da Companhia de Jesu do Estado do Brasil*, Lisbon, 1865, I, 82, p. 133.
16 Soares de Souza, "Tratado descriptivo do Brasil en 1857," pp. 157, 152.
17 De Magalhães Gandavo, *The Histories of Brazil*, Vol. II, chap. 10, p. 89.
18 Other indications on the familial organization of the ancient Tupi may be found in Alfred Métraux, *La Religion des Tupinamba*, Paris, Leroux, 1928, *passim*; Lafone Quevedo, "Guarani Kinship Terms as an Index of Social Organization," *American Anthropologist*, 21 (1919), pp. 421–40; Paul Kirchhoff, "Die Vemandschaftsorganisation der Urwaldstämme Südamerikas," *Zeitschrift für Ethnologie*, 63 (1931), ch. 15, p. 182.
19 Yves d'Evreux, *Voyage dans le nord du Brésil*, ed. F. Denis, Paris, 1864, II, p. 14.
20 Ibid., XXVIII, p. 109.
21 De Léry, *Voyage faict en la terre du Brésil*, II, chap. 20, p. 133. See also Fernão Cardim, *Tratados da terra e gente do Brasil*, Rio de Janeiro, 1925, pp. 169–70.
22 The widespread South American custom of using kinship terms to express social relationships is attested to by Karl von den Steinen (*Unter der Naturvölkern Zentral-Brasiliens*, 2nd edn, Berlin, 1897, p. 286), who was called "elder brother" by the Bakairi and "maternal uncle" by the Mehinaku. We have just established the equivalence of the terms "maternal uncle" and "brother-in-law" in a system of cross-cousin marriage combined with avuncular marriage. Regarding the use of the term "elder brother," two observations should be made. First, in a kinship system such as that of the Bororo, not far distant from the Xingu, each generation is to some extent split into two layers, the elder half being assimilated to the younger half of the generation above and the younger half to the elder half of the generation below. In such a system, an "elder brother" may well be a true uncle and a potential brother-in-law.

The use of the term "brother" for social purposes may also be understood in another way. Among the Nambikwara, there is a special term, sometimes used to designate a sibling of the same sex, the meaning of which is "the other one." This term is applied not only to describe a familial relationship but is also used to name objects belonging to a class which includes several units (for instance, the posts of the huts or the pipes of the whistles). Friendly groups may also consider themselves to be "brothers," and the exclamation, "You are no more my brother!" may often be heard in discussions between angry adversaries.

This suggests that the term "brother" possesses, in addition to its kinship significance, a very wide meaning, both logical and moral. Nevertheless, when the technical problem of establishing new social relationships is put to the Indians, it is not the vague "brotherhood" that is called upon, but the more complex mechanism of the "brother-in-law" relationship.

23 The same sociological derivation is expressed in English through the etymological origin of the word "gossip" (god-sib).
24 Jacques Soustelle, *La Famille Otomi-Pame du Mexique central*, Paris, Institut d'Ethnologie, 1937.
25 D'Evreux, *Voyage dans le nord du Brésil*, XI, p. 234.

Chapter XIV On Dual Organization in South America

1 Robert H. Lowie, "A Note on the Northern Gê Tribes of Brazil," *American Anthropologist*, 43/2 (1941), pp. 188–96.
2 Ibid., p. 195.
3 Lowie likened Lévi-Strauss's suggestion to the most audacious and least supported hypothesis of the German diffusionist school, which tended to assume a historical link for any case where a resemblance between two societies was observed. Thus, for example, analogies between certain forms of social organization in Australia and Tierra del Fuego was explained by postulating the existence of a "central" culture, now extinct, as their common origin [Editor's note].
4 Lowie, "A Note on the Northern Gê Tribes of Brazil," p. 195.
5 See chapter XIII.
6 Lowie, "A Note on the Northern Gê Tribes of Brazil," p. 195.
7 Curt Nimuendajú and Robert H. Lowie, "The Dual Organizations of the Ramko'kamekra (Canella) of Northern Brazil," *American Anthropologist*, 39/4 (1937), pp. 565–82, at p. 578.
8 I am well aware of the fact that what Professor Lowie defines as "the Bororo–Canella organization" is the dual organization with matrilineal moieties. On the other hand, the moieties of the Parintintin and Munduruku are patrilineal. But shall we try to account through entirely different processes for the matrilineal moieties of the Canella and for the patrilineal ones of the Šerente? This seems unlikely. The problem of dual organization in South America is to be taken as a whole. The matrilinear or patrilinear character of a given society has very important consequences, but not from the point of view of the dual organization itself. All that is necessary for the latter is a unilateral principle, which can be found in a unilateral theory of conception, prior to the elaboration of any theory of filiation. The two are not necessarily linked. Thus, the Talmud presents us with a maternal theory of conception and with a patrilineal

theory of filiation. The unilateral principle, once given, can develop in one direction or the other, either matrilineal or patrilineal. But this is a secondary phenomenon. Why else should patrilineal and matrilineal institutions be found closely associated in all areas of clan or moiety organization?

9 Karl von den Steinen, *Unter der Naturvölkern Zentral-Brasiliens*, Berlin, 1897, p. 581 of the Portuguese translation (Departamento de Culture, São Paulo, 1940).
10 Ibid., p. 580.
11 Antonio Colbacchini and César Albisetti, *Os Boróros Orientais*, São Paulo, 1942, pp. 66–8.
12 W. A. Cook, "The Bororó Indians of Matto Grosso, Brazil," *Smithsonian Miscellaneous Collections*, 50/7 (1908), pp. 48–62.
13 Vojtěch Frič and Paul Radin, "Contributions to the Study of the Bororo Indians," *Journal of the Royal Anthropological Institute*, 36 (1906), pp. 382–406, at pp. 391–2.
14 J. M. Cooper, "The South American Marginal Cultures," *Proceedings of the Eighth American Scientific Congress*, 2 (1940), pp. 147–60.
15 Erland Nordenskiöld, *The Changes in the Material Culture of two Indian Tribes under the Influence of New Surroundings*, Göteborg, 1930.
16 Von den Steinen, *Unter der Naturvölkern Zentral-Brasiliens*, p. 488 of the Portuguese translation.

Index

Page numbers in *italic* indicate illustrations.

Abbeville, Claude d' 174
acculturation 12, 88, 89, 90, 120, 181, 183
Achille-Delmas, François 40
affinity 4–5
aggression 16–17, 18, 19
  see also conflict and war
Algerian war 23
Allier, Raoul 41
American anthropology 7, 8, 9, 10, 11, 12, 83–91, 94, 128
  see also specific indigenous peoples
American Museum of Natural History 158–64
Amniapä 215, 216, 217, 218, 220, 221, 222, 225
Anchieta, José de 173–5
Année Sociologique group 9, 49, 57, 58–9
Apache 87–90
Apiacá 188
Aranda 143
Arawaiti 143
Arawaks 115, 183
Aricapu 215, 219, 222
art
  "The Art of the Northwest Coast at the American Museum of Natural History" 3–4, 158–64
  body paintings 151–7, *154*, *155*, *156*, 193, 205–6, 218
  dance masks 161–2, 222
  Guaporé River tribes 221
  Nambikwara 209–10
  textiles 158–9

artisanal specialization 105–6, 142
Arua 215, 220, 222, 225
Auetö 107
Australia 49–50, 115, 117, 134, 143, 144, 146
avuncular marriage 116, 168, 173, 174, 175, 176, 197, 208, 209
Aweti 143
Aztecs 181

Bakairi 105–6, 107, 186
Banks Islands 145
Barthes, Roland 30
basketry 185, 195, 206
Bastide, Roger 9, 41
Bataillon, Lionel 38
Bayet, Albert 39, 43
behaviorism 60
Bella Coola 159
Berbers 72
Bergson, Henri 16
Blanchot, Maurice 29, 31
Bloch, Marc 38
Blondel, Charles 39, 40
blood customs 146
blood kinship 69, 88
blood quarrels 73
Boas, Franz 90, 162
body paintings 151–7, *154*, *155*, *156*, 193, 205–6, 218
Boggiani, Guido 152
Bonald, Louis de 15, 55
book reviews
  An Apache Life-Way 87–90
  The Apinayé 90–1

The Cheyenne Way: Conflict and Case Law in Primitive Jurisprudence 85–7
Children of the People 88
The Eastern Timbira 90–1
The Navajo 88
The Šerente 90–1
The Social Organization of the Western Apache 87–90
Sun Chief: The Autobiography of a Hopi Indian 83–4
The Use of Personal Documents in History, Anthropology and Sociology 84–5
Bororo 7, 8, 11, 116, 119, 132–4, 181, 183, 186
  demographic collapse 184
  food and harvest rituals 132, 184
  shamanism 132
Bouglé, Célestin 8, 38, 44, 59
Brazil 19, 91, 103–16
  see also specific indigenous peoples
Brazzaville Conference (1944) 24
Breton, André 13, 27, 28
Briffault, Robert 69, 75
British anthropology 65, 71, 74
Burke, Kenneth 5

Cabahiba 188
Cabishinana 215, 221
Caillois, Roger 29, 38, 41–2
cannibalism 104, 221
Capitaine-Paul-Lemerle 27, 28, 29
Cardim, Fernão 178
Cayapo 119
Cayrol, Jean 29, 31
Cerae 133, 134
Chandler, Raymond 93
Chapacuran tribes 214, 215
Chemins du Monde (journal) 17
Cheyenne 85–7
chieftaincy
  chief–commoner relationship 129
  choice of 122, 137
  consent and 122, 123, 128, 208
  duties and responsibilities 122, 123, 125, 126, 130
  festivals 197–8
  generosity 124–5
  giving up 124
  Guaporé River tribes 220–1
  hereditary 196
  Nambikwara 18, 120, 121–8, 137, 139, 208
  "natural leadership" 130–1

polygyny 123, 126–7, 139, 168–70, 197, 208
reciprocity and 128–30
shamanism 125, 198, 211
Tupi-Kawahib 196, 197–8
childbirth 196, 209
Chilkat 158–9, 160
Chinook 159
Chiricahua 87
Choctaws 145
civic-mindedness 98
Clastres, Pierre 4
"closed society" 148
clothing and adornment
  Guaporé River tribes 216–18, *217, 218, 219*
  Nambikwara 112, 204–6, *204, 205, 207*
  Tupi-Kawahib 193–4, *193, 194*
Colbacchini, Antonio 132–3, 183
collective consciousness 56
Collège de France 14, 21, 22, 23
Collège de Sociologie 38
colonial question 24–5
Comanche 86
comics, American 96
"common humanity" notion 74
compérage 176, 177–8
Comte, Auguste 20, 35, 36, 39, 47, 48, 52
Condorcet, Nicolas de 52
conflict and war
  assimilation processes and 116
  conflict avoidance 96–7, 110–11
  economic exchanges and 17, 20, 104–5, 107, 110, 113, 114, 115, 141
  foreigner, concept of 138, 141, 144–5, 146
  Nambikwara 17, 111–12, 113–14, 140, 141, 142, 208–9
  pretexts for 113
  prisoners 104, 106, 220
  reciprocity and 104–5
  reconciliation inspections 112, 141
  Tupi-Kawahib 196
  "War and Trade among the Indians of South America" 4, 17, 103–16
  war expeditions 113–14, 209
  see also "The Foreign Policy of a Primitive Society"
Constant, Benjamin 20
contract law 43
Cook, Captain James 145, 160
Cook, W. A. 183
Cooper, J. M. 184–5

cooperation 17
   see also exchange relations
coton-assap 176, 177
Council of Trent 178
Creek 146
crime and punishment 85–7
cross-cousin marriage 116, 121, 126, 127, 168, 172, 173, 174, 175, 176, 180, 197, 208, 209
Cruz, Manuel 132–3
cultural history 36, 42, 49, 51, 120
curare 114, 125, 208, 220

dance masks 161–2, 222
Davy, Georges 38, 42, 43, 52
death customs 197, 209, 221
decolonization 23–4
dehumanization 27, 28
Demangeon, Albert 38
Devereux, Georges 9
Diderot, Denis 20, 36
diffusionist thesis 68, 69, 75
Dion, Robert 37
division of labor 19, 52, 59
   sexual 127, 169
domestic animals 190, 192, 198, 201–2, 216
Durkheim, Emile 4, 9, 11, 15, 20, 35, 36, 37, 42, 44–57, 59–60, 61, 65, 71, 118
   anthropological influence 41, 42, 54
   The Division of Labor and Society 42, 55
   The Elementary Forms of Religious Life 44–5, 49–50, 54, 55, 56, 61
   functional perspective 9, 45–6
   historical perspective 9, 45–6
   and Mauss, compared 53–4
   methodological principles 10, 42, 44–9, 54, 60
   morality, analysis of 42
   philosophical training 54, 57
   "La Prohibition de l'inceste" 41, 46
   on the psychic nature of social phenomena 39, 55
   The Rules of Sociological Method 35, 42, 46, 50, 52, 56
   and social facts 54, 60
   social typology 47
   sociology of law 42
   Suicide 39, 49, 51
   on symbolism 46, 55

Éboué, Félix 24, 131
École Coloniale 40

École Libre des Hautes Études 13, 14–15, 17, 23
economic sociology 43–4
The Elementary Structures of Kinship 3, 6, 11, 14, 19
entropy 25
Essertier, Daniel 39
ethnology 63–4
evolutionism 2, 8, 10, 11, 66, 67–8, 69, 70, 74–5
   moral 75
   social 48, 54, 67, 74
   unilinear 52, 74, 75
Evreux, Yves d' 103, 104, 173, 175–6, 178
exchange relations 17, 20, 104–5, 106, 107, 112–13, 114, 115, 139
   "barter auction" 107
   conflict and 17, 20, 104–5, 107, 110, 113, 114, 115, 141
   fairness, concept of 113, 141
   games, rituals and celebrations 107
   gifting 9, 10, 17, 50, 51, 52, 112–13, 124–5, 141
   see also reciprocity
exogamy 11, 91
Eyiguayegui 153, 154, 156–7

The Family and Social Life of the Namikwara Indians 4
farming 183–4, 185
   forest agriculture 185, 186
   Tupi-Kawahib 189
   see also foraging
Fauconnet, Paul 42–3, 52
Fawcett, P. H. 105, 181
Febvre, Lucien 38, 143
federalism 18, 24
fetishism of progress 25
fieldwork
   concrete realities of 9
   group expeditions 8
Fleury, Maurice de 40
folklore 40, 60, 66, 72
food preparation
   Guaporé River tribes 216
   Nambikwara 126, 201
   Tupi-Kawahib *190*, 191–2, *191*
food ritual 132
foraging 144, 186
   Nambikwara 108–9, 119, 137, 201
   Tupi-Kawahib 189–90
Ford, Clellan S. 83
"The Foreign Policy of a Primitive Society" 15, 16, 19, 25, 135–48

Index

foreigner, concept of 138, 141, 144–5, 146
France
  French Revolution 36
  immigration 23
  see also French sociology
Frazer, James G. 54, 57, 65, 67, 71
French sociology 35–62
  anthropology and 36, 40, 42
  birth of 20, 35
  distinctive characteristics 36–7
  economic sociology 43–4
  fieldwork, neglect of 9
  "French Sociology" 4, 8–10, 35–62
  principles and methods 44–59
  religious sociology 38, 41–2, 44–5, 61
  sociology of law 42–3, 58
  trends in 35–44
  universalism of 37, 38
Freud, Sigmund 63
Fric [Frič], Vojtěch 183–4
functionalism 10, 12, 13, 15, 45, 54, 64, 87

games 125, 146, 147, 197, 221
Gê 119, 180–1, 182, 186, 215
Gennep, Arnold van 40
genocide 30
geographical determinism 185–6
Germany, Year Zero (film) 31
Gestalt 48
ghosts, belief in 225
gifting 9, 10, 17, 50, 51, 52, 112–13, 141
  chieftains 124–5
Goodwin, Grenville, *The Social Organization of the Western Apache* 87–90
Gottmann, Jean 37
Gourou, Pierre 37
Granet, Marcel 38, 42
great apes 67–8
Griaule, Marcel 9, 42
Guaporé River tribes 214–26
  art and recreation 221–2
  chieftainship 220–1
  culture 215–25
  dress and adornment 216–18
  languages 215
  life cycle 221
  material culture 218–19
  religion, folklore and mythology 222, 225
  shamanism 222, 225
  social organization 220–1
  subsistence and food preparation 215–16
  tribal division 214–15
  weapons 220, *220*
Guaratägaja 215, 216, 217, 221, 222, 225
Guayaki 184
Guaycuru 151
Gurvitch, Georges 5, 8, 13, 41, 42, 43, 44, 57–9

Haida 159, 160
Halbwachs, Maurice 38, 39, 44, 51
Hammett, Dashiell 93
Handbook of South American Indians 7, 8
happiness 97, 98, 99
harpy eagles 192, 198
harvest ritual 184
Hertz, Robert 50
Hobbes, Thomas 20
Hoebel, Edward Adamson, *The Cheyenne Way: Conflict and Case Law in Primitive Jurisprudence* 85–7
homo economicus 43
homosexual relations 170, 176, 197, 208
Hopi 83–4, 145
houses
  Guaporé River tribes 216
  Nambikwara 108, 109, 138, 202, *203*
  Tupi-Kawahib 192
Huari 215, 216, 217, 220
Hubert, Henri 35, 38, 41, 51
human geography 37
humanism 26, 55
Hume, David 128
hunter-gatherers 181, 184, 185
Huvelin, Paul-Louis 41

immigration 23
"In Memory of Malinowski" 63–4
Inca empire 114, 115
incest taboo 11, 41, 46, 71–2, 129
India 6, 26, 28
"Indian Cosmetics" 4, 151–7
individualism 43, 55, 56
inner child 95, 96
Institut d'Ethnologie de Université de Paris 40
international division of labor 19
international relations 16, 18
  "The Foreign Policy of a Primitive Society" 15, 16, 19, 25, 135–48
intertribal relations 135–48
  see also conflict and war; exchange relations; marriage

Introduction to the Work of Marcel Mauss 4
Inuit 145
Ipotewát 189
Islam 6

Jabotifet 189
Jakobson, Roman 6, 30
jurisprudence in indigenous societies 85–7

Kaduveo graphic art 151–7
Kamayura 106
Karaja 119
Kepikiriwat 215, 216, 217, 220, 221
kinship 117, 121
  blood kinship 69, 88
  brother-in-law relationship 167, 169, 170, 171, 172, 173, 175–6, 176–7
  moiety system 133–4
  Nambikwara 115, 121, 142, 167–78, 180, 208
  "The Social Use of Kinship Terms among Brazilian Indians" 4, 167–78
  see also marriage
Kluckhohn, Clyde 6, 84–5
  Children of the People 88
  The Navajo 88
  The Use of Personal Documents in History, Anthropology and Sociology 84–5
Kroeber, Alfred 9, 10, 36, 49, 50, 52
Kustenau 106, 107
Kwakiutl 159, 162

Labrador, Sánchez 151–2, 153, 154, 155–7
L'Âge d'Or (journal) 17
Lalo, Charles 42
Lam, Wifredo 27
land ownership 142
  see also territory
language and dialects 114, 119
  Guaporé River tribes 215
  multilingualism 106–7, 142
  Nambikwara 138, 171, 180, 200
  Tupi-Kawahib 188
L'Année Sociologique (journal) 11
Laugier, Henri 19
law, sociology of 42–3, 58
Lazarus 29
Leenhardt [should be "Leenhardt", and in the text as well], Maurice 42

Leighton, Dorothea C.
  Children of the People 88
  The Navajo 88
Leiris, Michel 9
Leroy, Olivier 41
Léry, Jean de 103, 104, 173, 175, 176, 178
Lévi-Strauss, Claude
  cultural attaché 6, 15, 19, 21, 23
  experience of exile 12–13
  lack of peer recognition 14, 21
  New York period 6–13
  periods of crisis 21, 29–30
  political thinking and activism 14–15, 18, 20–2, 29
  UNESCO International Social Science Council member 21, 25–6
  wartime experiences 22–3
Lévy, Emmanuel 43
Lévy-Bruhl, Lucien 40–1, 55, 56–7, 60
linguistics 37, 48
  see also language and dialects
Llewellyn, Karl N., *The Cheyenne Way: Conflict and Case Law in Primitive Jurisprudence* 85–7
Lowie, Robert 8, 36, 65, 90, 91, 118–19, 131, 179, 180, 181
Luquet, Georges-Henri 42
Lyautey, Hubert 131

Machiavelli, Niccolò 20
Macurap 215, 219, 220, 221, 222
Magalhães Gandavo, Pero de 175
magic and religion 41, 66, 69, 71, 104, 125, 198, 210–11, 222, 225
Malinowski, Bronislaw 7, 10, 15, 35, 45, 60, 63–4, 87
  Crime and Custom in Savage Society 129
  ethnology 63–4
  functionalism 10, 15, 64, 87
  "In Memory of Malinowski" (Lévi-Strauss) 63–4
Manitsaua 106
Maori 160, 161
marriage 68, 91
  alliances 107, 141–2, 180
  avuncular 116, 168, 173, 174, 175, 176, 197, 208, 209
  cross-cousin 116, 121, 126, 127, 168, 172, 173, 174, 175, 176, 180, 197, 208, 209
  incest taboo 11, 41, 46, 71–2, 129
  polygyny 168–70
  widows 221
matrilineal moieties 179, 181, 182

Index

Maunier, René 40
Maurras, Charles 15
Mauss, Marcel 4, 8, 9, 17, 35, 38, 39, 40, 41, 42, 43, 49, 51, 52, 53, 57, 59, 60–1, 129, 160
  anthropological influence 41
  and the Durkheimian tradition 53–4
  Kroeber's critique of 9, 49, 50
  methodology 54, 59
  on the psychic nature of social phenomena 55
  on sacrifice 51
Maya 182
Mead, Margaret 5, 94
mechanical solidarity 52
medicine 211, 225
Mediterranean civilization 75
Mehinaku 106, 107
Meillet, Antoine 37
Mendès-France, Pierre 24
method of concomitant variations 59
Métraux, Alfred 9, 26, 42
Mexico 19, 177, 181, 182
Meyer, Hermann 105
Mialat 189, 190, 192, 197
Mirkine-Guetzévitch, Boris 15
modernity, Western 25, 29
Mojo–Chiquito culture 214
Monbeig, Pierre 37
Monnet, Georges 14
monogamy 50, 70, 74, 75, 127, 208
monographs, indigenous 83–91
Montaigne, Michel de 20, 36, 122
Montesquieu 20
morality 70–2
  moral evolution 15, 75
  moral judgments 66, 70
  moral maxims 70
  moral values 41, 76
  social observation 70
  theoretical 66
Moret, Alexandre 42
Morgan, Lewis H. 52, 69–70, 74
Morocco 72, 74
moste 177
Mundurucú 183, 188, 200
Musée de l'Homme 23, 40
music and dance 197–8, 198, 210, 222
musical instruments 198, 210, 222, *223–4*
Mythologiques 22, 30
mythology 162–4, 181, 211, 222, 225

Na Dené 160
Nahukuá 105–6, 107, 143

Nambikwara 7, 77–9, 108–14, 118, 119–20, 136–42, 199–212
  art and recreation 209–10
  band relationships 121–2, 137, 139, 141–2
  chieftainship 18, 120, 121–8, 129–30, 137, 139, 208
  culture 108–14, 200–12
  demographic collapse 120, 137, 170–1, 200
  economic cooperation and exchange *see* exchange relations
  farming 108, 137, 201
  folklore, lore and learning 211–12
  foreign policy 16, 25, 142
  homosexual relations 170, 176, 208
  hostilities 17, 111–12, 113–14, 140, 141, 142, 208–9
  intergroup contact 110–14, 140–3
  kinship system 115, 121, 142, 167–78, 180, 208
  language and dialects 138, 171, 180, 200
  life cycle 209
  magic and religion 209, 210–11
  material culture 112, 119, 138, 139, 140, 206–7
  "The Nambikwara" 199–212
  "The Name of the Nambikwara" 11, 77–9
  nomadic behaviours 108–10, 119, 120, 137, 139, 201
  polygyny 126–7, 129–30, 139, 168–70, 175, 208
  shamanism 125, 209, 211
  social and political organization 118, 120–31, 137, 138, 141–2, 171, 208–9
  subsistence 108–10, 200–2
  territory 19, 119, 136–7, 143–4, 167, 199
  tribal divisions 199–200
  war expeditions 113–14, 209
naming of native tribes 11, 77–9
narcotics and beverages 197, 210, 222
nation-state model 18, 25
national insurance schemes 18, 130
national sovereignty 24
nationalism 24
natural selection 67
nature–culture distinction 3, 74
Nazi Germany 16
Nimuendajú, Curt 7, 188, 189
  The Apinayé 90–1
  The Eastern Timbira 90–1
  The Šerente 90–1

Nóbrega, Manoel de 175
Nootka 159
Nordenskiöld, Erland 185
Nourry, Emile 40

"On Dual Organization in South America" 11, 179–87
Ona 145
ontological pluralism 58
Opler, Morris E., *An Apache Life-Way* 87–90
optimistic sociology 97, 99
organic solidarity 52

Pakistan 6, 26
Palikur 183
Palmella 215
Pantanal 151
Parain, Brice 1
Paranawát 189
Paressi 200, 202
Parintintin 183, 188
Parsons, Talcott 6, 36
patu mere 160, 161
Paulme, Denise 9
Pavlov, Ivan 55
Pawumwa 216, 220
petroglyphs 182
Petrullo, Vincenzo 105
"phoneme zero" 30–1
phonemics 48
physics 52–3
Pires de Campos, Antonio 77
poisons 114, 125, 208, 211, 220
political anthropology 4
Politique etrangère 15–16
polyandry 197
polygyny 123, 126–7, 129–30, 139, 168–70, 175, 197, 208
Polynesia 145, 160, 161
Popper, Karl 16
  The Open Society and its Enemies 16
post-war renewal 16, 17, 20
potlatch 43
  see also gifting
pottery 105–6, 110, 139, 140, 195, 206, 219
power
  and consent of the group 18
  political power 118, 128
  "The Theory of Power in a Primitive Society" 4, 15, 24, 117–31
  see also chieftaincy
pre-Columbian America 104, 114, 120, 160–1, 182

"primitive thought" 40–1, 56, 57, 60, 136, 144–5
"primitiveness" 117–18, 119, 120, 135–7
promiscuity theory 66, 67, 68, 69, 73–4, 75–6
Proudhon, Pierre-Joseph 57
providentialism 87, 118
psychoanalysis 55, 63, 97
psychology, sociology and 11, 12, 39, 48, 55, 67, 68, 69, 70, 71–5, 84, 131
puberty rituals 209
Puruborá 215

Quain, Buell 105, 106–7

Race and Culture 30
Race and History 25, 26, 29
racial conflicts 98
Radcliffe-Brown, Alfred 35, 65, 67, 72–3
  The Andaman Islanders 35
Radin, Paul 83
Ray, Jean 43
reciprocity 10, 11, 18, 19, 52
  chieftaincy and 128–30
  conflict and 104–5
  and group cohesion 19, 129
  international level 19
  moiety system 132–4
  mutual obligations 18
  qualitative/quantitative 129
  "Reciprocity and Hierarchy" 11, 132–4
  see also exchange relations
Redfield, Robert 35, 36
religious beliefs *see* magic and religion
religious sociology 38, 41–2, 44–5, 61
Renaissance (journal) 17
responsibility 43, 75, 130
retributive emotions 70
Révolution Constructive 14
Rivers, W. H. R. 66, 71, 72, 73, 75
Rivet, Paul 23, 40, 41, 161
Rockefeller Foundation 6, 8
Roman, Monique 21
Rondon, General Cândido Mariano da Silva 77, 107, 108, 120, 188, 189, 196, 199
Roquette-Pinto, Edgar 199–200, 202
Rossellini, Roberto 31
Rougemont, Denis de 5
Rousseau, Jean-Jacques 18, 20, 36, 128
Runyon, Damon 93

sacrifice 50, 51
Salish 159

Sapir, Edward 160
Saussaye, Chantepie de la 35
Saussure, Ferdinand de 37
The Savage Mind 3, 30
savannal culture 185–6
Schaden, Egon 77
Schmidt, Max 105
Schuhl, Pierre-Maxime 42
Seghers, Anna 27
Serge, Victor 27
sexual division of labor 127, 169
shamanism
  Bororo 132
  Guaporé River tribes 222, 225
  Nambikwara 125, 209, 211
Shoah 26, 27, 28, 29, 30
Simiand, François 37, 38, 43–4
Simmons, Leo W. (ed.), *Sun Chief: The Autobiography of a Hopi Indian* 83–4
Sion, Jules 37
Sirionó 200
skyscrapers 99
Smith, Elliot 75
Snethlage, Emil 225
Soares de Souza, Gabriel 174, 175
social and political organization 114–15
  "The Foreign Policy of a Primitive Society" 15, 16, 19, 25, 135–48
  Guaporé River tribes 220–1
  moieties 115, 116
  Nambikwara 118, 120–31, 137, 138, 141–2, 171, 208–9
  "On Dual Organization in South America" 11, 179–87
  Timbira 91
  Tupi-Kawahib 196
  see also chieftaincy
social citizenship 18
social contract 128
social evolution 48, 54, 67, 74
social facts 54, 60, 71, 85
social monetarism 44
social morphology 44, 47, 52
social philosophy 20, 36, 48
social rights 43
"The Social Use of Kinship Terms among Brazilian Indians" 4, 167–78
Soustelle, Jacques 9, 23, 24
Spencer, Herbert 47, 48, 50, 74
Staden, Hans 103, 104, 174
Steggerda, Morris 77
Steinen, Karl von den 105, 106, 115, 183, 184, 186
Steward, Julian H. 7, 8

Stoczkowski, Wiktor 26
The Story of Lynx 30
structural anthropology, genesis of 13–14
Structural Anthropology
  article selection 3–4, 5, 6, 21
  prehistory of 3–6
  publication of 1–2, 14
  thematic organization 1–2
Structural Anthropology, Volume II 2
subsistence
  Guaporé River tribes 215–16
  Nambikwara 200–2
  Tupi-Kawahib 189–92
suicide 9, 10, 39–40, 52
  altruistic 51
  anomic 51
  egoistic 51
supernatural world 84
  see also shamanism
survival principle 69
Suya 106
Swanton, J. R. 163
symbolic activity 9
symbolism 3, 46, 55
syncretism 182, 187

Takwatip 189, 192, 196
Talayesva, Don 83–4
Tapanyuma 200
Tarde, Gabriel 39
tattooing 46–7, 151, 152, 193
"Techniques for Happiness" 5, 6, 17, 18, 92–9
Tereno 183
territory 106, 143–4
  fluidity 144
  Nambikwara 19, 119, 136–7, 143–4, 167, 199
  Tupi-Kawahib 188–9
textiles 138, 158–9, 195, 206, 218–19
"The Theory of Power in a Primitive Society" 4, 15, 24, 117–31
Thevet, André 103, 175
Tiahuanaco 181
Tlingit 159, 160, 162, 163
tobacco smoking 210
totemism 46, 198
transportation
  Guaporé River tribes 218
  Nambikwara 206
  Tupi-Kawahib 194
"Tribes of the Right Bank of the Guaporé River" 214–26

Tristes Tropiques 1, 3, 4, 5, 6, 7, 14, 16, 18, 21, 23, 24, 26, 27, 28, 29, 30
Trumai 106
Tschudi, Johann Jakob von 160–1
Tsimshian 159
Tucumanfét 189
Tugaregue 133, 134
Tuparí 215, 217, 220, 221, 222
Tupi 77, 78, 178, 186
  kinship system 173–6
  mythology 181
Tupi-Kawahib 107, 116, 125, 183, 188–98, 200
  art and recreation 197–8
  chieftaincy 196
  culture 189–98
  demographic collapse 188, 189
  dress and ornaments 193–4
  houses 192
  kinship 196
  language 188
  life cycle 196–7
  material culture 195–6
  music 198
  shamanism 198
  social and political organization 196
  subsistence 189–92
  territory 188–9
  transportation 194
  tribal divisions 188–9
  "The Tupi-Kawahib" 188–98
  warfare 196
Tupinamba 103, 104
Twentieth Century Sociology 8
Tylor, Sir Edward Burnett 57, 65, 67

unconscious mind 47
UNESCO 25
  Declaration on Race 25
  International Social Science Council 21, 25–6
unilinear evolution 52, 74, 75
Union Française 23, 24
United Nations 19
United States 18, 19, 92–9
  American anthropology 7, 8, 9, 10, 11, 12, 83–91, 94, 128
  civic-mindedness 98
  collective discipline 95–6, 98
  conservatism 94
  happiness, techniques for 97, 98, 99
  immigration 23
  liberalism 93
  presidential elections 92

sociability, relentless 99
social philosophy 94–5
society 5–6, 92–9
universal principles, search for 17
USSR 18, 19

Vallois, Henri 23
Vasconcellos, Simão 175
vengeance, psychology of 73
venigaravi 146
The View from Afar 2–3, 5, 30

"War and Trade among the Indians of South America" 4, 17, 103–16
war dances 210
Warner, W. Lloyd 36, 49
Wauters, Arthur 22
Wayoro 215, 217, 220, 221, 225
We Are All Cannibals 5
weapons
  Guaporé River tribes 220, *220*
  Nambikwara 112, 114, 207–8
  Tupi-Kawahib 195
welfare state 18
Westermarck, Edward 10–11, 15, 54, 65–76
  Ethical Relativity 66, 76
  evolutionism and 66, 67–8, 69, 70, 74–5
  The History of Human Marriage 11, 65–6, 67, 71, 75
  The Origin and Development of the Moral Ideas 66, 70–2, 75, 76
  promiscuity thesis 66, 67, 68, 69, 73–4, 75–6
  psychological approach 67, 68, 69, 70, 71–5
  "The Work of Edward Westermarck" (Lévi-Strauss) 65–76
Willems, Emilo 77
Wiraféd 189
"The Work of Edward Westermarck" 65–76
Workers' International 14
"writing degree zero" 30–1

Xingu 105, 142, 143

Yabuti 215, 220, 222
Yawalapiti 106, 107, 143
Yolngu 146

zero signifier 30–1